THE DIGITAL TRANSFORMATION PLAYBOOK

THE DIGITAL
TRANSFORMATION
PLAYBOOK

Rethink your business for the digital age

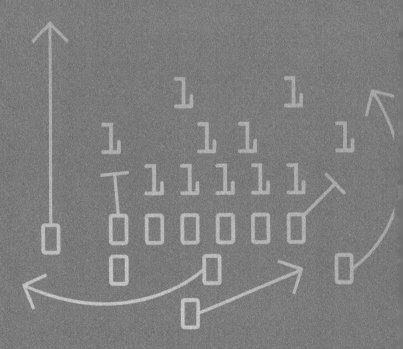

DAVID L. ROGERS

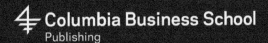

Columbia Business School
Publishing

Columbia University Press
Publishers Since 1893
New York   Chichester, West Sussex
cup.columbia.edu

Library of Congress Cataloging-in-Publication Data
Names: Rogers, David L., 1970– author.
Title: The digital transformation playbook : rethink your business
for the digital age / David L. Rogers.
Description: New York : Columbia University Press, [2016] |
Includes bibliographical references and index.
Identifiers: LCCN 2015037126| ISBN 9780231175449 (cloth : alk. paper) |
ISBN 9780231541657 (e-book)
Subjects: LCSH: Technological innovations—Management. |
Information technology—Management. | New products. | Strategic planning.
Classification: LCC HD45 .R6335 2016 | DDC 658.4/062—dc23
LC record available at http://lccn.loc.gov/2015037126

Columbia University Press books are printed on permanent and
durable acid-free paper.
This book is printed on paper with recycled content.
Printed in the United States of America

c 10 9 8 7 6 5 4 3 2 1

Jacket design: Elliot Strunk/Fifth Letter

For my parents, two writers who got me writing

CONTENTS

PREFACE

The rules of business have changed. In every industry, the spread of new digital technologies and the rise of new disruptive threats are transforming business models and processes. The digital revolution has turned the old business playbook upside down.

In my own work, teaching and advising business leaders from companies around the world, I repeatedly hear the same urgent question: How do we adapt and transform for the digital age?

Businesses founded before the rise of the Internet face a stark challenge: Many of the fundamental rules and assumptions that governed and grew their businesses in the pre-digital era no longer hold. The good news is that change is possible. Pre-digital businesses are not dinosaurs doomed to extinction. Their disruption is not inevitable. Businesses can transform themselves to thrive in the digital age.

In this book I explore the phenomenon of digital transformation: What separates businesses that manage to adapt and thrive in a digital world from those who fail?

In pursuing the answers to this question, I have been privileged to draw on the insights, perspectives, and questions of an amazing range of executives and entrepreneurs, both through my consulting and keynote speaking, and in my Columbia Business School executive programs on digital marketing and digital business strategy. I have been able to conduct research studies on big data and marketing metrics, mobile shopping behaviors, the Internet of Things, and the future of data sharing. And for nine years, as founder of the BRITE conference, I have convened C-suite leaders from global brands, technology firms, media companies, and fast-growing startups to discuss the evolving digital business landscape.

One central insight emerged and shaped the development of this entire book: *Digital transformation is not about technology—it is about strategy and new ways of thinking.* Transforming for the digital age requires your business to upgrade its strategic mindset much more than its IT infrastructure. This truth is apparent in the changing roles of technology leadership within business. A Chief Information Officer's traditional role has been to use technology to optimize processes, reduce risks, and better run the existing business. But the emerging role of a Chief Digital Officer is much more strategic, focused on using technology to reimagine and reinvent the core business itself.

Digital transformation requires a holistic view of business strategy. In my last book, *The Network Is Your Customer*, I focused on the impact of digital technologies on customers—their behaviors, interactions, and relationships with businesses and organizations of all kinds. In this book, I take a broader scope, looking at five domains of business strategy: customers, competition, data, innovation, and value.

Like my previous books, *The Digital Transformation Playbook* focuses on practical tools and frameworks that readers can apply in making decisions and formulating strategies for their own business, no matter their size or industry. I have packed the text with case studies that illustrate the concepts and illuminate the strategies. My hope is that you, the reader, will bring the playbook into action by applying its lessons and discovering the next stage of value creation and growth for your business.

Acknowledgments

No book is possible without the help of many generous contributors.

I thank all the many business leaders and writers whose work is cited in the book, especially those who shared their experiences with me in detail in the classroom, onstage at conferences, or in interviews.

This book would not have happened without my agent, Jim Levine, and my publisher, Myles Thompson, championing the project at every stage from the very beginning. They both have my enduring gratitude. My editor, Bridget Flannery-McCoy, provided invaluable feedback in crafting the pitch and structure of the book. Rita Gunther McGrath, a fellow faculty member and co-conspirator at Columbia Business School, provided both rich intellectual inspiration for many ideas and critical feedback towards the end of the writing process, helping me hone the book's focus and core message. Karen Vrotsos was the perfect editor of the final draft, sharpening each turn of phrase, tightening the prose, and ensuring that every idea would be clear to readers approaching it for the first time.

Columbia Business School has been the greenhouse for my work for over fifteen years. Mike Malefakis has been a great champion of my teaching as a member of the Executive Education faculty. Bernd Schmitt and Matthew Quint supported my research at the Center on Global Brand Leadership for many years. Schmitt and my speaking agent, Tom Neilssen, provided excellent advice during the initial planning of the book. Alisa Ahmadian contributed expert background research, and Oded Naaman designed the playbook's five handsome icons. Stephen Wesley at Columbia University Press and Ben Kolstad at Cenveo answered all my questions and worked arduously to keep the publication on track at every perilous turn of the process.

Lastly, I thank my wife, Karen, and son, George. They kept me going, inspired my creativity, and picked up my slack during the weeks I spent absorbed in writing. Their love is the inspiration behind all my work.

David Rogers
Montclair, New Jersey

THE DIGITAL TRANSFORMATION PLAYBOOK

1

The Five Domains of Digital Transformation
Customers, Competition, Data, Innovation, Value

You may remember the *Encyclopædia Britannica*. First published in 1768, it represented the definitive reference resource in English for hundreds of years before the rise of the Internet. Those of us of a certain age likely remember thumbing through the pages of its thirty-two leather-bound volumes—if not at home, then in a school library—while preparing a research paper. In the initial debate about *Wikipedia*, and in the later stories of its amazing rise, that vast, online, community-created, freely accessible encyclopedia for the digital age was always compared to the *Britannica*, the traditional incumbent that it was challenging.

When, after 244 years, Encyclopædia Britannica, Inc., announced it had printed its last edition, the message seemed clear. Another hidebound company born before the arrival of the Internet had been *disrupted*—wiped out by the irrefutable logic of the digital revolution. Except that wasn't true.

Over the preceding twenty years, Britannica had been through a wrenching process of transformation. *Wikipedia* was not, in fact, its first digital challenger. At the dawn of the personal computing era, Britannica sought to shift from print to CD-ROM editions of its product and suddenly faced competition from Microsoft, a company in a totally different industry: Microsoft's *Encarta* encyclopedia was a loss leader, given away free on CD-ROM with purchases of Windows software as part of a larger strategy to position personal computers as the primary educational invest-ment for middle-class families. As CD-ROMs gave way to the World Wide Web, Britannica faced competition from an explosion of online informa-tion sources, including *Nupedia* and later its exponentially growing, crowd-sourced successor, *Wikipedia.*

Britannica understood that customers' behaviors were changing dra-matically with the adoption of new technologies. Rather than trying to defend its old business model, the company's leaders sought to understand the needs of its core customers—home users and educational institutions, increasingly in the K–12 market. Britannica experimented with various delivery media, price points, and sales channels for its products. But, sig-nificantly, it maintained a focus on its core mission: editorial quality and educational service. With this focus, it was able not only to pivot to a purely online subscription model for its encyclopedia but also to develop new and related product offerings to meet the evolving needs for classroom cur-ricula and learning.

"By the time we stopped publishing the print set, the sales represented only about 1% of our business," explained Britannica President Jorge Cauz on the anniversary of that decision. "We're as profitable now as we've ever been."[1]

The story of Britannica may seem surprising precisely because the setup is so familiar: powerful new digital technologies drive dramatic changes in customer behavior. Once started, the digitization of a product, interaction, or medium becomes irresistible. The old business model is invalidated. Inflexible and unable to adapt, the "dinosaur" business gets wiped out. The future belongs to the new digital pioneers and start-ups.

But that's not what happened with Britannica, and that's not how it has to be for your business.

There is absolutely no reason upstart digital companies have to sup-plant established firms. There is no reason new businesses have to be the only engines of innovation. Established companies, like Britannica, can set the pace. The problem is that—in many cases—management sim-ply doesn't have a playbook to follow to understand and then address the competitive challenges of digitization. This book is that playbook, intended to help you understand, strategize for, and compete on the digi-tal playing field.

Overcoming Your Digital Blind Spots

An analogy may be helpful here. Back during the first wave of the Industrial Revolution, factories were dependent on fixed sources of power—first, water power from waterwheels located along rivers and, later, steam power from coal-fired engines. Although these power sources enabled the rise of mass production, they set fundamental constraints as well. At the outset, they dictated where plants could be located and how productive they could be. Furthermore, because both waterwheels and steam engines demanded that all equipment in a factory be attached to a central drive shaft—a single long motor that powered every machine—these power sources dictated the design of factories and the way work could be done within them.

With the spread of electrification to factories at the end of the nineteenth century, all of this changed. Electrical power eliminated all the constraints that had defined factories up until that point. Machinery could be arranged in the optimal order of work. Lines of production could feed into each other, like tributaries to a river, rather than all fitting in along one line shaft. Factory size was no longer limited by the maximum length of line shafts and belts. The possibilities for entirely new plant designs were breathtaking. And yet the incumbent plant owners were largely blind to these opportunities. They were so used to the assumptions and constraints of hundreds of years of plant design that they simply could not see the possibilities before them.

It fell to the new electrical utilities, the "start-ups" of the electrification era, to evangelize for innovation in manufacturing. These new firms loaned electric motors for free to manufacturers just to get them to try the new technology. They sent trainers and engineers, also for free, to train the managers and workers at plants so that they could see how electric motors could transform their business. Progress was slow at first, but it turned out the utilities could teach some old dogs new tricks. By the 1920s, a new ecosystem of factories, workers, engineers, products, and businesses had taken shape, with electrical power at its center.[2]

Today, our digital-born businesses (such as Google or Amazon) are like the electrical companies of the early electrification era. And our savvy digital adopters (such as Britannica) are like the factories that learned to retool and advance into the next industrial age. Both types of businesses recognize the possibilities created by digital technologies. Both see that the constraints of the pre-digital era have vanished, making new business models, new revenue streams, and new sources of competitive advantage not only possible but also cheaper, faster, and more customer-centric than ever before.

Let's take a closer look at that world.

Five Domains of Strategy That Digital Is Changing

If electrification was transformative because it changed the fundamental constraints of manufacturing, then the impact of digital is even bigger because it changes the constraints under which practically every domain of business strategy operates.

Digital technologies change how we connect and create value with our customers. We may have grown up in a world in which companies broadcast messages and shipped products to customers. But today the relationship is much more two-way: customers' communications and reviews make them a bigger influencer than advertisements or celebrities, and customers' dynamic participation has become a critical driver of business success.

Digital technologies transform how we need to think about competition. More and more, we are competing not just with rival companies from within our industry but also with companies from outside our industry that are stealing customers away with their new digital offerings. We may find ourselves competing fiercely with a long-standing rival in one area while leveraging that company's capabilities by cooperating in another sector of our business. Increasingly, our competitive assets may no longer reside in our own organization; rather, they may be in a network of partners that we bring together in looser business relationships.

Digital technologies have changed our world perhaps most significantly in how we think about data. In traditional businesses, data was expensive to obtain, difficult to store, and utilized in organizational silos. Just managing this data required that massive IT systems be purchased and maintained (think of the enterprise resource planning systems required just to track inventory from a factory in Thailand to goods sold at a mall in Kansas City). Today, data is being generated at an unprecedented rate—not just by companies but by everyone. Moreover, cloud-based systems for storing data are increasingly cheap, readily available, and easy to use. The biggest challenge today is turning the enormous amount of data we have into valuable information.

Digital technologies are also transforming the ways that businesses innovate. Traditionally, innovation was expensive, high stakes, and insular. Testing new ideas was difficult and costly, so businesses relied on their managers to guess what to build into a product before launching it in the market. Today, digital technologies enable continuous testing and experimentation, processes that were inconceivable in the past. Prototypes can be built for pennies and ideas tested quickly with user communities. Constant learning and the rapid iteration of products, before and after their launch date, are becoming the norm.

Finally, digital technologies force us to think differently about how we understand and create value for the customer. What customers value can change very quickly, and our competitors are constantly uncovering new opportunities that our customers may value. All too often, when a business hits upon success in the marketplace, a dangerous complacency sets in. As Andy Grove warned years ago, in the digital age, "only the paranoid survive." Constantly pushing the envelope to find our next source of customer value is now an imperative.

Taken together, we can see how digital forces are reshaping five key domains of strategy: customers, competition, data, innovation, and value (see figure 1.1). These five domains describe the landscape of digital transformation for business today. (For a simple mnemonic, you can remember the five domains as CC-DIV, pronounced "see-see-div.")

Across these five domains, digital technologies are redefining many of the underlying principles of strategy and changing the rules by which

Figure 1.1
Five Domains of Digital Transformation.

companies must operate in order to succeed. Many old constraints have been lifted, and new possibilities are now available. Companies that were established before the Internet need to realize that many of their fundamental assumptions must now be updated. Table 1.1 sets out the changes in these strategic assumptions as businesses move from the analog to the digital age.

Let's dig a bit more deeply into how digital technologies are challenging the strategic assumptions in each of these domains.

Customers

The first domain of digital transformation is customers. In traditional theory, customers were seen as aggregate actors to be marketed to and persuaded to buy. The prevailing model of mass markets focused on achieving efficiencies of scale through mass production (make one product to serve as many customers as possible) and mass communication (use a consistent message and medium to reach and persuade as many customers as possible at the same time).

In the digital age, we are moving to a world best described not by mass markets but by customer networks. In this paradigm, customers are dynamically connected and interacting in ways that are changing their relationships to business and to each other. Customers today are constantly connecting with and influencing each other and shaping business reputations and brands. Their use of digital tools is changing how they discover, evaluate, purchase, and use products and how they share, interact, and stay connected with brands.

This is forcing businesses to rethink their traditional marketing funnel and reexamine their customers' path to purchase, which may skip from using social networks, search engines, mobile screens, or laptops, to walking into a store, to asking for customer service in a live online chat. Rather than seeing customers only as targets for selling, businesses need to recognize that a dynamic, networked customer may just be the best focus group, brand champion, or innovation partner they will ever find.

Competition

The second domain of digital transformation is competition: how businesses compete and cooperate with other firms. Traditionally, competition

Table 1.1

Changes in Strategic Assumptions from the Analog to the Digital Age

	From	To
Customers (chapter 2)	Customers as mass market	Customers as dynamic network
	Communications are broadcast to customers	Communications are two-way
	Firm is the key influencer	Customers are the key influencer
	Marketing to persuade purchase	Marketing to inspire purchase, loyalty, advocacy
	One-way value flows	Reciprocal value flows
	Economies of (firm) scale	Economies of (customer) value
Competition (chapter 3)	Competition within defined industries	Competition across fluid industries
	Clear distinctions between partners and rivals	Blurred distinctions between partners and rivals
	Competition is a zero-sum game	Competitors cooperate in key areas
	Key assets are held inside the firm	Key assets reside in outside networks
	Products with unique features and benefits	Platforms with partners who exchange value
	A few dominant competitors per category	Winner-takes-all due to network effects
Data (chapter 4)	Data is expensive to generate in firm	Data is continuously generated everywhere
	Challenge of data is storing and managing it	Challenge of data is turning it into valuable information
	Firms make use only of structured data	Unstructured data is increasingly usable and valuable
	Data is managed in operational silos	Value of data is in connecting it across silos
	Data is a tool for optimizing processes	Data is a key intangible asset for value creation
Innovation (chapter 5)	Decisions made based on intuition and seniority	Decisions made based on testing and validating
	Testing ideas is expensive, slow, and difficult	Testing ideas is cheap, fast, and easy
	Experiments conducted infrequently, by experts	Experiments conducted constantly, by everyone
	Challenge of innovation is to find the right solution	Challenge of innovation is to solve the right problem
	Failure is avoided at all cost	Failures are learned from, early and cheaply
	Focus is on the "finished" product	Focus is on minimum viable prototypes and iteration after launch
Value (chapter 6)	Value proposition defined by industry	Value proposition defined by changing customer needs
	Execute your current value proposition	Uncover the next opportunity for customer value
	Optimize your business model as long as possible	Evolve before you must, to stay ahead of the curve
	Judge change by how it impacts your current business	Judge change by how it could create your next business
	Market success allows for complacency	"Only the paranoid survive"

and cooperation were seen as binary opposites: businesses competed with rival businesses that looked very much like themselves, and they cooperated with supply chain partners who distributed their goods or provided needed inputs for their production.

Today, we are moving to a world of fluid industry boundaries, one where our biggest challengers may be asymmetric competitors—companies from outside our industry that look nothing like us but that offer competing value to our customers. Digital "disintermediation" is upending partnerships and supply chains—our longtime business partner may become our biggest competitor if that partner starts serving our customers directly.

At the same time, we may need to cooperate with a direct rival due to interdependent business models or mutual challenges from outside our industry. Most importantly, digital technologies are supercharging the power of platform business models, which allow one business to create and capture enormous value by facilitating the interactions between other businesses or customers.

The net result of these changes is a major shift in the locus of competition. Rather than a zero-sum battle between similar rivals, competition is increasingly a jockeying for influence between firms with very different business models, each seeking to gain more leverage in serving the ultimate consumer.

Data

The next domain of digital transformation is data: how businesses produce, manage, and utilize information. Traditionally, data was produced through a variety of planned measurements (from customer surveys to inventories) that were conducted within a business's own processes—manufacturing, operations, sales, marketing. The resulting data was used mainly for evaluating, forecasting, and decision making.

By contrast, today we are faced with a data deluge. Most data available to businesses is not generated through any systematic planning like a market survey; instead, it is being generated in unprecedented quantities from every conversation, interaction, or process inside or outside these businesses. With social media, mobile devices, and sensors on every object in a company's supply chain, every business now has access to a river of unstructured data that is generated without planning and that can increasingly be utilized with new analytical tools.

These "big data" tools allow firms to make new kinds of predictions, uncover unexpected patterns in business activity, and unlock new sources of value. Rather than being confined to the province of specific business intelligence units, data is becoming the lifeblood of every department and a strategic asset to be developed and deployed over time. Data is a vital part of how every business operates, differentiates itself in the market, and generates new value.

Innovation

The fourth domain of digital transformation is innovation: the process by which new ideas are developed, tested, and brought to the market by businesses. Traditionally, innovation was managed with a singular focus on the finished product. Because market testing was difficult and costly, most decisions on new innovations were based on the analysis and intuition of managers. The cost of failure was high, so avoiding failure was paramount.

Today's start-ups have shown us that digital technologies can enable a very different approach to innovation, one based on continuous learning through rapid experimentation. As digital technologies make it easier and faster than ever to test ideas, we can gain market feedback from the very beginning of our innovation process, all the way through to launch, and even afterward.

This new approach to innovation is focused on careful experiments and on minimum viable prototypes that maximize learning while minimizing cost. Assumptions are repeatedly tested, and design decisions are made based on validation by real customers. In this approach, products are developed iteratively through a process that saves time, reduces the cost of failures, and improves organizational learning.

Value

The final domain of digital transformation is the value a business delivers to its customers—its value proposition. Traditionally, a firm's value proposition was seen as fairly constant. Products may be updated, marketing campaigns refreshed, or operations improved, but the basic value a business offered to its customers was assumed to be constant and defined by its industry (e.g., car companies offer transportation, safety, comfort, and status, in varying degrees). A successful business was one that had a clear value proposition, found a point of market differentiation (e.g., price or branding), and focused on executing and delivering the best version of the same value proposition to its customers year after year.

In the digital age, relying on an unchanging value proposition is inviting challenge and eventual disruption by new competitors. Although industries will vary as to the exact timing and nature of their transformation by new technologies, those who assume it will be a little farther down the road are most likely to be run over. The only sure response to a shifting business environment is to take a path of constant evolution, looking to every technology as a way to extend and improve our value proposition to our customers. Rather than waiting to adapt when change becomes a matter of life or death, businesses need to focus on seizing emerging opportunities, divesting from declining sources of advantage, and adapting early to stay ahead of the curve of change.

A Playbook for Digital Transformation

Faced with transformation in each of these five domains, businesses today clearly need new frameworks for formulating their own strategies to successfully adapt and grow in the digital age.

Each of the domains has a core strategic theme that can provide you with a point of departure for your digital strategy. Like the engineers who trained the traditional factory managers, these five themes can guide you, revealing how the constraints of your traditional strategy are changing and how opportunities are opening up to build your business in new ways. I call this set of strategic themes the digital transformation playbook.

Figure 1.2 depicts this playbook on one page, along with many of the key concepts we will explore in this book as we examine each theme in detail. In doing so, it illustrates how the building blocks of your playbook for digital transformation fit together. Let's look at each of the five themes to understand them a bit better.

Domains	Strategic themes	Key concepts
Customers	Harness customer networks	• reinvented marketing funnel • path to purchase • core behaviors of customer networks
Competition	Build platforms, not just products	• platform business models • (in)direct network effects • (dis)intermediation • competitive value trains
Data	Turn data into assets	• templates of data value • drivers of big data • data-driven decision making
Innovation	Innovate by rapid experimentation	• divergent experimentation • convergent experimentation • minimum viable prototype • paths to scaling up
Value	Adapt your value proposition	• concepts of market value • paths out of a declining market • steps to value prop evolution

Figure 1.2
The Digital Transformation Playbook.

Harness Customer Networks

As customers behave less like isolated individuals and more like tightly connected networks, every business must learn to harness the power and potential of those customer networks. That means learning to engage, empower, and co-create with customers beyond the point of initial purchase. It means leveraging the ways that happy customers influence others and drive new business opportunities.

Harnessing customer networks may involve collaborating with customers directly, like the fans of Doritos snack chips who create its award-winning advertisements or the drivers using Waze who provide the input that powers its unique mapping system. It may involve learning to think like a media company, like cosmetics giant L'Oréal or industrial glassmaker Corning, both of whose content has been spread far and wide by networked customers. Other organizations, like Life Church and Walmart, are connecting with customers by finding the right moment in their digital lives for the value each organization is offering. Long-established companies, from Coca-Cola to Maersk Line, are sparking social media conversations with internal and external customers in industries as diverse as soft drinks and container shipping services.

Today, creating an effective customer strategy requires that you understand such key concepts as customers as strategic assets, the reinvented marketing funnel, the digital path to purchase, and the five core behaviors of customer networks (accessing, engaging, customizing, connecting, and collaborating).

Build Platforms, Not Just Products

To master competition in the digital age, businesses must learn to cope with asymmetric challengers who are reshuffling the roles of competition and cooperation in every industry. They must also understand the increasing importance of strategies to build platforms, not just products.

Building effective platform business models may involve becoming a trusted intermediary who brings together competing businesses, as Wink brought together Philips, Honeywell, Lutron, and Schlage. It may require opening up a proprietary product for other companies to build on, like Nike did with its wearable fitness devices and Apple did with its iPhone. Or, as in the case of Uber and Airbnb, it may mean building a business whose value is created largely by its partners, with its platform acting as the critical connection point. Sometimes it may mean combining the best elements of both traditional and platform business models, as Best Buy and Amazon have each done. Firms may have to establish new partnerships to leverage platforms for distribution, as The New York Times Company has done with Facebook. Other firms may have to learn to renegotiate their relationships with channel partners they have long relied on, as HBO and Allstate Insurance have done. Still other firms may have to learn when and where to cooperate with their fiercest competitors, as Samsung does with Apple.

Developing a digital-age competitive strategy requires that you understand these principles: platform business models, direct and indirect network effects, co-opetition between firms, the dynamics of intermediation and disintermediation, and competitive value trains.

Turn Data Into Assets

In an age when data is in constant surplus and often free, the imperative for businesses is to learn to turn it into a truly strategic asset. That requires both assembling the right data and applying it effectively to generate long-term business value.

Building a strong data asset may begin with effectively collaborating with data partners, as Caterpillar does with its sales distributors and The Weather Company does with its most avid customers. A data asset may yield value in the form of new market insights: the unstructured conversations of car customers revealed the trajectory of Cadillac's brand; social media showed Gaylord Hotels what motivated customer recommendations. Data can add value by helping to identify which customers require the most attention, as it did for priority guests of Intercontinental Hotels and for high-needs patients served by the Camden Coalition of Healthcare Providers. In other cases, data can be used to help businesses personalize their communications to customers, whether it is Kimberly-Clark talking to the right family about the right product or British Airlines identifying its most valued business class fliers even when they are riding in coach class with their families. Sometimes the value of data can be found in identifying contextual patterns, as when Opower shows utility customers their electricity usage or when Naviance helps high school students understand their odds for admission as they apply to different colleges.

To create good data strategy, you must begin with an understanding of the four templates of data value creation, the new sources and analytic capabilities of big data, the role of causality in data-driven decision making, and the risks around data security and privacy.

Innovate by Rapid Experimentation

Because digital technologies make it so fast, easy, and inexpensive to test ideas, firms today need to master the art of rapid experimentation. This requires a radically different approach to innovation that is based on validating new ideas through rapid and iterative learning.

Rapid experimentation can involve continuous A/B and multivariate testing, like the tests Capital One uses to refine its marketing and the ones Amazon and Google use to refine their online services. Other experiments may use minimum viable prototypes to explore new products: Intuit tested the concept for a mobile finance app with a manager holding reams of paper and a dumb phone. Experiments should involve rigorous testing of an innovation's assumptions as Rent The Runway did before launching its online fashion service and JCPenney failed to do before launching its catastrophic store redesign. Once an idea has been validated through experiment, it requires careful piloting and rollout, as Starbucks has done with its new store features and Settlement Music House did with its community music programs. And any business that commits to rapid experimentation must learn to encourage smart failures within its organization, as Tata has done with its Dare to Try initiative.

Innovating in the digital age requires that you have a firm understanding of both convergent experiments (with valid samples, test groups, and controls) and divergent experiments (designed for open-ended inquiry). To bring the results to market, you need to understand both minimum viable prototypes and products and master the four paths to scaling up an innovation.

Adapt Your Value Proposition

To master value creation in the digital age, businesses must learn how to continuously adapt their value proposition. That means they need to learn to focus beyond their current business model and zero in on how they can best deliver value to their customers as new technologies reshape opportunities and needs.

Continuous reconfiguration of a business may involve discovering new customers and applications for its current products, as when Mohawk Fine Papers found new digital uses for its products and the publisher of *The Deseret News* discovered new online audiences for its content beyond its traditional local market. It may mean evolving a business's offering while its old business model is under severe threat: Encyclopædia Britannica, Inc., has reenvisioned itself as an educational resource; The New York Times Company has reimagined what it means to be a news source. Adaptation may mean aggressively developing a new suite of products in anticipation of rapid customer changes, as Facebook did during its pivot to mobile platforms. Or it may mean experimenting with new ways to engage a business's customers while they are still loyal to it, as the Metropolitan Museum of Art has done, building an array of digital touchpoints to deepen the cultural experiences of patrons near and far.

To proactively adapt your value proposition, you need to understand these elements: the different key concepts of market value, the three possible paths out of a declining market position, and the essential steps to take to effectively analyze your existing value proposition, identify its emerging threats and opportunities, and synthesize an effective next step in its evolution.

Getting Started on Your Own Digital Transformation

Where do you get started on digital transformation if you are an established firm?

Many books on digital innovation and strategy focus heavily on start-ups. But the challenges of launching a blank-slate, digital-first business are quite different from those of adapting an established firm that already has infrastructure, sales channels, employees, and an organizational culture to contend with.

In my own experience—advising executives at centuries-old multinational firms as well as today's digital titans and brand-new seed-funded start-ups—I have seen that these leaders face very different challenges. The same strategic principles—of customers, competition, data, innovation, and value—apply. But the path to *implementing* these principles is different, depending on the point from which one starts. That is why this book focuses primarily on enterprises that were established before the birth of the Internet and looks at how they are successfully transforming themselves to operate by the principles of the digital age.

The book includes case examples from dozens of companies to illustrate how each of the strategies discussed plays out in a variety of industries and contexts. We will examine a few relevant examples from digital titans (like Amazon, Apple, and Google) and from digital rising stars (like Airbnb, Uber, and Warby Parker). But mostly we will look at existing enterprises founded before the Internet and learn how they are adapting. These companies vary in size and come from a diverse range of industries: automotive and apparel, beauty and books, education and entertainment, finance and fashion, health care and hospitality, movies and manufacturing, and real estate, retail, and religion, among others.

In addition to frameworks, analysis, and numerous cases, the book includes a set of nine strategic planning tools:

9 TOOLS FOR DIGITAL TRANSFORMATION

- Customer Network Strategy Generator (chapter 2)
- Platform Business Model Map (chapter 3)
- Competitive Value Train (chapter 3)
- Data Value Generator (chapter 4)
- Convergent Experimental Method (chapter 5)

- Divergent Experimental Method (chapter 5)
- Value Proposition Roadmap (chapter 6)
- Disruptive Business Model Map (chapter 7)
- Disruptive Response Planner (chapter 7)

These tools can be categorized as follows:

- *Strategic ideation tools*: Tools for generating a new solution to a defined challenge by exploring different facets of a strategic phenomenon (Customer Network Strategy Generator, Data Value Generator)
- *Strategy maps*: Visual tools that can be used to analyze an existing business model or strategy or to assess and explore a new one (Platform Business Model Map, Competitive Value Train, Disruptive Business Model Map)
- *Strategic decision tools*: Tools with criteria for evaluating and deciding among a set of generic options available for a key strategic decision (Disruptive Response Planner)
- *Strategic planning tools*: Step-by-step planning processes or methods that can be used to develop a strategic plan tailored to a specific business context or challenge (Convergent Experimental Method, Divergent Experimental Method, Value Proposition Roadmap)

These tools have been developed based on feedback from strategy workshops that I have conducted with hundreds of companies around the world. They are practical tools meant to help you directly apply the concepts in this book to your own work, whatever your industry or business.

Each tool is presented briefly in the text of the book, tied to analysis and cases that show how and where it may be useful. A more detailed explanation of some tools, with step-by-step guidance for applying them to your business, can be found in the Tools section of my website at http://www.davidrogers.biz.

Of course, you will need to do more than just adopt the right strategic thinking, planning frameworks, and tools for action. Pursuing digital transformation in an established company will also force you to grapple with important issues of organizational change.

Throughout the book, I have ended each chapter with a section that discusses these organizational issues and hurdles. That's because digital transformation is not just about having the right strategy; it's also about making that strategy happen. My discussion involves questions of leadership; company culture; changes to internal structures, processes, or skills; and changes to external relationships. I draw on the perspectives of specific business leaders who have grappled with these issues. The right approach for you depends on the history and character of your organization. My aim is mostly to shed light on some of the trickier hurdles that may impede change because experience shows that digital transformation doesn't simply proceed on its own momentum, even if the company has decided on the right strategy.

A Guide to the Rest of This Book

The next five chapters in the book are designed to focus your team on how digital technologies are changing the traditional rules in each of the strategy domains that I've introduced here. The chapters also show your team what to do about these changes. You will learn how to apply each of the core strategic themes and see examples of all kinds of businesses that are using them to rethink their orientation in the digital age. As we saw with Encyclopædia Britannica and will see in many other cases, the future is not about new start-ups burying long-established enterprises. It's about new growth strategies and business models replacing old ones as established companies learn new ways of operating.

However, even if you embrace all these strategies and tools, there are no crystal balls in business. You could still find your business model under sudden threat due to an unforeseen and unexpected new challenger: disruption!

The last chapter of the book examines disruption—an oft-discussed but not always well understood phenomenon—and how it unfolds in the digital age. The chapter provides a tool to gauge whether or not an emerging challenger really is a disruptive threat to your business. It also includes a tool to assess your options if you are faced with a truly disruptive challenger: Is it best to fight back or get out of the way? Mastering disruption requires some rethinking and updating of Clayton Christensen's classic theory on this subject. Accordingly, we will examine a revised theory that reflects some key changes to disruption in the digital age. And we will see how disruption is rooted in the five domains of digital transformation that we will examine throughout the book.

The book's conclusion reflects on the remaining hurdles organizations must clear to truly adopt the new strategic thinking at the heart of the digital transformation playbook. Sadly, not every business follows Britannica's example. For every Britannica, there is a Kodak or a Blockbuster—a business that failed to recognize that the rules of the game had changed and that did not manage to change its strategy to match digital reality. Here we will examine why and how some institutions have failed to keep up. Finally, the book provides a self-assessment tool with questions to help you judge the readiness of your own business for digital transformation.

We live in what is commonly referred to as a digital age. An overlapping ecosystem of digital technologies—each one building on those before and catalyzing those to come—is transforming not only our personal and communal lives but also the dynamics of business for organizations of every size in every industry.

Digital technologies are transforming not just one aspect of business management but virtually every aspect. They are rewriting the rules of customers, competition, data, innovation, and value. Responding to these changes requires more than a piecemeal approach; it calls for a total integrated effort—a process of holistic digital transformation within the firm. Fortunately, this process is clearly achievable. We are surrounded now by examples of businesses whose own lessons, learned as they adapted to their own very particular challenges, shed light on the universal principles that apply to businesses in general. By mastering these lessons—and by learning to apply this digital transformation playbook—any business can adapt and grow in the digital age.

2

Harness Customer Networks

CUSTOMERS

When he joined Life Church in Oklahoma as a pastor, Bobby Gruenewald was only two years out of college, but he had already built and sold two Web-based businesses, including an online community for fans of professional wrestling. At Life Church, he focused on a community of a different kind. He was brought on as Innovation Leader to help the three-year-old evangelical church find new ways to reach a contemporary audience and engage them in Christianity.

Many churches today use podcasts or streaming broadcasts of their weekly sermons to reach parishioners on their commute, at home, or wherever they can listen. Life Church has gone much further, building a "digital mission" that includes on-demand and live-streaming video services at LifeChurch.tv and a platform of technology tools for other churches to use as well. During the heyday of the Second Life online community, Gruenewald built a virtual church to reach believers in their 3D avatar forms. He has bought Google ads to reach people searching for pornography and steer them to a church experience instead. As he tweeted, "We'll do anything short of sin 2reach ppl who don't know Christ. 2reach ppl no one is reaching we'll do things no one is doing."[1]

Gruenewald's biggest impact, though, may be in creating YouVersion, the world's most popular Bible app for smartphones. With more than 168 million downloads, the app rivals some of the biggest mobile games and social networks. YouVersion allows users to read the Bible in over 700 languages, from Eastern Arctic Inukitut to Hawaiian English Creole; it is the only mobile app in the world that includes such obscure languages as Bolivian Guarani. Within a given language, there are numerous translations, including 30 versions in English—from the King James Bible, to the New International, to the ultramodern "The Message." Readers can pick and choose a translation, search for any passage or phrase, and highlight, bookmark, and share what they are reading with others. Readers share more than a hundred thousand verses a day, directly from the app. User Jen Sears, a human resources manager in Oklahoma City, says that when she wants to pray, she now reaches for her mobile phone. Since she installed YouVersion, she says, "I have my print Bible sitting on my dresser at home, but it hasn't moved."[2]

Every Sunday, screens are aglow in the hands of parishioners at nearly 2,000 churches that use YouVersion to conduct their services. As ministers preach, LifeChurch.tv's servers track 600,000 requests per minute and register which verses are most popular in different communities. That helps Life Church choose the daily Bible verse that is sent out to all 168 million users of the app. Other preachers, from megachurch founder Rick Warren to Reverend Billy Graham, use YouVersion to distribute their own custom reading plans to followers anywhere around the world. Geoff Dennis, one of the publishers whose translation appears on YouVersion, says, "They have defined what it means to access God's word on a mobile device."[3]

Rethinking Customers

On-demand, customizable, connected, shareable—the same qualities that LifeChurch.tv offers to engage its digital-age parishioners are what customers seek from every business today.

As we begin to build our playbook for digital transformation, the first domain of strategy that we need to rethink is customers. Customers have always been essential to every business as the buyers of goods and services. In order to grow, companies have targeted them with mass-marketing tools designed to reach, inform, motivate, and persuade them to buy. But in the

Table 2.1
Customers: Changes in Strategic Assumptions from the Analog to the Digital Age

From	To
Customers as mass market	Customers as dynamic network
Communications are broadcast to customers	Communications are two-way
Firm is the key influencer	Customers are the key influencer
Marketing to persuade purchase	Marketing to inspire purchase, loyalty, advocacy
One-way value flows	Reciprocal value flows
Economies of (firm) scale	Economies of (customer) value

digital age, the relationship of customers to businesses is changing dramatically (see table 2.1).

Another industry where this changed relationship is crystal clear is the music business. Not long ago, the only role of the customer was to buy a copy of the latest product (a CD or an LP). To sell their products, record labels relied on a few mass channels for promotion (radio airplay, MTV) and distribution (chain record stores, Walmart). Today, customers expect to listen to any song at any time, streaming from a variety of services on a variety of devices. They discover music through search engines, social media, and the recommendations of both friends and algorithms. Musicians may skip the record label and go directly to the customers themselves. They ask customers to help fundraise for an album before it is even recorded, to share it on their playlists, and to connect their favorite bands to peers in their social networks.

Customers in the digital age are not passive consumers but nodes within dynamic networks—interacting and shaping brands, markets, and each other. Businesses need to recognize this new reality and treat customers accordingly. They need to understand how customer networks are redefining the marketing funnel, reshaping customers' path to purchase, and opening up new ways to co-create value with customers. Businesses need to understand the five core behaviors—access, engage, customize, connect, and collaborate—that drive customers in their digital experiences and interactions. And they need to leverage these behaviors to invent new communications, products, or experiences that add value to both sides of the business-customer relationship.

This chapter explores how and why the relationship to customers is changing in every industry and what the challenges are for enterprises that developed in the mass-media era. It presents a framework for understanding customers' networked behaviors and motivations. And it introduces the Customer Network Strategy Generator, an ideation tool for developing breakthrough strategies to engage your networked customers and achieve specific business objectives.

Let's start by looking more closely at how and why the relationship of customers to businesses is changing so fundamentally.

The Customer Network Paradigm

Today, customers' behavior—how they find, access, use, share, and influence the products, services, and brands in their lives—is radically different than in the era in which modern business practices arose.

In the twentieth century, businesses of all kinds were built on a mass-market model (see figure 2.1). In this paradigm, customers are passive and are considered in aggregate. Their only significant role is to either purchase or not purchase, and companies seek to identify the product or service that will suit the needs of as many potential customers as possible. Mass media and mass production are used to deliver and promote a company's offerings to as many customers as possible. Success in the mass-market model hinges on efficiencies of scale. And for decades, it worked! Throughout the twentieth century, this approach built the world's largest and most successful companies.

Today, however, we are in the midst of a profound shift toward a new paradigm that I call the customer network model (see figure 2.2).[4] In this model, the firm is still a central actor in the creation and promotion of goods and services. But the new roles of customers create a more complex

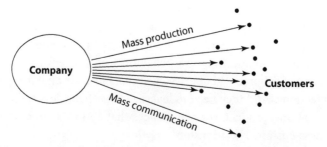

Figure 2.1
Mass-Market Model.

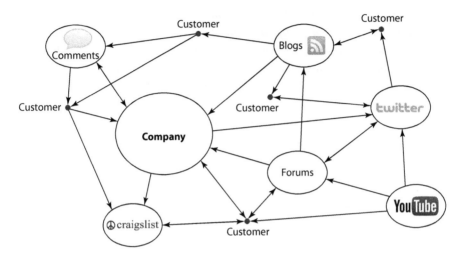

Figure 2.2
Customer Network Model.

relationship. No longer are they relegated to a binary role of "buy" or "do not buy." In the customer network model, current and potential customers have access to a wide variety of digital platforms that allow them to interact, publish, broadcast, and innovate—and thereby shape brands, reputations, and markets. Customers are just as likely to connect with and influence each other as they are to be influenced by the direct communications from a firm. Borrowing from the rich theories of network science (which date back to eighteenth-century mathematics and have been applied to model the spread of language and disease and the structures of railroads and nervous systems), we can see customers as nodes in a network, linked together digitally by various tools and platforms and interacting dynamically.

In a market defined by customer networks, the roles of companies are dramatically different as well. Yes, the firm is still the greatest single engine for innovation of products and services, and still the steward of its brand and reputation. But while delivering value outward to customers and communicating to them, the firm also needs to engage with its customer network. It needs to listen in, observe the customers' networked interactions, and understand their perceptions, responses, and unmet needs. It needs to identify and nurture those customers who may become brand champions, evangelists, marketing partners, or cocreators of value with the firm.

One of the main points in the model of customer networks is that a "customer" can be *any key constituency* that the organization serves and relies on. Customers may be end consumers purchasing a product or businesses purchasing professional services. For a nonprofit, they may be donors or grassroots volunteers. In many cases, it is important to look at a range of interconnected constituencies that are all within an organization's customer network: end consumers, business partners, investors, press, government regulators, even employees. All of these types of customers are critical to the business of a firm, and all of them now exhibit dynamic, networked behaviors in relating to the firm and to each other.

A Different Take on Brands

The broad shift in the balance of power between companies and networked customers is redefining brand relationships. A brand is no longer something that a business alone creates, defines, and projects outward; it is something that customers shape, too, and the business needs their help to fully create it. Many customers want to do more than just buy products and brands; they want to co-create them.

PepsiCo is one of many brand-focused traditional enterprises that has rethought the role of its customers in its brands. Brand communications used to come solely from the business, but now some of its best communications are created by the customers themselves. By eschewing professional ad agencies and inviting customers to compete to make the funniest thirty-second ads themselves, PepsiCo's Doritos brand has consistently won awards for the most liked, talked about, and effective ads during the Super Bowl. PepsiCo's Lay's brand of potato chips has even let customers help reinvent the product. Millions of them have nominated or voted on new potato chip flavors as part of the brand's Do Us A Flavor social media contests.

Brands taking this approach are responding to a broad shift in customer expectations. A global study of 15,000 consumers by Edelman, in 2014, found that most customers want more than a "transactional" relationship; they expect brands to "take a stand" on issues and invite consumer participation. When they see a brand reaching out to them, they are more willing to advocate for that brand, defend it from criticism, share personal information, and purchase from the brand.[5]

Clearly, a strong brand today is much more than a business's crisp logo and a powerful positioning statement; it is a shared creation, bolstered by customer networks.

The Marketing Funnel and the Path to Purchase

The marketing funnel (sometimes called the purchase funnel) is one framework for understanding how customer networks have such great impact on businesses' relationships to customers. This classic strategic model is based on "hierarchy of effects" psychological research dating to the 1920s.[6] It maps out the progression of a potential customer from awareness (knowledge that a product or company exists) to consideration (recognition of potential value) to preference (intent to purchase or choice of a preferred company) to action (purchase of a product, subscription to a service, voting for a political candidate, etc.). At each stage, the number of potential customers inevitably diminishes (more will be aware than consider, etc.)—hence the tapering shape of the funnel. In recent years, a further stage, loyalty, was added. It is almost always more efficient to invest in retaining customers than in attempting to acquire new ones.

The enduring utility of the marketing funnel stems from the fact that it is a *psychological* model, based on a progression of psychological states (awareness, etc.). As a result, the funnel can still be applied even as customer behaviors change dramatically—for example, due to the rise of customer networks.

In the mass-market era, businesses developed an array of "broadcast" marketing tools to reach and influence customers at different stages of the funnel (see figure 2.3). Television advertising, for example, is extremely effective at driving awareness, with some impact at later stages. Direct mail coupons and promotions help drive customers from choice of a brand (preference) to sale (action). Reward programs—offering incentives for everything from collecting a product's box tops to having a card punched at a local diner—help nudge customers from initial sale (action) to repeat business (loyalty).

Today, all of these broadcast tools are still in play, and each can be quite useful in a given instance. If a business needs to rapidly boost awareness of a new product across a very broad mass audience, television advertising is still the most powerful tool (although expensive). Out-of-home billboards, direct mail, newspaper advertising—all of these still have a potential role for reaching customers. But depending on whom you are trying to reach, you may find these broadcast tools becoming less effective over time (especially given the changing media habits of younger consumers) and therefore less cost effective. (The price per thousand viewers of a U.S. television

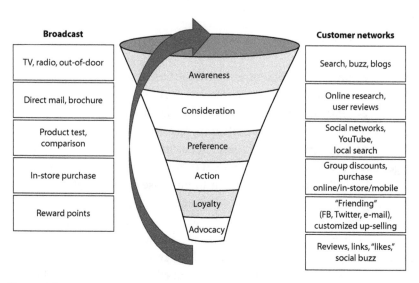

Broadcast

	Customer networks
TV, radio, out-of-door	Search, buzz, blogs
Direct mail, brochure	Online research, user reviews
Product test, comparison	Social networks, YouTube, local search
In-store purchase	Group discounts, purchase online/in-store/mobile
Reward points	"Friending" (FB, Twitter, e-mail), customized up-selling
	Reviews, links, "likes," social buzz

Funnel stages: Awareness, Consideration, Preference, Action, Loyalty, Advocacy

Figure 2.3
Rethinking the Marketing Funnel.

ad continues to rise each year, despite the increasing fragmentation of that audience outside of a few huge live events like the Super Bowl.)

At the same time, however, at each stage of the marketing funnel, today's customers are also influenced by customer networks (also shown in figure 2.3). Search engine results are now one of the biggest drivers of customer awareness for any new brand or business. Customer reviews, posted on sites such as Amazon or TripAdvisor, are hugely influential in the consideration stage as consumers evaluate different brands. These third-party reviews are influential even when customers are purchasing offline, in a physical store. With the Internet at their fingertips via smartphones, customers are engaging in online research for products that were once "impulse" buys—purchases driven solely by shelf placement and packaging. As customers progress to brand preference, they often turn to social networks like Facebook, asking if any friends have visited this vacation destination or purchased that brand of refrigerator. At the action stage, they may purchase from a retail business on its website, in its store, on a mobile device, or even on a mobile device while standing in its store. After purchase, companies now have many more ways—from e-mail marketing to social media—to maintain a relationship with these customers and drive them to loyalty.

Today's customer networks, however, make their biggest impact on the marketing funnel through an additional level, which I call advocacy. At this psychological stage, customers are not just loyal; they advocate for the brand and connect the brand to people in their network. These customers post photos of products on Instagram, write reviews on TripAdvisor, and answer friends' product questions on Twitter. Thanks to search engine algorithms, this type of customer expression is heavily weighted to influence search results. Each customer's advocacy thus feeds back up to the top of the funnel and has the potential to increase the magnitude of awareness, consideration, and so on through the funnel. (This extended, or looped, marketing funnel is sometimes renamed the customer journey, with new names invented for the same stages of the funnel, ending in advocacy. But the model is the same.)

Now every business needs to go beyond driving potential customers to the stages of purchase (action) and repeat purchase (loyalty). Businesses need also to engage, nurture, and inspire repeat customers to enter the stage of advocacy, where they will contribute to the growth of the business in the rest of its customer network.

At the same time that the funnel is influenced by customers' networked behaviors, their range of possible touchpoints with a company is increasing dramatically. In addition to advertisements, store shelves, and possibly a call center, today's customers may be consulting a search engine, the company's website, a mobile app, a local map search, a physical retailer, online retailers, peers on social media, the company's own social media accounts, instant chat, and customer review sites. Customers are increasingly proactive in taking advantage of all these resources. Customers who are standing in a store looking at a product display are likely to use a mobile device to check prices, additional product details, and customer reviews. They may also check shipping options if they don't want to carry the product home. And they may be instant messaging a quick snapshot to their friend or spouse before making a final decision on color or model. In a study at Columbia Business School on "Showrooming and the Rise of the Mobile-Assisted Shopper," we observed all these behaviors and more.[7]

These touchpoints open multiple paths to a purchase. To effectively market to customers, businesses must think about the specific needs that will lead customers to take one path to purchase versus another: How quickly do they need the product? How price sensitive are they? Do they already have a preferred brand? How close are they to physical retailers? And so on. Businesses can increase their influence by mapping and optimizing the customer experience on each path. They begin this process by developing an "omni-channel" view of the customer—based on an understanding that the same customer may be using a tablet app and a desktop computer and walking into a store. Designing each touchpoint experience

---

What Is a Customer Worth?

One of the most important questions any business must face today is, How much are my customers worth?

As customer interactions expand across more digital touchpoints, measuring the return of marketing investments requires new financial tools. Chief among them is a model of customer lifetime value—the profitability of each customer for your bottom line over the long term. For any business, some customers are more profitable than others, and some may even be costing you money. Customer lifetime value can be shaped by various factors: frequency of purchase, volume of purchase, price point, reliance on discounting, and loyalty or attrition rate. To build a model, you will need historical data and the involvement of your finance team. (To get started, you can read *Managing Customers as Investments* by Sunil Gupta and Don Lehmann.[8]) Once you have a customer lifetime value model, it is extremely helpful in segmenting your customers, defining objectives for new customer strategies, and measuring the impact of things like customer engagement and advocacy.

In a networked world, though, customers add value in more ways than just their transactions over time. Increasingly, new business models are being built where the customers' participation, data, and collective knowledge are a business asset and a key competitive advantage.

This more intangible value of customer networks can even be a factor in the financial valuation of firms. Customer participation is a key driver of stock price for social networks such as Facebook or LinkedIn. When Yahoo paid $1 billion for the popular blogging platform Tumblr, it was not for Tumblr's paltry revenue but for its large network of young, active, creative users. Of course, the challenge in acquiring a firm for its customer network is that continued customer loyalty is not assured. When Google purchased Waze for $1.1 billion, it was critical to maintain the participation of Waze's customer network to justify the full price of the acquisition. Google immediately announced that Waze would not be rolled into Google Maps but would be kept as a separate product run by the original Israeli team that started it. Customer networks are extremely valuable, but they are intangible assets that can't be swapped and leveraged as easily as real estate or factory equipment.

in isolation, as if it were for a different customer, dilutes and disrupts the brand experience. An omni-channel experience uses design to integrate the path to purchase as it moves from one touchpoint to the next.

Whereas the funnel is a macro tool for thinking very broadly about customers' psychological states, the path to purchase is a lens for looking at customer behaviors much more specifically. Both perspectives illustrate the necessity of understanding customer motivations and needs more deeply than ever. They also point to two striking new imperatives for every business: create compelling experiences at each step of the path to purchase, and drive customer advocacy at the end of the funnel so as to engage and co-create value with the most involved customers. These imperatives raise important questions: How do you engage customers in their networked world? What motivates them? What are they looking for?

Five Customer Network Behaviors

In the research for my book *The Network Is Your Customer*, I sought to answer this question: What kinds of digital offerings most deeply engage customers in their digital lives? I started by looking at hundreds of cases—across consumer and B2B industries—of the products, services, communications, and experiences that had been embraced and adopted by customers during the first two decades of the World Wide Web and the mobile Internet. What I found was a recurring pattern of five behaviors that drive the adoption of new digital experiences. I call these the five core behaviors of networked customers:

- *Access*: They seek to access digital data, content, and interactions as quickly, easily, and flexibly as possible. Any offering that enhances this access is incredibly compelling. Think of text messaging on early mobile phones, which revolutionized communications with the ability to receive and send messages from anywhere at any time. From the convenience of e-commerce to today's latest instant messaging apps, customers are drawn to anything that provides the immediacy of simple, instant access.
- *Engage*: They seek to engage with digital content that is sensory, interactive, and relevant to their needs. From the early popularity of Web portals, to the spread of online video, to next-generation virtual realities—their digital desires are marked by a thirst for content. The old media adage that "content is king" is at least half right. Although

content makers may struggle to earn profits in the digital era, there is no question that the desire to engage with content is a key driver of customer behavior.

- *Customize*: They seek to customize their experiences by choosing and modifying a wide assortment of information, products, and services. In a generation, customers have gone from having a handful of television channel options to a digital world with more than a trillion webpages. They have been trained by their digital networks to expect ever more options for personal choice, and they like this. From Pandora's personalized radio streams to Google's search bar that anticipates their search terms when they type just a few characters, they are drawn to increasingly customized experiences.
- *Connect*: They seek to connect with one another by sharing their experiences, ideas, and opinions through text, images, and social links. This behavior has driven the entire explosion of social media—from blogging, to social networks like Facebook or LinkedIn, to online niche communities that gather around a shared passion, vocation, or viewpoint. All of these incredibly popular platforms are driven by the behavior of individuals using small bits of text and images to signal to others that "here is where I am, what I'm thinking, what I see."
- *Collaborate*: As social animals, they are naturally drawn to work together. Accordingly, they seek to collaborate on projects and goals through open platforms. This is the most complex and difficult of these five behaviors, but it doesn't stop them from trying. Whether building open-source software together, raising money for causes they believe in, or organizing write-ins and protests around the world, they seek collaboration.

As illustrated in figure 2.4, these customer behaviors can be leveraged strategically through a set of corresponding customer network strategies. These can be used for strategic planning for any industry, business model, or customer objective. I have used them in executive strategy workshops with hundreds of companies facing widely varying customer challenges. By starting with a strategy rooted in customer behavior, businesses can avoid the trap of technology-first thinking (What's our Twitter video strategy?) and focus instead on value to the customer and the business.

Let's take a look at each of the five strategies in depth, with examples. Then I will present a tool that you can use to choose which customer network strategy is best for a given business scenario.

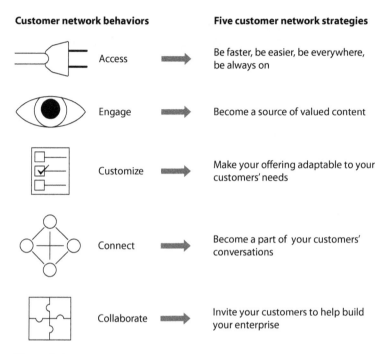

Customer network behaviors		Five customer network strategies
Access	⟹	Be faster, be easier, be everywhere, be always on
Engage	⟹	Become a source of valued content
Customize	⟹	Make your offering adaptable to your customers' needs
Connect	⟹	Become a part of your customers' conversations
Collaborate	⟹	Invite your customers to help build your enterprise

Figure 2.4
Five Customer Network Behaviors and Customer Network Strategies.

Access Strategy

The access strategy for business is to be faster, be easier, be everywhere, and be always on for your customers. We know that standards of speed, ease, and ubiquity may shift over time: where an access strategy might have once meant offering e-commerce for the first time, today it might mean providing a mobile-optimized website, more rapid delivery, or order tracking. My research on mobile showrooming with Matt Quint and Rick Ferguson found that the same customers may, at different times, choose to buy a product online or in a store (even choosing the more expensive option), depending on which method gives them greater convenience. And that convenience depends on context: Am I buying something I want to use right now? Is it something heavy that is easier to have shipped to my home? Can I afford to wait a day or two for delivery?[9] The use of cloud computing, mobile devices, and location-based geo-targeting has brought a wave of new innovations that grant greater access to consumers and business customers alike.

An access strategy may therefore take a variety of approaches, including mobile commerce, omni-channel experiences, working in the cloud, and on-demand service.

- *Mobile commerce*: Travelers are already accustomed to using QR codes on their phone screens as tickets to board planes and trains. Hotel chains like Starwood are developing room doors that guests can unlock with a swipe of their smartphone. Tesco launched its stores in South Korea by putting up posters of popular grocery items on subway platforms and allowing customers to order home delivery right from their phone just by scanning the item they wanted (milk, biscuits, 32 oz. Snapple). With mobile payment systems and in-store targeting, customers can receive discounts, redeem coupons, purchase, and recommend, all from their small screen.

- *Omni-channel experiences*: Increasingly, businesses are recognizing that customers are looking for an integrated experience across all digital and physical touchpoints. Walmart, for example, has developed a mobile shopping app with different features designed for when customers are in a Walmart store versus using the same app at home. An additional feature auto-detects when a customer opens the app while in one of its four thousand North American stores, to provide the right version. After implementing this enhanced mobile app, Walmart found that 12 percent of its online sales came from customers who purchased from Walmart.com while in the store aisle.

- *Working in the cloud*: With the shift from downloaded MP3s on iTunes to streaming music services like Spotify, consumers are quickly becoming accustomed to paying for products that reside entirely in the cloud. Likewise, businesses are shifting more and more of their work processes to the cloud with software-as-a-service (SaaS) providers like Google Apps, Salesforce, Dropbox, and Evernote. The result is much lower IT costs for businesses and greater flexibility for an increasingly mobile and collaborative workforce.

- *On-demand services*: Increasingly, services that used to require the customer to be in a specific location at a specific time are now accessible to customers anywhere at any time. Retail banks that used to advertise the number of local ATMs they had are now touting all the banking services customers can manage via their phone (including scanning a paper check to deposit it). Start-ups like the Khan Academy, Coursera, and EdX are pushing the limits of on-demand education. Health care is just beginning to take advantage of telemedicine, where customers receive nonurgent care and consultation remotely by text, e-mail, and live videoconferencing with a physician.

The keys to an access strategy are simplicity, convenience, ubiquity, and flexibility. Offering a product or service one step closer, easier, or faster helps your business to continuously create additional value for customers and win their loyalty.

Engage Strategy

The engage strategy for business is to become a source of valued content for your customers. Businesses today face an increasingly challenging environment in seeking to communicate with their customers. The profusion of media channels and forms (from YouTube, to gaming consoles, to news via mobile apps) has fragmented the audience for traditional media, where brands historically placed advertising. In this context, businesses must expand their approach beyond interruption advertisements—messages that customers see only because they piggyback on or interrupt content that customers are genuinely interested in. Businesses need to adopt a different mindset and learn to create their own content that is relevant enough for customers to seek it out, consume it, and even share it within their networks. At the same time, this content must add value to businesses by enhancing their customer relationships.

An engage strategy may take a variety approaches, including product demos, storytelling, utility, and brands as publishers.

- *Product demos*: Content that demonstrates the value proposition of a business or product in a compelling and engaging way can be extremely effective. When L'Oréal was looking to raise the profile of a niche brand, the tattoo cover-up Dermablend, the company produced a long-form music video featuring Rick Genest (aka "Zombie Boy"), a Canadian artist and model whose entire body is covered in tattoos. The video starts with an apparently untattooed Genest, but as the Dermablend covering his skin is gradually removed, viewers witness a startling transformation. The video was placed on YouTube with virtually no media budget to promote it and became a sensation, with over 25 million views. Like the famous "Will it blend?" videos that popularized premium blender brand Blendtec, the Zombie Boy video is effective because the drama is entirely about the product's performance.

- *Storytelling*: In other cases, brands can reach a broader audience by creating an emotionally compelling story that is less product-specific. Industrial glass manufacturer Corning used a six-minute video called "A Day Made of Glass" to depict its vision of a future full of interactive glass surfaces, touchscreens, and display technologies. The video was viewed more than 20 million times, and Corning launched a follow-up series of videos and content around its technologies.
- *Utility*: Content isn't always about stories and emotions, however. It can also be about utility. Brands can effectively engage customers by providing useful content at just the right time. Columbia Sportswear connects to consumers interested in an active, outdoor life by creating mobile apps that range from a handy guide to tying rope knots (with examples from sailors, fishermen, and mountaineers) to a GPS Portable Activity Log (designed to help customers rapidly journal their most memorable outdoor experiences using a mix of videos, geo-tags, notes, photos, and records of distance traveled, time, and elevation).
- *Brands as publishers*: In some cases, brands move beyond individual pieces of content and engage customers by becoming publishers in their own right. Luxury department store Barneys New York has a website for e-commerce, but it has also become publisher of *The Window*, an online magazine that tells the stories of designers, fashion models, and craftspeople and of the products themselves—offering the kind of interviews and style guides you'd expect in a fashion magazine, not a product catalog. The company evaluates its return on investment (ROI) for *The Window* by comparing the purchasing patterns of customers who spend time on it to those of its general customer population.

The key to an engage strategy is to think like a media company, focused every day on earning the attention of your audience. First, know your customers and create content that is relevant, compelling, or useful to them; then strategize about how to use this engagement to strengthen your customer relationship. Meanwhile, measure the impact on your business.

Customize Strategy

The customize strategy for business is to make your offering adaptable to your customers' needs. Customization is increasingly possible due to the spread of e-commerce; automation in inventory and shipping;

digitization of media products; advances in 2D and 3D printing technologies; and the accessibility of big data on consumers' preferences, location, and behaviors. As customers seek more choice and more personalized experiences, businesses need to find ways to meet their demands without overwhelming them with choice or unnerving them with excessively personal messaging.

A customize strategy may take a variety of approaches, including recommendation engines as well as personalized interfaces, products and services, and messages and content.

- *Recommendation engines*: To help viewers find what to watch from its large catalog of streaming television and movie titles, Netflix uses a combination of behavioral data (What kinds of shows has this user watched on prior Wednesday nights at 10:00 P.M.?) and a system of micro-tags that human staff apply to all of its content. The result is a constantly changing, personalized set of playlists served up every time the user logs in. The micro-genres (more than 76,000 by one estimate) range from "Mother-Son Movies from the 1970s" to "Cerebral Suspenseful Dramas Starring Raymond Burr."[10] The impact of these recommendations can be measured by how infrequently customers bother to use the search bar to find a show to watch. Their success is striking: 75 percent of customers' viewing hours are spurred by Netflix's personalized recommendations.[11]
- *Personalized interfaces*: Lancôme's magic mirror on its Facebook page allows customers to select one of their Facebook photos and then try out various beauty products, virtually applying them to the photos to see how they look on the customers' own features, complexion, and hair. Increasingly, customers are expecting more personalized interfaces, whether online, in retail spaces, or moving between them.
- *Personalized products and services*: Coke sales were declining among young adults in Australia when Coca-Cola introduced its personalized Share a Coke cans there. The company chose the 150 most popular names for young adults in Australia and printed those names on the cans in place of the brand's own name—but in the same recognizable script. Customers with less common names could print personalized cans of Coke at kiosks in major shopping centers or share a personalized virtual can on Facebook. The customized cans were so popular that young adult consumption grew 7 percent in the Australian market, and Coca-Cola extended the campaign to eighty countries worldwide.[12]

With 3D printing being applied to prosthetic limbs, automobile chassis, and running shoes, the opportunities for customized products are rapidly expanding.

- *Personalized messages and content*: One of the easiest ways to customize an offering for customers is through media and messaging. As publishers transition from print to digital, they are able to deliver only the most appropriate content for each customer. They can invite readers to indicate their interests (thumbs up or down), directly observe what customers spend time on, and then promote future articles likely to be of highest relevance. Customized messages improve marketing as well. Microsoft increased the conversion rates of one e-mail marketing campaign by 70 percent by targeting the specific offer based on the recipient's location, age, gender, and online activity.[13]

The keys to a customize strategy are identifying the areas where your customers' needs and behaviors diverge and finding the right tools to either personalize on their behalf or empower them to personalize their own experiences.

Connect Strategy

The connect strategy for business is to become a part of your customers' conversations. With Facebook, which has surpassed 1.5 billion active users, and other huge platforms like Sina Weibo, Twitter, and LinkedIn, social media have become a global standard for how customers communicate with each other. They are also increasingly where customers expect to communicate with businesses of all kinds. Whether answering customers' questions, solving their problems, or providing product news, businesses are expected to be present, responsive, and active in social media conversations.

A connect strategy may take a variety approaches, including social listening, social customer service, joining the conversation, asking for ideas and content, and hosting a community.

- *Social listening*: Customer conversations can be a tremendous source of market insight for businesses, which can listen and learn with the help of numerous tools. Insights can range from product problems to drivers of positive customer comments. Many brands have used social insights to inform new branding and ad campaigns. Cable provider

Comcast has used social listening to identify regional outages even before its engineering teams do.

- *Social customer service*: Many businesses find that social media can serve as an effective channel within their customer service mix, alongside call centers, instant chat, and other tools. If a business is able to answer questions successfully, it can impress not only one customer but a network of others as well (a customer who experiences a problem but has it resolved well is the most likely to evangelize on behalf of the company). Of course, not all issues can be resolved in a social media exchange, but effective training can make a big difference. After building up its social media leadership team, Citibank was able to resolve 36 percent of its customers' Twitter queries within that social media channel versus only 11 percent for Wells Fargo and 3 percent for Bank of America.[14]

- *Joining the conversation*: Maersk Line, a container shipping company with 25,000 employees, decided to test whether social media could help its corporate communications. As an experiment, the company began engaging in conversations and sharing videos and photos from its ships around the world, using platforms as diverse as Facebook, Instagram, LinkedIn, YouTube, Sina Weibo, and Pinterest. Within a year, the project had helped defuse a PR crisis involving a dead narwhale, uncover historical video from the company's archives, and build a large and engaged following of customers, suppliers, shipping experts, and employees. Among the most tangible benefits for Maersk were new networks for hiring and recruiting, new sales leads, and improved satisfaction among both customers and employees.[15]

- *Asking for ideas and content*: Many times, companies will connect with customers by using social media to ask them for ideas, suggestions, or content in the form of photos or videos. Action camera brand GoPro built its reputation entirely by asking customers to share their most amazing videos filmed with the product, whether surfing, hang gliding, or bike riding. Other companies, from Dell to Starbucks, have used tools like the IdeaStorm platform to solicit customer suggestions and have then used these suggestions for product development and service improvements. This kind of responsiveness can be a powerful way to make customers feel a sense of ownership and contribution to a company's success.

- *Hosting a community*: In some cases, it may make sense for a business to host its own online community around a shared topic of interest.

Technology provider SAP hosts the SAP Community Network so customers, business partners, employees, and others can share insights and discuss questions related to their overlapping technology needs. The network has over a million unique visitors per month. Procter & Gamble had difficulty marketing feminine hygiene products, so it built BeingGirl.com, a forum where teen girls can discuss the experiences and challenges of young womanhood. Letting customers lead the conversation, P&G found that BeingGirl delivered a sales ROI several times higher than that for their TV ads for Tampax and Always brands.[16]

The keys to a connect strategy are focusing on the social media your customers use and engaging in conversations to solve problems, learn about your market, and become closer to your customers. The goal is not conversation for its own sake but value creation for your business.

Collaborate Strategy

The collaborate strategy for business is to invite your customers to help build your enterprise. A collaborate strategy is distinct from a connect strategy in that the company invites customers not just to share information but also to work together in a focused way toward a shared goal or objective, using open platforms. *Wikipedia* is still the touchstone example of digital collaboration that most people are familiar with—an unmatched public resource, generated almost entirely by the volunteer efforts of contributors around the world. But *Wikipedia* has evolved only through careful iterations of its editorial process to ensure its reliability and usefulness. Mass collaboration does not happen without careful attention to creating the right context and the right motivations for participants to take action and to feel they are being fairly treated.

We see a few well-established broad approaches to a collaborate strategy, including passive contribution, active contribution, crowdfunding, open competitions, and collaborative platforms.

- *Passive contribution*: Sometimes collaboration can involve as little as customers' consent so that actions they are already taking can be used to power a collective project. The Waze navigation app is one such collaborative tool; simply by driving a car with the mobile app running, each customer provides real-time data on the speed of traffic and best routes to destinations. Duolingo, a free language-learning app, includes translation homework for students—and then uses those homework assignments to power the second part of its business, a Web translation tool.

- *Active contribution*: In other cases, customers are invited to contribute their efforts directly to a cause, taking on a small part of a large project. CNN's iReport allows anyone to contribute photos, videos, or eyewitness reports to a crowdsourced journalism website. When the images or stories are particularly newsworthy, they are picked up and included in the main CNN news broadcast, with credit given to the "iReporter" who happened to be on the scene.

- *Crowdfunding*: A type of active contribution that has become quite widespread, crowdfunding is the process of seeking collaborators to contribute to and raise funds for a new project, product launch, or initiative. Crowdfunding started as a way for artists to raise funds but quickly spread as a means to raise seed capital for new businesses (including start-ups Oculus Rift and Pebble Watch) and diverse other ventures. In some markets, crowdfunded projects are legally allowed to grant equity directly to funders. This approach has been used by real estate crowdfunder Prodigy Network to raise the capital for and begin construction of the tallest building in Colombia, the BD Bacatá skyscraper.

- *Open competitions*: Some problems cannot be easily divided among contributors. In these cases, competitions can be used to enlist a diverse group to find the best answer or solution. Cisco has invested in a variety of innovation competitions, from an I-Prize business model competition, to hackathons for outside programmers to develop technical solutions, to the Internet of Things. InnoCentive hosts a network of over 300,000 "solvers"—scientists, engineers, and technical experts around the world—who can be tapped by any company seeking to run a competition to solve an intractable R&D challenge.

- *Collaborative platforms*: In this approach, the business creates a context for collaboration but lets the network of collaborators define the challenges to be addressed. In the iPhone's second year on the market, Apple opened up the operating system as a platform for collaboration. This experiment triggered the explosion of outside innovation that is the App Store. A good collaborative platform doesn't try to define what the next crop of projects should be; it focuses on providing a structure on which others can build. (We'll see much more on platform business models in the next chapter.)

The keys to a collaborate strategy are understanding the motivations of your contributors, giving everyone a stake (so no one feels exploited), allowing participants to contribute at their proper level of expertise, and offering freedom for contributors to bring their own ideas while providing enough guidance to shape an effective final outcome.

We now have a clear understanding of the five customer network strategies. But how do you choose between them and know which to apply in a given business situation? That is the aim of this chapter's tool, which we will see next.

Tool: The Customer Network Strategy Generator

The Customer Network Strategy Generator is designed to help you develop new strategic ideas for engaging and creating value with networked customers. It does this by linking your own business objectives to the core behaviors of customer networks that we have examined in this chapter. It can be used to generate new marketing communications and customer experiences as well as new product and service innovations.

The tool follows a five-step process for generating new strategic ideas (see figure 2.5). Let's look at each of the steps in detail.

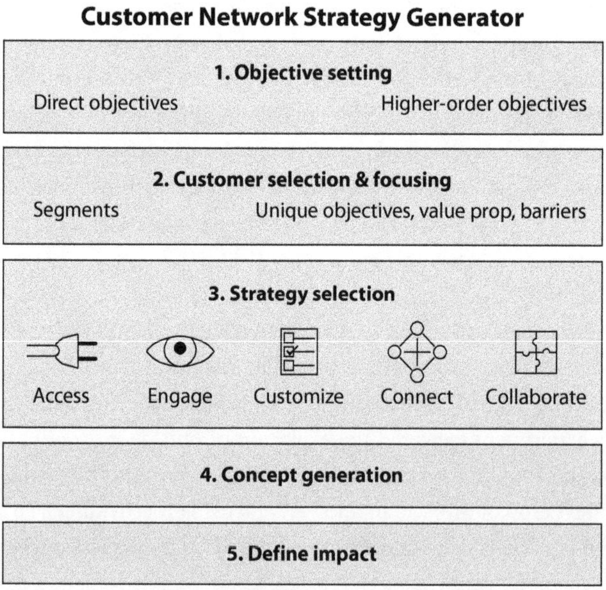

Customer Network Strategy Generator

1. Objective setting
Direct objectives   Higher-order objectives

2. Customer selection & focusing
Segments   Unique objectives, value prop, barriers

3. Strategy selection
Access   Engage   Customize   Connect   Collaborate

4. Concept generation

5. Define impact

Figure 2.5
The Customer Network Strategy Generator.

Step 1: Objective Setting

The first step of this process is to define the objectives you are hoping to achieve for your business with any new customer strategy you develop. It is valuable to define objectives at two levels: direct objectives and higher-order objectives.

- *Direct objectives:* These are the objectives that you are directly responsible for addressing in your project. For example, if you were leading customer service, you might be seeking to develop new strategies that leverage customers' digital behaviors to increase the speed of response to customer queries, reduce attrition of dissatisfied customers, or turn customer service into a source of customer insights. If you were responsible for developing direct-to-consumer sales for the first time via e-commerce, you might be seeking to drive awareness and product discoverability, reduce friction in the purchase decision, and engage lead customers as evangelists for your new sales channel.
- *Higher-order objectives:* It is also important to identify what overarching, or higher-order, objectives you are seeking to support through your initiative. These are objectives that you are not solely responsible for but that your project should support. In the e-commerce example above, you might identify developing richer data sets about customers across all channels as a firm-wide objective that your initiative should support. This would impact how you plan for your initiative to support that data collection and integration.

Step 2: Customer Selection and Focusing

The next step is to get a clear picture of the customers that you are seeking to address. This starts with selecting which customer segments are most relevant to your stated objectives. For example, if your key project objective were to reduce customer attrition, you might select customer segments with the highest rates of attrition and high-value segments whose losses pose the greatest risk. If your project were aimed at increasing the acquisition of a group of customers who are often influenced by opinion leaders, you would want to include both these segments in your plan.

Then you need to focus on these segments to understand them in the context of your project's specific objectives. That involves answering three key questions:

What is my *unique objective* for each customer segment? If you are focusing on different segments to launch your new e-commerce service, how does your objective differ—even slightly—for each of them? Perhaps, for one segment, the objective is simply to drive early adoption; for another highly active segment, you want not just adoption but also customer feedback and assistance in iterating the platform; for a third segment, you want to convince customers to set up recurring contracts with the new service.

What is my *unique value proposition* for each customer segment? It is important to see how the value proposition (the reason for customers to give you their time, attention, and money) varies among segments. For one customer segment, the value proposition of your e-commerce service may be simplicity in placing orders; for another, it may be a better selection of products; for another, it may be better record keeping for past and future orders.

What are the *unique barriers to success* for each customer segment? Barriers could vary from lack of awareness of a new offer to indifference, price sensitivity, technical hurdles, or risk aversion, among others. For each customer segment, try to articulate what the biggest barrier is and see how it differs from the others.

Step 3: Strategy Selection

Now that you know your objectives for your customer strategy and have a strong understanding of the customers you are trying to reach, you are ready to start the strategy ideation process.

You should begin by looking back at the five core customer network behaviors and the broad strategies that derive from them:

- *Access*: Be faster, be easier, be everywhere, and be always on for your customers.
- *Engage*: Become a source of valued content for your customers.
- *Customize*: Make your offering adaptable to your customers' needs.
- *Connect*: Become a part of your customers' conversations.
- *Collaborate*: Invite your customers to help build your enterprise.

Although all five strategies can be valuable for your business in the abstract, you are now looking to generate ideas for a specific project. Consider the objectives you have set and the customers you are trying to reach (including their needs, barriers, etc.). Use these objectives and target customers to select one or more of the five strategies that seem best suited for the task.

For example, if you are launching an e-commerce platform and one of the key motivators of your customer segments is a simple and frictionless interface, then you should think about generating ideas for an access strategy. If you are seeking to capture ideas from the customer service interactions of your customers, then a focus on conversation in a connect strategy would be appropriate. If you are aiming to recruit a group of customer evangelists to beta test a new product and help introduce it to markets, then a collaborate strategy would fit.

You may decide that more than one of the five broad strategies make sense for your goals—for example, an access and a customize strategy or an engage and a connect strategy. But I would advise against selecting all five, as the goal here is to set a focused direction before concept generation begins.

Step 4: Concept Generation

Now you are ready to start generating specific strategic concepts based on the broad strategies, objectives, and customers you have selected. A concept is a specific, concrete idea for a product, service, communication, experience, or interaction you design for customers. For example, if you are pursuing an engage strategy (becoming a source of valued content) as part of introducing a new premium VIP service to customers of your travel booking service, you should consider creating a variety of kinds of content: an "explainer" video showing how the new service works simply and easily via your mobile device, short lifestyle reports on up-and-coming travel recommendations that customers can subscribe to based on their travel interests, a news alert service to tell them about travel safety conditions in regions on their upcoming agenda, and so on. Even if you have chosen only one broad strategy, you should aim to generate several different strategic concepts.

As you begin this step, you may want to look back at the different cases and approaches given earlier in the chapter for each of the strategies. For example, if you are looking at a customize strategy, you may want to consider ideas related to recommendation engines, personalized interfaces, personalized products and services, and personalized messages and content.

This step is fundamentally a creative, idea-generating effort. You will want to bring together a diverse group of people who are ready to push themselves to generate new thinking. A small team (about five people) from different backgrounds and areas of the organization is ideal. Make sure everyone is steeped in the project objectives and the customer segments as you've defined them. Look for benchmarks and creative ideas from outside your industry. And be honest about whether you are just trying to catch up with your competitors or looking to create a compelling and differentiating new offering.

Lastly, it is critical to keep the focus on how your new ideas can create value for the customer. If they don't, they are unlikely to succeed. Following are some questions to keep you focused on customer value.

FOR AN ACCESS STRATEGY

- How could you make the experience faster, simpler, easier for customers?
- How could you better integrate different interactions?
- How could you make the service more accessible, more on-demand, more self-serve?

FOR AN ENGAGE STRATEGY

- How could you earn the attention of your audience?
- What problem could you solve for your customers with the right content or information at the right time?
- Would anyone not working at your company recommend this content to a friend?

FOR A CUSTOMIZE STRATEGY

- Where do your customers' needs and interests differ most from each other?
- Why would your customers want a more personalized experience? For better utility? For unique interests? For self-expression?
- How could you make it easy, and not overwhelming, for your customers to make the right choice for themselves?

FOR A CONNECT STRATEGY

- What conversations are your customers already having that are relevant to your objectives?
- How could you enable, facilitate, or enhance those conversations rather than intruding on them?
- What could you learn from your customers' conversations?
- What could you contribute to these conversations that your customers would value?

FOR A COLLABORATE STRATEGY

- What skills could your customers bring to bear, and what are the limits in their ability to contribute successfully?
- What would most motivate customers? Excitement about your brand, cause, or project? Social recognition? Monetary rewards? Or some combination of these?
- How could you make sure customers feel validated and rewarded?

Step 5: Defining Impact

At this point, you should bring each of your ideas back to the business objectives you set for yourself in step 1. For each strategic concept, you need to answer these questions: If you do proceed with this, how will you know if you have achieved the objectives you set? For example, if your objective is to reduce customer attrition, will the strategy you have developed address this? If so, how will you measure its impact? If your objective is to drive product awareness and discoverability and you have developed a series of content initiatives as part of an engage strategy, how will you know if they are achieving your goal? The point here is to articulate a measurable benefit to your company and clarify how you think the strategic concepts you have developed will achieve this outcome.

Having completed all five steps, you should now have a set of compelling new customer strategies for your team to consider for implementation. These should be strategies rooted in a deep understanding of your specific customers, based on their own networked behaviors, designed to add real value for these customers, and able to drive the objectives most important to your business.

This tool has been designed for strategic ideation. Still to come would be any planning to test your strategic concepts, validate them, allocate resources to them, refine their metrics, and (if appropriate) move to a public launch. We will talk more about how to test and learn from new strategic ideas in chapter 5.

Before we leave the domain of customer strategy, though, let's consider some of the challenges that a traditional, pre-digital-era enterprise may face in rethinking its assumptions about customers.

Organizational Challenges of Customer Networks

Joseph Tripodi knows something about customer networks. Over the course of his career, he has served as the chief marketing officer at Allstate Insurance, The Bank of New York, MasterCard, Seagram, and Coca-Cola. When I spoke to him about his view of the changing relationship of organizations to customers, he told me, "For any large organization, this is definitely a journey. We're waking up to the fact that we've been too passive by trying to engage with consumers in more traditional ways. How do you build an infrastructure for ongoing, real-time consumer engagement? It's a challenge for behemoth companies who operate around the world."[17]

For some time, Tripodi has been thinking about customer networks in terms of three different networks. One network is end consumers. Another is business customers, whether retailers, analysts, or opinion elites who influence your industry and regulations. The third is your own employees.

Enabling the Network Inside

A firm's internal customer network—its own employees—is critical to the digital transformation of a business. That transformation begins with applying the same customer network strategies we have seen to help internal teams achieve their goals. As workforces become more mobile, businesses need to help employees *access* their work more easily and flexibly. Employees need to be able to *engage* with the right content, information, and resources to stay informed for their job. They need tools that allow them to *customize* their workflow around flexible travel, roles, and schedules. They need to *connect* with each other—to share knowledge and to ask and answer questions—using various modes of communication (e-mails, instant messages, videoconferences) without confusion. And they need to be able to *collaborate* using tools that allow them to share projects and files while working remotely and asynchronously.

As big a challenge as all this may be, the bigger challenges are often cultural. As Tripodi told me, "We have to evolve to be a much more permeable hierarchy, where information is collected, gathered, analyzed, and shared at all levels."

Reducing hierarchical control is rarely easy. Many times, distrust of employees and fear of risk can lead organizations to wall off digital connections and restrict employees from using online tools effectively. The head of human resources for a billion-dollar business unit of a large multinational firm confessed to me that even she was not able to access YouTube while at work. The IT department forbade tablet computers and sealed off employees behind a tight firewall. If she wanted to find educational content for her own staff, she had to search from her home computer on the weekends. So much for using technology to educate and connect your workforce! Walling off employees because you fear their freedom to connect digitally is a losing strategy.

Nurturing an effective employee network is all the more important as the size of a firm increases, as its geographical disparity increases (making casual face-to-face interactions more difficult), and as its employees' and executives' jobs change more rapidly.

Adding New Skills and Replacing Old Habits

In order to leverage customer networks outside the firm, businesses are having to acquire a host of new skills, particularly in their customer-facing divisions, including marketing, communications, sales, and service.

These skills include social media and community management, journalistic content creation, new media buying and measurement, e-commerce, and more. The challenge for established businesses is to avoid outsourcing these tasks to expert agencies—a quick and easy but shortsighted way to bridge the skills gap. Outsourcing delays the process of integrating new skills into the organization, and integration is essential to developing strategic thinking and new ideas that go beyond what competitors are doing.

In many companies, these new networked skills exist but are unevenly distributed. I have worked with global firms facing a wide gap in digital skills and perspectives among executives at the same level of leadership.

These companies have employees with great digital skills, but they are scattered across departments and isolated at different levels of seniority (not just among young millennials). Among the key challenges for such firms are sharing best practices internally and quickly bringing employees to a baseline level of shared knowledge.

Many organizations simply find that old habits die hard. The employees who have been most successful and earned their stripes with the old tools of broadcast marketing (buying TV ads and sending out print mailings) may be the ones most resistant to adopting a new, more networked approach to customers. "Getting the corporation to apply its energy to reskilling the team is difficult culturally," Tripodi says. "It's a new world order, but the challenge is that people want to rely on what got them there before." It is often much easier to keep spending money where you used to (even without clear measures of ROI) than to shift spending into new tactics for engaging customers.

Bridging Silos

Another challenge for organizations is that customer networks affect every department of the organization. This can lead to tensions over who leads customer interactions across digital touchpoints. It can be as mundane an issue as who owns the company's Facebook presence: Marketing? Communications? Customer service? IT? Should that presence be managed by global headquarters or devolved to local business units, each with its own page? Even if one department is responsible for the "voice" of the company in a given social media platform, the strategy needs to be able to support the diverse needs of the entire business. I have seen a global telecom company struggle because the department that had ownership of social media was inflexible when an external crisis led to another department's asking for support for its own objectives.

As technology becomes more central to all customer interactions, rivalries can arise between the marketing and IT departments. (Numerous studies have been conducted about the changing relationship of the chief marketing and chief information officers.) It is critical that the two disciplines learn to work together effectively, despite differences in culture, budget, and priorities. At Kimberly-Clark, for example, the solution was to create liaison positions on both sides: a vice president of IT focused entirely on partnering with the global marketing team and an equivalent leadership position on the marketing side focused on partnering with IT.[18] Some firms, like Motorola, have gone so far as to merge the CMO and CIO into a joint position.

The strongest argument for bridging the traditional silos of a company is the need to integrate the total customer experience with a firm and its brand. When Frank Eliason came to Citibank to take on the role of senior vice president of social media, he faced this challenge. "Inside your business, you may see yourselves as lots of different units: we're in mortgages; business loans is someone else, and personal checking is different altogether. But from the point of view of the customer, we're all just one brand, Citi. And when they interact with your brand on social media, they expect to be able to ask about any part of their experience with your company."[19]

To adapt and thrive in the digital age, businesses must learn to view customers differently, understanding the dynamic, networked ways in which they interact, now both with businesses and with each other. By learning to think about customers as networks and to think differently about the path to purchase and the marketing funnel, any business can begin to transform its customer strategies. It can meet customers where they are and add value to both sides of the relationship by helping them to access, engage, connect, and even collaborate with the business.

But relationships with individual customers are not the only ones that are changing in the digital age. The interactions between businesses are being similarly transformed. What used to be fairly simple, even binary relationships (partner or competitor) have become more complex and interconnected. This shift requires new thinking about how businesses interact with each other and new models for creating value when one business becomes a platform for others. This will be the focus of the next chapter.

3

Build Platforms, Not Just Products

COMPETITION

In 2007, two recent graduates of the Rhode Island School of Design, Brian Chesky and Joe Gebbia, were struggling to pay the rent on their apartment in San Francisco. When they heard that the city's hotels were fully booked during an upcoming design conference, they had an entrepreneurial idea: Why not rent out a bit of their space? They bought three airbeds (inflatable mattresses), put up a website, and, within six days, found three guest lodgers. Each one paid $80 a night. "As we were waving these people goodbye, Joe and I looked at each other and thought, there's got to be a bigger idea here," Chesky said.[1] By the following year, they had teamed up with another friend, computer science graduate Nathan Blecharczyk, and started a business that they later named Airbnb.

By 2015, Airbnb had served 25 million travelers, providing them with lodging in over 190 countries around the world. But it doesn't look like a typical global corporation in the business of providing lodging and hospitality. Instead of building hotels and hiring employees to serve customers, the three founders built a platform that brings together two distinct types of people: hosts with homes to rent (whether a spare room or their whole home while they are away) and travelers who are looking for someplace to stay. The company has minimal assets. In fact, it doesn't own a single rental property. Yet it can offer travelers their choice of more than 1 million listings, ranging from a sofa or tiny guest room up to an actual castle (more than 600 are available to rent). The company takes a cut of the rental fee on each transaction.

Airbnb has only a few hundred employees but manages to book 40 million guest-nights per year because its platform is built to be as simple and self-service as possible for both homeowners and travelers. Its staff focuses on building a Web interface and mobile apps that make it as easy and frictionless as possible for a host to offer lodging or for a traveler to find a place to stay.

Much of Airbnb's success comes down to building trust between the two parties. (Who wants to have their apartment trashed by out-of-town guests when they are on vacation? Who wants to show up at a dump that doesn't match what you booked online?) Building trust begins with mutual ratings and reviews for both hosts and travelers but goes far beyond that. The company waits to release rental payments to the host until after the renter has checked in and verified they are happy with the property; it likewise holds onto the renter's deposit until after they have left and the host has verified their home is in good shape. As further assurance, it provides each host with $1 million in insurance for damages. It has also added verification of both parties through detailed user profiles, ID verification, and links to social networks like Facebook. Travelers looking for options in a destination city can search by neighborhood, can read the company's curated recommendations on where to stay, and can even use Facebook to find "friends of friends" who are renting out spaces. Its founders were even able to mix trust building and marketing: by hiring photographers to take pictures of lodgings for any host who requested it (for free), they offered better visuals for the host while guaranteeing visitors that the company had verified the location they were renting. This innovation alone rapidly increased growth in bookings.

Airbnb has grown at a phenomenal rate, with more rooms for rent than Hilton, InterContinental, or Marriott[2] and nearly $4 billion in gross bookings in 2014.[3] During that year's World Cup games, out of 600,000 attendees who came to Brazil from around the world, 25 percent stayed at an Airbnb rental. Today, the company operates in over 190 countries.

"Every country other than North Korea, Iran, Syria, and Cuba," Chesky cheerfully told television host Stephen Colbert in a 2014 interview.[4] That list has since been updated: when the United States reestablished ties with Cuba in 2015, Airbnb was one of the first American companies to announce it had launched a presence there.[5]

Rethinking Competition

Airbnb is an example of a platform—a class of businesses that are rethinking which competitive assets need to be owned by a firm (e.g., rental properties and trained service staff) and which can be managed through new kinds of external relationships.

These platform businesses are part of a broad transformation of the domain of competition and the relationships between firms. In the past, competition took place between similar rival businesses and within clearly defined industries with stable boundaries. Businesses created value within their own organization and in partnership with their suppliers and sales channels. But in the digital age, the boundaries between industries are blurring, and so is the distinction between partners and competitors. Every relationship between firms today is a constantly shifting mix of competition and cooperation.

Think of the television business. In the traditional view, a network like HBO partners with cable companies for distribution, and it competes with networks like Showtime or AMC—companies with the same business model and a similar offering for customers. But as digitization has transformed media, HBO has found itself competing with Netflix, an asymmetric challenger that is going after the same customers with a different pricing model and a completely different means of distribution. As the boundaries of the "television" industry have been redefined, HBO must compete for leverage against its distribution partners, cable companies like Comcast and Time Warner (which previously owned HBO's parent company). It also must compete for leverage against some of its own star talent, who now have the option to work with firms like Netflix or Amazon as they develop their own original programming for direct distribution to viewers. At the same time, three of the biggest broadcast television networks—ABC, NBC, and Fox—have put aside their rivalry to cooperate in creating Hulu, a digital channel that aggregates all their content for online viewing with a mix of advertising and subscriber revenue. Clearly, the shape of inter-firm competition and cooperation in the world of television has gotten very complicated.

The digital revolution is redefining competition and relationships between firms in several ways. It is supercharging the growth of platform businesses like Airbnb. For businesses like HBO, it is disintermediating and reshuffling channel and partner relationships. More broadly, it is shifting the locus of competition: competition is happening less within industries and less between similar companies that seek to replace each other; it is happening more across industries and between partners who rely on each other for success. Lastly, digital technology is increasing the importance of "co-opetition," where companies that compete directly in some arenas find it valuable to act as partners in other areas. (See table 3.1.)

This chapter explores the changing dynamics of competition and inter-firm relationships and their particular impact on platform businesses. It also presents two strategic planning tools. The first is the Platform Business Model Map, which can be used to analyze or design new platform businesses by understanding how they exchange value between different kinds of part-ners. The second is the Competitive Value Train, which provides a lens for understanding the simultaneous competition and cooperation among sup-ply chain partners, traditional rivals, and asymmetric competitors and for planning strategic moves to increase a business's competitive leverage.

Let's start by looking more deeply at the concept of platform busi-nesses and what they tell us about the shifting roles of competition and cooperation.

Table 3.1
Competition: Changes in Strategic Assumptions from the Analog to the Digital Age

From	To
Competition within defined industries	Competition across fluid industries
Clear distinctions between partners and rivals	Blurred distinctions between partners and rivals
Competition is a zero-sum game	Competitors cooperate in key areas
Key assets are held inside the firm	Key assets reside in outside networks
Products with unique features and benefits	Platforms with partners who exchange value
A few dominant competitors per category	Winner-takes-all due to network effects

Rise of the Platform

Airbnb is just of one of many new digitally powered businesses that act as platforms—bringing together two or more parties to create and exchange value *through* the business rather than trying to create all the value themselves.

Marketplaces like eBay, Etsy, or Alibaba's Taobao bring together buyers and sellers of goods of all kinds in direct sales or auctions. Matchmaking services like Uber or Didi Kuaidi provide taxi services not by purchasing vehicles and hiring drivers but by providing a platform to connect drivers in their own cars with people nearby needing a car service. Media companies from YouTube to Forbes.com operate by bringing together independent content creators, content consumers, and advertisers—each of whom is seeking out the other. Mobile operating systems like Apple's iOS, Google's Android, and Xiaomi's MIUI compete by attracting the best software developers to create apps, which, in turn, draw consumers to buy their smartphones.

Platform businesses are everywhere, appearing in a wide range of industries:

- *Retail*: Taobao, eBay, Amazon Marketplace
- *Media*: YouTube, Forbes.com
- *Advertising*: Google, Baidu, Craigslist
- *Finance*: PayPal, Kickstarter, Alipay
- *Gaming*: Xbox, PlayStation
- *Mobile computing*: iOS, Android, Xiaomi
- *Business software*: SAP, Salesforce
- *Home appliances*: Philips, Nest
- *Hospitality*: Airbnb, TripAdvisor
- *Transportation*: Uber, Didi Kuaidi
- *Education*: Coursera, Udemy
- *Recruiting and job search*: LinkedIn, Glassdoor
- *Freelance work*: Upwork, Amazon Mechanical Turk
- *Philanthropy*: Kiva, DonorsChoose

Platforms represent a fundamental shift in how businesses relate to each other—from linear to more networked business models. Platform businesses can often be very light in assets but generate large revenues. Instead of building features and seeking to get customers to use their own products, they build ecosystems by getting customers to interact with each other. Rather than simply paying for services received, customers both provide value and receive value. As a result, the value of a platform grows as more people use it.

What Is a Platform Business Model?

Vagueness abounds in the current use of the word *platform*, whose most general meaning is "something on which you can build." In tech circles, a platform may be any underlying software on which additional programs are built. In media industries, it may mean a distribution channel. In marketing, it may refer to any brand or product line that could be used to launch additional products. In the context of this chapter, however, we will be discussing platforms in a specific sense—as a kind of business model.

Origins of Platform Theory

The idea of platforms as business model has its origins in the economic theories of two-sided markets developed by Jean-Charles Rochet and Nobel laureate Jean Tirole,[6] along with Thomas Eisenmann, Geoffrey Parker, Marshall Van Alstyne,[7] and others. Their work examines pricing and competition in markets where one business serves two different types of customers that are dependent on each other. They found that the two sides often show different price sensitivity and that in efficient markets one side often subsidizes the other (e.g., advertisers subsidize the cost of media for consumers, and merchants cover the transaction costs of credit cards for the shoppers using them).

The study of two-sided markets led, in turn, to the realization that the same effects could be seen in markets with more than two types of customers (Visa and MasterCard, for example, bring together not just the consumers who use credit cards and the merchants who accept them but the credit-issuing banks that back them as well). This led to the more general concept of multisided markets. At the same time, the theory began to shift from looking at the market dynamics (i.e., who will pay what price in equilibrium with others) to looking at the kind of businesses that make them possible (i.e., what distinguishes the business model of a Visa or Master-Card and what its success factors are).

The term in economics for the business model at the center of a multi-sided market is a *multisided platform*, or just *platform*. Going forward, you can take my use of the term *platform* to refer to these multisided platform business models.

It is by applying these economic theories that we can begin to understand the power and unique value of businesses like Airbnb, Uber, or Xiaomi.

A Definition of Platforms

The most precise and illuminating description of what constitutes a platform comes from the work of Andrei Hagiu and Julian Wright.[8] To condense their thinking, I offer this definition:

> *A platform is a business that creates value by facilitating direct interactions between two or more distinct types of customers.*

Three key points from Hagiu and Wright that I include in this definition are worth noting:

- *Distinct types of customers*: To be a platform, the business model must serve two or more distinct sides, or types, of customers. (These can be buyers and sellers, software developers and consumers, merchants and cardholders and banks, etc.) The need for distinct sides explains why a pure communication network (such as Skype, fax, or telephone) is not a platform: although it connects customers to each other, the customers are all of the same type. The unique dynamics of platforms arise because they bring together different parties that each play different roles and contribute and receive different kinds of value.
- *Direct interaction*: Platforms must enable these two or more sides to interact directly—that is, with a degree of independence. In a platform such as Airbnb or eBay, the two parties are free to create their own profiles, set and negotiate pricing, and decide how they want to present their services or products. This is a critical distinction between a platform and a reseller or sales channel. The independence of interaction is why our definition of platforms does not include a supermarket connecting brands with shoppers or a vertically integrated consulting firm connecting clients with its hired employees.
- *Facilitating*: Even though the interactions are not dictated by the platform business, they must take place through it and be facilitated by it.

This is why our definition of platforms does not include a franchise business like McDonald's or H&R Block, which provides brand licensing, training, and support services to individual owners who open branch businesses. Although franchisors do, in some sense, enable commerce between the franchisees (e.g., restaurant owners) and end consumers (e.g., restaurant patrons), that commerce does not flow through the original corporation, and only one party (the franchisee) is in any way affiliated with the original franchisor company.

In table 3.2, we can see how a number of different platforms bring together distinct types of customers and create value by facilitating their direct interaction.

Table 3.2
Platforms and the Customers They Bring Together

Platform	Distinct customers, interacting directly, facilitated by the platform
Airbnb	Hosts Renters
Uber	Freelance drivers Riders
DonorsChoose	Schoolteachers seeking grants Donors
PayPal	Account holders Merchants Banks
YouTube	Video viewers Video creators Advertisers
Google search	Search engine users Website creators Search advertisers
Forbes.com	Independent writers (not employees) Readers Advertisers
Android operating system	Phone and tablet users Hardware manufacturers App developers In-app advertisers
Salesforce.com	Software users App developers creating additional integrated services

Four Types of Platforms

Platform business models are not new to the digital age, although (as we shall see) digital technologies are fueling their increasing spread and dominance. But even before the rise of mobile computing or the Internet or even information technology, platform business models could be seen in a variety of forms.

David S. Evans and Richard Schmalensee identify four broad types of platform businesses (see table 3.3):[9]

- *Exchanges*: These types of platforms (sometimes also called marketplaces) bring together two distinct groups of customers for a direct value exchange, with each group attracted by the number and quality from the other side. One familiar example would be real estate brokers, who bring together buyers and sellers. Another would be a shopping mall, which promotes itself as a shopping destination to consumers and rents space to various vendors. Digital exchanges can bring together buyers and sellers of products (such as eBay) as well as services (such as Airbnb).

Table 3.3
Four Types of Platforms

Type of platforms	Pre-digital examples	Digital examples
Exchange	Real estate brokers Shopping malls Nightclubs	Product marketplaces (eBay, Etsy) Service marketplaces (Airbnb, Uber) Dating websites (eHarmony)
Transaction system	Credit cards Debit cards	Digital payment systems (PayPal) Digital currencies (Bitcoin)
Ad-supported media	Newspapers (subsidized or free due to ads) Broadcast TV	Websites with ads Social networks with ads
Hardware/software standard	Color TVs (RCA vs. CBS) Videocassettes (VHS vs. Betamax) Motor fuels (diesel vs. ethanol)	Videogame consoles (Xbox, PlayStation) Mobile operating systems (iOS, Android)

- *Transaction systems*: These platforms act as an intermediary between different parties to facilitate payments and financial transactions. Issuers of both credit cards and debit cards provide this service, linking together cardholders, merchants, and banks. New digital payment systems, whether PayPal or Apple Pay, are based on the same model. To succeed, a transaction system must get sufficient numbers on board from each party: merchants will install card readers and accept the fees owed to the platform only if they see a sizable number of customers using the system; customers will be more likely to sign up if they see that the service is widely accepted by merchants that they buy from.
- *Advertising-supported media*: In this case, the platform typically plays an additional role of creating (or sourcing) media content that is attractive to consumers. For example, a printed newspaper or an online news publication hires writers to create professional content. Once the value of the content attracts an audience, the platform can charge advertisers who are eager to present their messages to that audience. As the platform attracts more people, its value to advertisers increases. The advertisers, in turn, provide value to the audience by reducing or eliminating the cost of the content for them.
- *Hardware/software standards*: These platforms provide a uniform standard for the design of subsequent products to enable their interoperability and benefit the ultimate consumer. At the birth of color television, a struggle took place between RCA and CBS to determine which would establish the standard used by broadcasters and television set manufacturers (RCA won). Later the introduction of videocassette tapes resulted in a competition between the VHS and Betamax standards for hardware (VHS won). But not every standards competition ends with a single winner. Today's smartphone market is roughly divided between Apple's iOS and Google's Android. Each of these operating systems is a software platform vying to attract more software developers that will build apps; in addition, Android serves as a hardware platform for handset manufacturers like Samsung that are seeking to compete with Apple's iPhone.

This list is not exclusive; new platform businesses could well arise that don't quite fit any of these four types. But these categories provide a useful way of thinking about the differences among current platform businesses.

Direct and Indirect Network Effects

One of the key features of platforms is that their value increases as more customers use them. This phenomenon is commonly called network effects, but there are actually two different kinds of network effects that can impact the growth of a business.

Direct network effects (or "same-side" network effects) occur when the increasing number of customers or users of a product drives an increase in value or utility for that same type of user. In communications theory, this is commonly dubbed Metcalfe's law. When the first user purchased a fax machine, the utility was zero: Who could they dial? As the number of users increases, each additional user leads to an exponential increase in the number of potential connections that can be made in the network (connections = $n(n - 1)/2$). Direct network effects occur in platforms such as Facebook, which is a platform because (unlike a fax machine) it brings together not just users but advertisers, publishers, and app developers as well.

For platforms, the more common type of network effect is indirect network effects (or "cross-side" network effects). These occur when an increase in the number and quality of customers on one side of the platform drives increasing value for customers on the *other* side of the platform. You don't sign up for Visa because it has lots of other cardholders (no direct network effect), but the presence of lots of Visa cardholders does make it more attractive for a merchant to accept Visa (strong indirect network effect).

Are indirect network effects reciprocal? Not always. In advertising-supported media, the indirect network effects usually run only one way: as the number of readers increases for a newspaper, its value to advertisers increases as well, but increasing the number of ads in each issue does not directly increase the value for readers. (The one exception would be classified ads, where the ads really are the "content" that the audience goes to the publication to read.) For media companies, that imbalance is critical in determining pricing for both sides.

But for platforms other than ad-supported media, the indirect network effects usually do work both ways. Airbnb renters like to see more hosts to choose from, and hosts want to see more potential renters on the site. When indirect network effects happen both ways, they drive a virtuous cycle, with new customers on each side increasing the attractiveness to the other side. This is what drives extremely rapid growth and a highly defensible market position for a platform like Airbnb or PayPal that becomes a leader in its category.

The Platform Spectrum

Any business today faces a strategic choice of whether to pursue a platform model or a more traditional business model. Should you build a store or a marketplace? Should you hire a group of experts or cultivate a network of them? But the choice is not a simple "all or nothing" decision. The right business model may be somewhere on a spectrum from platform to nonplatform.

Consider the second defining quality of platforms: they allow direct and independent interaction between the parties they bring together. In practice, this independence may happen by degrees. Both Uber and Relay-Rides allow owners of cars to provide mobility to those without them (in the former, the car comes with a driver; in the latter, you borrow the car and drive it yourself). But whereas RelayRides lets riders offer their own price, Uber imposes standardization around rates. Within the category of electronic gaming, both consoles like Microsoft's Xbox and app stores like Google Play act as platforms, bringing together designers who have games to sell and gamers who are looking to buy. However, the console makers exert more control on the interaction: although the game developers set the pricing, the actual purchase contract is between the gamer and Microsoft. On the Google Play store, the parties are given more independence: the gamer buys the app from the third-party designer, but Google maintains quality review.[10]

Some companies successfully employ a mix of platform and nonplatform business models, even within the same business unit. Amazon.com started as a pure e-commerce business, buying and selling products just like a physical retailer. But it later launched Amazon Marketplace, which allows independent stores to offer goods for sale on Amazon's website, greatly expanding its product breadth and enhancing Amazon's margins. The platform and nonplatform businesses sit side by side; in fact, products from both appear in the same search result on Amazon's website. In the retail world, electronics chain Best Buy was long a traditional reseller, controlling all aspects of how products are priced, displayed, and sold in its stores. More recently, though, it has allowed major brands such as Samsung, Microsoft, Sony, Google, and Apple to lease space in its retail stores and operate independent, branded mini-stores that are designed, stocked, and even staffed with salespeople from the brand itself. With its mini-stores, Best Buy is using a platform model that connects shoppers with the brands directly.

In some cases, both parts of the business may be significant: in 2014, Amazon reported that 42 percent of its units sold were from its Marketplace partners. When India's laws prevented foreign companies from conducting direct sales in e-commerce, Amazon entered the market with a 100 percent platform strategy, allowing local retailers to sell products through Amazon.in and its fulfillment services. In other cases, one business model may serve only particular customers. Evernote provides cloud-based note-taking software to 100 million users (I'm one of them). It also has an Evernote Platform that allows independent developers to build additional apps for Evernote users and an Evernote Market for independently made hardware and accessories; these offerings skew mostly toward customers with enterprise licenses, further widening the customer base.[11]

The decision whether to pursue a platform business model can shift over time. Shoe retailer Zappos.com started as a platform (a marketplace for designer shoe brands and consumers) but pivoted its strategy to become a direct reseller. Apple famously lost the desktop wars to Microsoft because it sought to control the development of software and hardware, whereas Microsoft aggressively pursued a platform strategy for Windows, seeking out as many partners (both PC makers and software developers) as possible. Apple almost made the same mistake with the iPhone before a major strategic change in its second year, when Steve Jobs allowed outside developers to begin writing apps for the new phone. Sales increased 245 percent that year, and the iPhone as a multisided platform business went on to make Apple the most valuable company in the world.

How Digital Impacts Platforms

As we have seen, multisided platforms have been around in various forms for many years. The basic model of an exchange probably dates back to the earliest markets where a landlord or municipal government owned the property and leased out stalls or patches of dirt to merchants who could peddle their wares to customers drawn by the market's promise.

So why are platform businesses so important now? Why are they growing so quickly and influencing so many sectors? Digital technologies are supercharging the growth and power of multisided platforms. These enabling technologies include the Web; on-demand cloud computing; application program interfaces (APIs), which increase the interoperability of data and functionality; social media; and mobile computing devices.

Together, these digital technologies are driving four key elements of platforms:

- *Frictionless acquisition*: Thanks to the Web, APIs, and software development kits (SDKs), the process of acquiring new customers for a platform is increasingly frictionless. There is no longer a need to negotiate terms for each additional participant in a multisided platform, removing a critical bottleneck to growth. For example, to place an ad on a television program, an advertiser needs to meet and negotiate directly with the network (or via a media buyer as intermediary) and may even need to commit to the purchase months in advance during an up-front purchase period. By contrast, to place an ad on Google to be seen by customers searching on specific keywords, an advertiser simply goes to the Google AdWords website, enters its credit card information, and begins using a self-service tool to test, launch, and optimize its advertising campaign in real time.
- *Scalable growth*: Cloud computing now allows any size business to rapidly scale the size of its platform as fast as it can acquire new customers. By taking a physical service like car transport or lodging reservations and moving it to a cloud-based platform, companies like Uber and Airbnb can expand with virtually no ceiling on their growth. A traditional night-club may thrive as a platform that attracts mutually attractive customers, but if it grows quickly, it will always reach a capacity cap until it can invest in renting or buying a new venue. By contrast, MeetUp.com, a cloud-based platform business that allows users to organize spontaneous social gatherings anywhere in the world, has no obvious limit to its scale. (MeetUp has 21 million members in 181 countries. As I type this, there are nearly 4,000 meet-ups happening simultaneously around the world.)
- *On-demand access and speed*: Mobile computing means that every platform now can be accessible to all of its customers anywhere at any time. As Airbnb founder Brian Chesky has remarked, "Imagine Uber, if every driver didn't have a phone . . . they have a laptop. And every driver had to drive home to check the laptop to see when a ride was available. Think about how much friction Uber would have! In our business, if a seller has a mobile device, it could simulate the responsive and the up-to-dateness of a hotel. This is why mobile is transformational for our business. It means a seller can act like a company, in the best possible way."[12]
- *Trust*: Anonymity is great for facilitating some kinds of interactions on the Web, but it isn't very helpful for a platform business. The rise

of dominant social networks and the ability to authenticate customers through their Facebook, Google, Twitter, or LinkedIn identities make it much easier for even a small start-up to use a verification system for new customers on its platform. That same trust allows for the rapid spread of recommendations and referrals through social media distribution, which is critical to growing a new platform business.

The biggest impact of digital technology on platforms may be in the size of the businesses involved. Before the digital age, platform businesses used to be mostly large enterprises—credit card companies, shopping malls, media companies—because of the resources required to attract sufficient numbers of participating partners. This is the downside of network effects for platforms: it can take a lot of capital to bring parties to the table at sufficient scale (economists dub this the chicken-and-egg problem). With the help of the digital tools described above, the chicken-and-egg problem is much more easily surmounted. Today, multisided platforms are no longer the domain only of large enterprises; they are the preferred launch pad for entrepreneurial ventures of all sizes, from large innovative companies to the smallest but most ambitious entrepreneurs.

Competitive Benefits of Platforms

Three of the five most valuable companies in the world—Apple, Google, and Microsoft—have built their businesses on platform business models. The secret to their success—and that of many other companies—is that platforms provide several powerful benefits to the companies that can build them effectively.

Light in Assets

When Chinese e-commerce and online marketplace titan Alibaba conducted its IPO, I was interviewed by the *Wall Street Journal* on the import of what was the largest IPO ever ($25 billion raised). One of the things I observed was Alibaba's rise among other mega-platform businesses, each with relatively light assets for its market valuation. As Tom Goodwin, a senior vice president at Havas Media, commented a few months later, "Uber, the world's largest taxi company, owns no vehicles. Facebook, the world's most popular media owner, creates no content. Alibaba, the most valuable retailer, has no inventory. And Airbnb, the world's largest accommodation provider, owns no real estate. Something interesting is happening."[13]

Because platforms give their customers the job of creating much of their value, they tend to be light in assets. Both capital and operating costs are low at businesses like Airbnb. These companies also tend to have few employees for the revenue they generate because their customers do much of the work that employees would do in a vertically integrated business. As a result, platform businesses can achieve extremely high operating margins on a percentage basis.

Scaling Fast

Platform businesses can grow extremely quickly. Their low operating costs, combined with a scalable cloud computing architecture, make this possible. A line chart of Airbnb's user growth looks like a hockey stick, with listings shooting up 1,000 percent in three years.[14] The ability of platforms to increase revenue with relatively slow employee growth is likely another factor. Airbnb reached $4 billion in gross bookings with only 600 employees.[15]

Since the rise of the Internet, the list of the fastest-growing new companies around the world is dominated by those using platform business models. In fact, eight of the ten most valuable global companies founded since 1994 are platform companies (see table 3.4).[16]

Table 3.4
Ten Most Valuable Public Companies Founded Since 1994

Company	Type of platform	Market value, 9/5/15 (in billions)	Year founded	Country
Google	Ad-supported media	$425.40	1998	United States
Facebook	Ad-supported media	$248.30	2004	United States
Amazon.com	Exchange	$235.70	1994	United States
China Mobile	—	$232.63	1997	China
Alibaba Group	Exchange, transaction system	$167.00	1999	China
Tencent Holdings	Exchange, ad-supported media	$150.87	1998	China
Sinopec	—	$73.62	1998	China
Priceline Group	Exchange	$62.86	1994	United States
Baidu	Ad-supported media	$52.40	2000	China
Salesforce.com	Software standard	$45.45	1999	United States

Source: Companies selected from Forbes Global 2000 list, published May 6, 2015.

Winner Takes All

Once a platform is widely established in its category, it is extremely hard to launch a direct challenger with a similar service—a result of the power of network effects. Customers would rather sign up for a platform that already has broad acceptance or many other users. It would be very hard for a direct competitor to catch up with Facebook (in social networking) or Google (in search) or to launch a new credit card challenger to Visa, MasterCard, and American Express. This defense is weaker in ad-supported media, where network effects are only one-sided (advertisers care about the number of readers, but readers don't care about the number of advertisers). But in a platform with network effects for all parties, new challengers face a formidable barrier to entry. In most cases, this leads toward consolidation around a few very dominant players holding the large majority of the market (e.g., credit cards, search engines).

In certain cases, markets will tend toward a true winner-take-all scenario where only one platform is viable. One example is the platform war between Sony's Blu-Ray and Toshiba's HD DVD to become the hardware standard for high-definition movie discs. Sony won, and Blu-Ray became the sole standard used by Hollywood studios and DVD players alike.

This kind of winner-take-all total consolidation is likely to happen when three factors are present:

1. Multihoming—using more than one platform—is hard for the customer (e.g., nobody wants to buy two DVD players, whereas carrying two credit cards is easy).
2. Indirect network effects are strong (e.g., viewers care what format Hollywood will release movies on, and Hollywood cares what format viewers use).
3. Feature differentiation is low (e.g., there were never going to be major differences in features among DVD players—product differentiation would mostly reside in the TV sets).

This anticompetitive aspect of platforms can be alarming because it can appear to reinforce monopoly behavior. But rather than a few monopolies striding over a handful of very broad industries, the future seems more likely to hold lots of (near) monopolies occupying shifting categories until they vanish (very soon no one will care who won the DVD wars). Facebook is extremely well protected against another challenger trying to launch an equivalent social networking tool (even Google Plus failed at this). But its challenge is that other platforms will establish dominant positions in slightly different categories of social media interaction—a dominant platform for photos or for messaging or for more ephemeral communications. (This is why Facebook bought Instagram and WhatsApp and tried to buy Snapchat.) The real threat to Google is not that another company will develop a similar search engine (e.g., Bing) but that users and advertisers will be drawn away to other kinds of search tools, like voice search via Siri, product search on Amazon, or other specialized search tools for travel, clothing, or other categories.

Economic Efficiency

One of the most striking benefits of platform business models is that they enable the efficient usage of distributed pockets of economic value (labor, assets, skills) that otherwise could not be effectively used.

The result is a profusion of platforms that bring together lone actors and empower them to contribute economically. These can be micro-retailers who are now able to sell their own craft products on Etsy or their music on CD Baby or micro-resellers who can find buyers for their used goods on eBay or Craigslist. They can be micro-donors on a platform like DonorsChoose or Kiva or micro-patrons of the arts who find that with just $25 they can help fund an independent documentary film on Kickstarter. They can be micro-investors on Lending Club or Funding Circle who are helping to finance others' small businesses. They can be micro-software–companies consisting of a single developer building an app for the most popular computing platforms in the world. They can be micro-freelancers, offering their services as a driver on Uber, a handyman on TaskRabbit, or a spell-checker on Amazon Mechanical Turk. Or they can be micro-renters, renting out their homes on Airbnb or cars on RelayRides. None of these roles would be possible without platforms. The individual actor would never have the resources to find the right matching project, need, or customer. But by reducing the transaction costs and aggregating a community of partners, platforms can unleash untapped economic capacity.

This phenomenon is often mislabeled the "sharing economy." In actual fact, very few platforms have been established to share assets or labor free of charge, and those that do (Freecycle, NeighborGoods, etc.) are all small.

The popular platforms that are commonly cited as evidence of the sharing economy are, in fact, better described as a "rental economy" (renting assets on Airbnb), a "resell economy" (selling used assets on eBay), or a "freelance economy" (selling labor on Uber). The societal benefits of unlocking these pockets of resources might be great. Uber, for example, has argued that its services reduce the total number of vehicles on the road in crowded cities. And Airbnb prides itself on helping homeowners better themselves as micro-entrepreneurs. But the benefits of this economic efficiency seem to accrue only when selling, rather than sharing, is the rule.

Competition Between Platforms

Platforms don't compete just with traditional businesses (Uber vs. a traditional car service). They also compete against other platforms. (Uber competes with Lyft in the United States and with Didi Kuaidi in China; all three are platforms.)

But how do platforms compete with each other in the same category? Not on the same factors—features, benefits, price, location—that differentiate traditional products and services. Instead, platforms tend to compete on five areas of value (see table 3.5):

Table 3.5
Points of Differentiation Between Competing Platforms

Area of value	Examples
Network-added value	More participants (network effects)
	Quality of goods and services from participants
	Data shared by participants
Platform-added value	Unique features and benefits
	Free content
Open standards	Web or app interfaces
	Software development kits and application program interfaces
	Platform control points
Interaction tools	Targeting and matchmaking tools
	Transaction enablers
Trust enablers	Identification systems
	Reputation systems
	Financial safeguards
	Noncompetitive assurances

- *Network-added value*: This is the most obvious way that platforms compete. Due to network effects, the platform with the most current customers is often the one most likely to draw future customers. But the network of participating customers can add benefits beyond sheer numbers. The quality of goods and services customers offer is often important as well. (Etsy has built a platform for selling handmade goods by nurturing a community of craftspeople making quality goods of a kind you may not find on eBay.) The data provided by one group of customers can also increase the ability of a platform to attract customers of another group. (The amount of social, demographic, and personal-interest data that users provide to Facebook is precisely the reason the company can charge advertisers relatively high rates.)
- *Platform-added value*: In some cases, the value provided by the various types of customers is not enough to make a platform competitive. The platform itself has to develop unique features and benefits to attract customers. Google attracts users to Android phones with its Google Now personal assistant and the seamless integration of its popular Maps, Calendar, and Gmail. Its competitor Apple attracts users with its own software, like iTunes and the Siri personal assistant, and the unique hardware design of its iPhones. For ad-supported media platforms, the biggest area of competition is their platform-added value—that is, the content they create to attract their audience. That content may be subsidized or provided entirely free to the consumer, thanks to advertiser revenue. Although a video channel or blog competes with its peers by trying to make attractive content, its real business model is to sell the audience to advertisers.
- *Open standards*: Another important way that a platform competes is by offering more-open and easier-to-use standards than its competitors. The rapid growth of platforms like YouTube is aided in large part by the self-service Web or app interfaces they offer, which make it easy for anyone to upload content or join a platform's network. For customers who need more technical control, platforms will use SDKs and APIs to provide self-service access. Openness is relative, however, and never completely absolute. Google's Android platform is more open than Apple's iOS, but even Android puts restrictions on phone manufacturers who wish to use its services like Google Maps, Calendar, and Search. (This is why Xiaomi and others use the unrestricted, open-source version of Android instead.) Standards offer access to outside parties, but they also act as control points by which platform owners restrict what

data and functionality outside parties can and cannot access. The only totally open platform is a public design standard. These facilitate interaction by all sides but afford no control or monetization to a central owner. The Internet itself is a set of such standards.

- *Interaction tools*: Once a platform has attracted customers and made it easy for them to come on board, it can compete by providing them with the best tools to find and interact with the right partners. Dating sites like eHarmony or OKCupid compete on the algorithms and data science they use to help men and women find the right match (rather than scrolling through thousands of random entries). Other interaction tools focus on enabling transactions between users. Airbnb added an Instant Book option that allows travelers in a hurry to instantly confirm a reservation—as they would on a hotel website—rather than waiting for a host to reply to their inquiry. eBay provides sellers the option to offer their products via an auction or at a fixed price. Amazon Marketplace provides fulfillment services for its sellers (they don't have to mail packages to the customer like an eBay seller); it also provides order tracking for purchasers.

- *Trust enablers*: The last way that platforms compete to attract customers is by offering better methods to enable trust among the parties they bring together. These can include identification systems, such as social log-ins through Facebook, Google, Twitter, or LinkedIn. (Although the early Internet thrived on anonymity, platforms thrive on identity.) Another enabler is reputation systems, typically in the form of customer reviews. In some platforms, reviews are mutual, but in others, they are only one-way (customers reviews the restaurant where they ate after making a reservation on OpenTable, but the restaurant doesn't review the diners). Trust can also be enabled by financial safeguards, such as insurance to cover losses incurred by customers or mediation of billing disputes by transaction platforms like PayPal. In other cases, noncompetitive assurances are critical to creating trust in a platform. Numerous manufacturers, from Samsung to Philips to Google's Nest, have begun developing "smart" products like lightbulbs, refrigerators, and thermostats for the "connected home." Consumers have been waiting for a single interface rather than having to use a different app for every appliance in the home. But none of the manufacturers was willing to use its competitor's software standard as a platform. This created an opportunity for Wink, a start-up that provides an elegant control interface for any device in the connected home. Because Wink does not make its own competing appliances, it has been able to attract big manufacturers like GE, Philips, Lutron, Honeywell, Schlage, and Nest to connect to its platform. Sometimes the small platform can win.

Before we move on from the subject of platforms to other changes in the landscape of competition, let's take a look at a strategic mapping tool that can be used to gain insights into any platform business.

Tool: The Platform Business Model Map

The Platform Business Model Map is an analytic and visualization tool designed to identify all the critical parties in a platform and analyze where value creation and exchange take place among the different customers and with the platform business itself. The logic of platforms is quite different from that of traditional product, service, or reseller businesses. It is therefore very important that you understand the value exchange among customers in order to see the strategy behind any successful platform.

In figure 3.1, we see how a Platform Business Model Map displays the various components of Facebook's business model.

Shapes indicate the key parties within the business model:

- *Circle*: The platform
- *Diamonds*: The payers (customers that provide revenue to the platform)
- *Rectangle*: The sweeteners (customers that provide no revenue but help to attract other valuable customers)
- *Spikes*: The number of other customer types that are attracted (e.g., publishers have one spike because they attract only users, but users have four spikes because they attract publishers, advertisers, app developers, and more users like themselves)
- *Double-borders*: The linchpin (the customer type with the most spikes; the king of network effects)

Arrows indicate value exchange:

- Arrows in each direction show the value provided, or received, by each customer type.
- Value in boldface is monetary value.
- Value in parentheses is provided by the platform itself or to the platform itself (e.g., the platform's share of revenues).
- Value not in parentheses is passed through the platform and is provided to other customers.

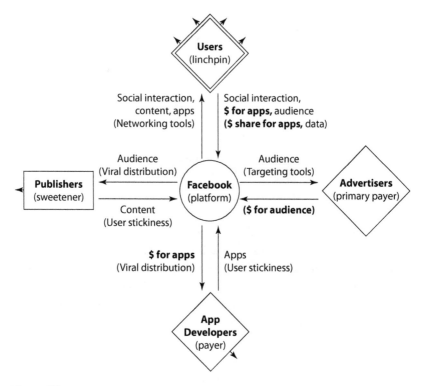

Figure 3.1
The Platform Business Model Map: Facebook.

We can learn several things about Facebook's business model through this tool. Facebook brings together four types of customers on its platform: social network users, advertisers, app developers, and news and content publishers. The business model is a mix of two of our four types of platforms: ad-supported media and software standard (for the app developers). The platform is fueled by cross-side network effects (different types of customers are attracted to each other) and also by same-side network effects (users are attracted by more of their own kind).

What about the relative importance of different types of customers to Facebook's platform? The prime importance of users is clear because even though they pay no fees to Facebook, they are the linchpin that attracts everyone else to the platform. Advertisers, on the right, are the primary revenue source for the business model. The role of news publishers is clarified, too: although they provide no revenue, they add value for the linchpin customers and hence to the platform (they get users to spend more time on the service and therefore see more ads).

If you are launching your own platform, you can use the Platform Business Model Map to answer these important questions:

- Whom do you need to bring on board to make your platform work?
- How will you monetize?
- Who are your most important customers? (These are likely both the primary payer and the linchpin.)
- Is your business model in balance? Does each party receive enough value to attract its participation? Does each party contribute enough value to justify its inclusion?

You can also use the Platform Business Model Map to analyze other platforms—competitors in your industry, a benchmark from another industry, or a platform that is acting as an intermediary between you and your customers. Analyzing another firm's platform will help you to answer these important questions:

- Who are the platform's key customers?
- What is the role, or value contribution, of each customer type?
- What draws each party to the platform?
- How does the platform monetize?
- What value do you provide if you are a customer of the platform?
- How could you extract or leverage more value from the platform?

A detailed guide on how to draw, and use, the Platform Business Model Map can be found at http://www.davidrogers.biz under Tools.

The Shifting Landscape of Competition

Platforms offer a fundamentally different model for how businesses relate to each other—not as suppliers, distributors, and rivals but as networked partners. But even if it does not use a platform business model, every business faces a very different world of competition in the digital age.

In a traditional view, we think of competition as happening between rival businesses of the same kind in the same industry. We think of collaboration as occurring between a business and the firms that serve as its sales channels and suppliers. But in the digital era, any relationship between two businesses is a shifting mix of competition and cooperation.

This is because digital technologies are contributing to three major shifts in the competitive landscape. First, competition with rivals is changing, becoming less of a direct contest and zero-sum game. Second, industry definitions and boundaries are becoming more fluid, leading to conflict between more asymmetrical competitors. Finally, the relationships of businesses to their channel and supply chain partners are being regularly reshuffled and reorganized. Let's look at all three shifts.

Co-opetition

Traditional thinking about competition is dominated by metaphors from war and sports. The aim of business is to "win," to "be the best," and to "beat" the competition. As in sports contests, our enemies are similar to us (Ford vs. General Motors, Sony vs. Samsung), and we compete within a clear set of rules: the boundaries of our industry. In the "business as contest" view, competition is a zero-sum game: for one side to win, the other side must lose. As Gore Vidal wrote, "It is not enough to succeed. Others must fail."

Michael Porter, perhaps the most famous management thinker on competition, criticizes this view of "competition to be the best" and warns that it is a path to mediocre performance. Simplistic striving for market share (remember GE CEO Jack Welch's famous insistence on being #1 or #2 in every industry) leads to price wars and low profitability. Aiming to be the generic "best" (as in the rallying cry of General Motors CEO Dan Akerson, "May the best car win!") obscures the importance of finding a unique way of creating value for customers, as this presumes there is only one way. A zero-sum view of competition sets up a race to the bottom that no one can win.[17]

Real competition is far from a zero-sum contest. In many cases, effective strategy calls for even direct competitors to find ways to work together cooperatively in certain arenas. The term *co-opetition* was coined by Novell founder Ray Noorda and popularized by Adam Brandenburger and Barry Nalebuff in a book of the same name. The authors apply game theory to business relationships to show why the right strategy for rival businesses is often a mix of competition and cooperation on different fronts. For example, peer universities will compete fiercely during the admissions process to attract the same desirable student applicants and during the hiring process to attract the same promising faculty. Yet, at other times, they will work together to advance the standing and role of university education in the broader market. In Brandenburger and Nalebuff's view, rival companies must cooperate to "grow the pie" at the same time that they compete with each other to "divide the pie."[18]

Digital platforms are increasingly a factor in driving strategic cooperation among business rivals. If you examine today's leading consumer technology companies—Apple, Google, Facebook, Samsung, Amazon—it is clear that they are all competing fiercely on multiple fronts. Apple's hardware competes with Samsung's and Amazon's. Apple's operating system competes with Google's (which is running on Samsung phones), which also competes with Amazon (which is running a proprietary and competitive version of Android). Facebook is competing with all these operating systems to be the most dominant layer of customer interaction on mobile devices and the most valuable digital advertising platform. It is also competing with Google's YouTube to be the biggest platform for online video distribution. Amazon is striving to steal search engine traffic for products from Google and building an advertising platform of its own. Meanwhile, Amazon is striving to stay ahead of Google and Apple as the leading source for digital books, television shows, and movies while all three compete to distribute downloaded and streaming music.

We could easily expect these five companies to behave like the Five Families of organized crime at war with each other in the *Godfather* movies. But, in fact, all five are deeply enmeshed with each other, cooperating and linking their products and services. Apple devices have long run Google as their default search engine. Facebook is the most popular app on everyone's mobile devices. Amazon's media collections are available and popular on Apple and Android devices, despite competing directly with Apple's App Store and Google's Play. Samsung actually manufactures many of the critical components for the very Apple iPhones that are competing with its own phones. The reason for all this cooperation is clear: the power of platforms. The power of Google in search, Amazon in media distribution, Facebook in social networks, and Apple and Android in mobile operating systems means that none of these businesses can afford to cut off their competitors from their own customers.

In other cases, disruptive threats from new technologies are driving rival businesses to team together and cooperate to defend their turf. Television networks had already seen the impact of digital distribution and digital piracy on industries like music and books when they decided to team together to launch Hulu, an online streaming television service that combines the latest shows from the same networks that compete as direct rivals in traditional television distribution.

Fluid Industries and Asymmetric Competitors

Much of our thinking about competition takes the industry as the unit of analysis. Porter's five forces (the most famous framework for thinking about competition) provide a model for the overall level of competition within an industry: How intense is competition in the U.S. airline industry? Or the Mexican cement industry? Is it increasing or decreasing? And so on. But what happens if the definition and the boundaries of your industry are in flux?

Today, the boundaries of industries are much less static due to rapid technological change. When the electric car company Tesla entered the market, it seemed to clearly fit in the automotive industry, competing against other manufacturers of electric, gas, and hybrid vehicles, like Toyota, BMW, and General Motors. But in order to develop its cars, Tesla has had to focus on developing next-generation electric batteries as well as services for charging them. In 2015, Tesla announced that it might begin offering these same batteries for electric power storage in consumers' homes. If successful and if combined with home solar panels, these could become a challenger to traditional electric utilities in the home.[19] So is Tesla a car company or an electric battery company? We don't know yet.

Meanwhile, Alphabet (Google's parent company) is one of the leading companies developing software for self-driving cars, drawing on its strengths in massive data computation. When these cars become commercially viable, the company that is most known for its search engine might become one of the dominant players in an auto industry that is becoming as focused on data and artificial intelligence as it is on engines and chassis design. As digital sensors and connectivity become embedded in more and more objects (cars, tractors, jet engines, home appliances), the Internet of Things is likely to redefine the boundaries of many industries that were less transformed by the Internet than were media and information businesses.

Companies can expect to compete with more and more businesses that do not look much like them. We can think of this as a shift from symmetric to asymmetric competitors.

Symmetric competitors offer similar value propositions to customers. BMW and Mercedes-Benz have different brands and appeal to different drivers, but their offerings are broadly similar: ownership or lease of a private vehicle with many of the same features. Symmetric competitors also deliver that value with similar business models. One carmaker may be larger or smaller, with different economies of scale or other factors, but the broad model is the same—manufacturing plants, dealerships, pricing for sale and lease.

Asymmetric competitors are quite different. They offer similar value propositions to customers, but their business models are not the same. For an automaker like BMW, an asymmetric competitor might include a ride-sharing service like Uber—if customers buy fewer cars because Uber can fulfill their transit needs. (For many American teenagers, signing up for an Uber rider's account may replace getting a driver's license as the rite of passage upon turning 16 years old.[20]) If an electric utility's symmetric competitors are other companies providing energy to homes from the power grid, its asymmetric competitor could be a partnership between Tesla's home batteries unit and a solar panel company, which together could enable homeowners to unplug from the grid completely. If HBO's symmetric competitors are Showtime and AMC (offering programs to consumers through the same cable bundles), then its asymmetric competitors would include Hulu and Netflix, which provide viewing options and original content through digital devices and outside of the cable intermediary.

Rita McGrath advises thinking about competition less in terms of industries and more in terms of arenas—companies that have a similar offer, for the same market segment, in the same geographic location.[21] Russell Dubner, U.S. CEO of Edelman, the world's largest independently owned PR firm, thinks a lot about asymmetrical competitors, or "substitutes," as he calls them. "We always look at substitutes—how else can our client spend their money to achieve that same goal? If you just look at direct competition, someone can eat your lunch and you'll never see them coming."[22]

Disintermediation and Intermediation

One of the biggest impacts of digital technologies has been on the relationships of businesses to the partners in their supply chain—the companies that supply critical inputs for the primary businesses' own products or that create additional value and distribute or sell those products to their eventual consumers.

This disruption and reconfiguration of business relationships is mostly talked about in terms of *disintermediation*—the removal of an intermediary or middleman from a series of business transactions. The Internet is widely known to have been a powerful force for disintermediation, as it has made it much easier for goods and services of all kinds to reach any audience that wants them.

Newspapers were disintermediated by classified websites like Craigslist or Monster.com. Individual advertisers were able to skip the middleman (an expensive print ad in the local newspaper) and reach the desired audience directly by posting a cheap or free ad on one of these popular websites. Retail bookstore chains like Barnes & Noble and Borders Books were disintermediated by the arrival of Amazon.com, which for the first time offered publishers another path by which to sell books to consumers (Borders eventually filed for bankruptcy). In these cases, a new, digital-first challenger arrived to act as intermediary, letting the supplier sidestep its traditional channel for reaching customers.

In other cases, companies trying to reach their ultimate consumers may build their own digital channel to sidestep, or disintermediate, their traditional partners. The insurance industry in many countries was built on an agency model, in which insurers sold their policies to individuals through independent agents. This reduced the employee overhead for the insurance companies but put a barrier between them and the users of their products, which inevitably reduces how much they know about those consumers and how effectively they can market to them. Insurance companies are extremely beholden to the intermediary, their agents, and this dependency hampers them in many markets when responding to consumers' increasing desire for self-service and online shopping and purchasing options. Newer insurance companies, such as Geico (owned by Berkshire Hathaway), have entered the market that are selling directly to consumers online. Allstate Insurance has maintained its insurance agents while at the same time acquiring Esurance, which sells directly to consumers like Geico does. Allstate is, in essence, maintaining and disintermediating its sales partners at the same time.

Digital platforms are also fueling a reverse phenomenon, which is best described as *intermediation*. In these cases, a new business manages to insert itself as an intermediary between the customers and a company that used to sell directly to them. Intermediation happens when a platform builds such a large customer base and becomes such a valuable interface to customers that other businesses cannot afford to skip the opportunity to reach customers through that platform. The benefit to the new intermediary is that it inevitably extracts a toll or platform benefit, often capturing a great deal of value.

Facebook, for example, has managed to insert itself as an intermediary between news readers and news publications that previously reached them directly, whether through printed editions or their own websites and apps. With social media driving over 30 percent of all traffic to publisher websites and Facebook delivering 75 percent of that social traffic, no publisher, from BuzzFeed to The New York Times Company, can afford to skip using Facebook as a means to promote its content.[23] That gives increasing leverage to Facebook, which is able to greatly influence the prominence and visibility of publishers' articles in the News Feed of its users. (In fact, Facebook became such a huge driver of publisher traffic only after reconfiguring its algorithm in December 2013 to give more priority to news stories.) As Facebook's leverage over publishers grows, it is expected to extract a share of the advertising revenue from the readers it delivers to news publishers.[24]

The same phenomenon of intermediation can be seen with other increasingly powerful platforms. Apple Pay, the mobile payment system for iPhones, iPads, and Apple Watches, was able to enlist Visa and Master-Card as partners for its launch, despite the fact that Apple Pay is inserting itself as an intermediary between these credit card companies and their own cardholder customers. Apple's huge and affluent customer base and its track record in designing digital interfaces that customers use make it too powerful to ignore in the growing mobile payments sector. When a consortium of 200 German publishers complained that Google was stealing value from them by including their articles in its search results, Google decided to simply exclude them from its searches. When they experienced a loss of traffic that they said could cause member publishers to go bankrupt, the consortium reversed course and asked Google to put their articles back in its search results.[25]

Tool: The Competitive Value Train

As the locus of competition expands from rivalries among similar firms to include asymmetric competitors and a firm's own suppliers and intermediaries, managers need new ways of visualizing their competitive landscape. The Competitive Value Train is a tool I designed to analyze competition and leverage between a firm and its business partners, direct rivals, and asymmetric competitors.

Let's avoid any confusion with two related terms. Porter's *value chain* is a popular tool for examining the various processes that add value to a product or service within a company's own operations (e.g., how the R&D, manufacturing, marketing, and sales departments each add value). The *supply chain* is a widely used tool for modeling the processes across different companies that contribute to a product's manufacture, distribution, and sale. Both these tools focus on operational design.

By contrast, the value train focuses on competition by looking at the leverage between the companies in a supply chain and their potential substitutes and by mapping how a particular product or service reaches a particular group of customers. For a business with many products, suppliers, sales channels, and types of customers, a single value train will show only one thread of its complete operations or business model. But this will allow managers to focus on the competitive and cooperative forces at work in delivering that particular stream of value.

A competitive value train starts with a horizontal train of firms leading to a final consumer on the right. The number of firms drawn will depend on your business model and means of distribution. Following are three broad types commonly seen as you move upstream from the final consumer:

- *Distributor*: Delivers the product or service to the consumer, although it may not manufacture the product or service (e.g., a retailer like Walmart or an e-tailer like Amazon)
- *Producer*: Creates the finished product, service, or offering paid for by the consumer (e.g., an insurance company, record label, book publisher, or laptop manufacturer)
- *Originator*: Creates unique elements or parts of the offering (e.g., a manufacturer producing operating systems or chips for laptops or a musician creating recordings for a record label)

Figure 3.2 presents an example of a simple value train with these three kinds of businesses.

The next element to add to a value train is competitors. Below each business, or "car," in the train, we indicate its symmetric competitors. Above the same car, we indicate any asymmetric competitors.

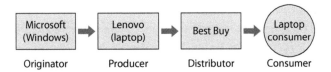

Figure 3.2
Simple Value Trains for Laptop Computers (Without Competitors).

Figure 3.3 represents a competitive value train for books sold through a retailer like Barnes & Noble. The books originate with the author (conceiving and writing the manuscript), who is contracted by the publisher (providing financing, marketing, distribution, and editorial services), and then are sold through a book retailer to the ultimate consumer, the reader. The competitive leverage of Barnes & Noble is shaped by the relative strengths of other physical retail chains and the dominant e-tailer, Amazon.

Understanding Competition as Leverage

By depicting both partners and their symmetric and asymmetric competitors, the value train aims to provide a multidimensional view of competition and cooperation.

Think of the newspaper industry. The *Washington Post* and the *New York Times* newspapers are clearly symmetric competitors—they provide similar value to overlapping readers. However, the biggest competitive threats to each newspaper may lie elsewhere.

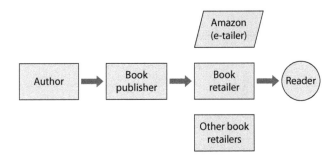

Figure 3.3
Competitive Value Train: Books Sold Through Retailers.

As we have already seen, as Facebook inserts itself between the newspapers and their readers, it is gaining competitive power as an intermediary (figure 3.4a). At the same time, classified websites have disintermediated the newspapers in the path from advertisers to readers (figure 3.4b). Lastly, these newspapers may face a threat from the reporters who write their articles (figure 3.4c). In the digital age, star journalists are able to cultivate brand visibility directly with their audience, particularly with the use of social media. Writer Ezra Klein quickly developed such a huge following as a political policy blogger at the *Washington Post* that the editors were reportedly loathe to critique his columns. Although the leadership of the paper supported Klein and tried to keep him on as a star employee, he eventually left to serve as founding editor-in-chief at a new digital-first news venture, Vox.com. The same process has been seen with several other star journalists in traditional media companies.

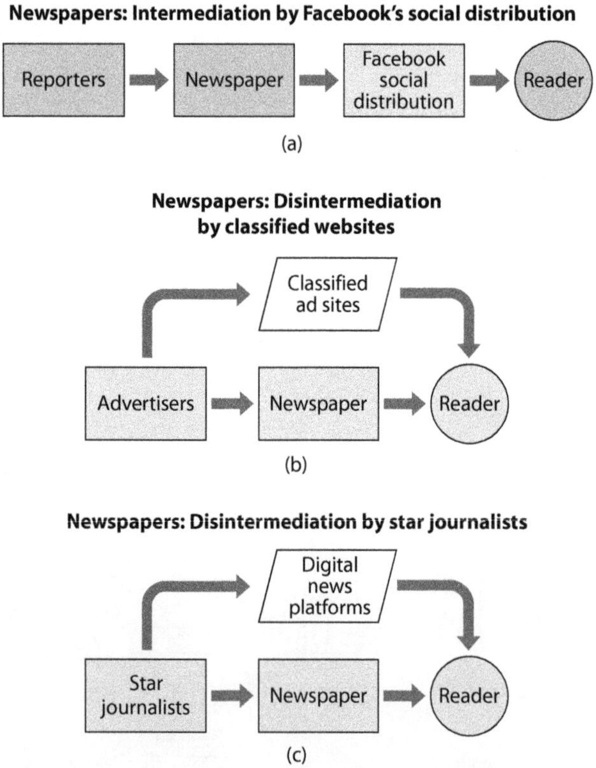

Newspapers: Intermediation by Facebook's social distribution

(a)

**Newspapers: Disintermediation
by classified websites**

(b)

Newspapers: Disintermediation by star journalists

(c)

Figure 3.4
Value Train Analysis of Three Competitive Threats to Newspapers.

The value train can be used to examine all three of these competitive dynamics for newspapers and the critical questions in each case: Who has leverage in the relationships in the value train? Where is disintermediation happening or possible? Where is intermediation happening? Looked at through the lens of the value train, it becomes clear that the goal for any business is not simply to defeat, or even outperform, its direct competitors (e.g., the *Washington Post* vs. the *New York Times*). The overriding competitive goal is to gain more leverage in its value train.

Two Rules of Power in Value Trains

More generally, we can identify two broad principles that determine who tends to gain power within value trains.

PRINCIPLE 1: POWER TO THE UNIQUE VALUE CREATOR

At every stage in the value train, each business needs to create unique value in order to exert competitive leverage on its partners upstream (to the left) and downstream (to the right). The more a business is able to distinguish itself from both symmetric and asymmetric competitors at its own stage in the value train, the more bargaining power it will maintain with its own partners and customers. All news publishers are losing influence to Facebook, but those whose products are more of a commodity have much less leverage than a publisher like The New York Times Company, which has continued to maintain a differentiated brand in the eyes of readers. Similarly, most reporters do not have the differentiated value to be able to disintermediate their own publication. It is the unique value of a writer like Ezra Klein (in the eyes of his readers) that gives him leverage over his publishers. Unique value can come from a variety of sources: intellectual property, brand equity, network effects, anything that creates additional value for the final customer in the value train.

PRINCIPLE 2: POWER TO THE ENDS

As industry redefinition leads to more asymmetric competitors, power in value trains is moving to the ends, where there is less opportunity to be skipped over by business partners. In a value train, the first creator and the final distributor to the end consumer each have additional influence by virtue of their positions. By contrast, the parties in the middle tend to be boxed in and lose influence relative to the creators and end distributors. Examples of original creators who gain more leverage are star journalists and brands manufacturing in-demand products (on the left side of the value train). Examples of strong final distributors are Walmart in physical retailing and Facebook as a media distribution layer (at the right side of the value train). This power imbalance was described in manufacturing by Acer founder Stan Shih's "smiling curve": profits are inevitably captured by the companies that originate key patents and those that brand and distribute products, but the fabricators and manufacturers in between them languish in a valley of low leverage and profitability.[26] Almost all digital platforms—whether Airbnb, Facebook, Google, or Apple Pay—seek to secure a position as the final interface to the end consumer because of the competitive leverage that it confers.

Applying the Competitive Value Train

You can use the tool to predict and assess possible moves by partners, competitors, and new entrants in your value train. You can also use it to analyze possible competitive moves that you are considering. It is particularly useful for understanding the dynamics of disintermediation and intermediation as well as any shifts in the relationships between your firm and its sales channels or its suppliers or both. This can include a business leapfrogging over its current partners—for example, launching a direct-to-consumer business to become its own distributor.

Figure 3.5 shows value train analyses of two examples seen earlier in the chapter. The first shows HBO's decision to launch a direct online service for viewers (branded HBO Now), despite the continued importance of cable companies as HBO's distributors to most consumers. The second depicts Allstate's acquisition of Esurance, an asymmetric competitor of its own affiliated insurance agents, while continuing to sell through the agents under the Allstate corporate brand name.

You can analyze other plans for intermediation, disintermediation, or channel substitution similarly in order to forecast their potential impact on competition and cooperation between firms.

A detailed guide on how to draw, and use, the Competitive Value Train can be found at http://www.davidrogers.biz under Tools.

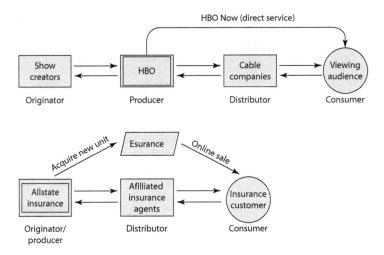

Figure 3.5
Value Train Analysis of Competitive Moves by HBO and Allstate.

Organizational Challenges of Competition

As businesses adapt to the growing importance of platforms and the shifting landscape of competition and cooperation between firms, many of the challenges that arise are not just strategic challenges but also organizational ones.

Shifting Roles Midstream

Reshuffling the roles and relationships of a company's value train can be difficult for an enterprise that has a long-standing business model and relationships with both upstream suppliers and downstream distributors. *Channel conflict* is the common term for the situation where a business is balancing both working with a key sales channel and going around it. Shifting channel strategies is particularly difficult for a business because of its vested interest in existing channels and the risk of cannibalizing its current sales in pursuit of a new opportunity.

The trade-offs are quite real. When e-commerce first offered the promise of selling directly to consumers, many brands embarked on plans to set up their own online stores. Most failed due to lack of sufficient demand (consumers didn't want to go to a different website to replace each item in their wardrobe or cabinet), lack of technical capability (to create a great online shopping experience), or both. Levi Strauss shifted course after spending millions of dollars on its e-commerce plans and chose to partner with traditional retailers like Macy's that were building online stores selling multiple brands.[27] Only later did Levi Strauss return to launch its own online channel. Other companies, like furniture maker Ethan Allen, have opted to use their offline sales partners to support order fulfillment for products sold directly to consumers. This allows them to establish an online channel but keep their existing offline partners invested.

When companies do launch a direct-to-consumer channel in competition with their primary sales channel, they need to establish clear boundaries. These may be geographic boundaries: some insurance companies that rely on sales agents have initiated their first direct-to-consumer sales in geographic markets where they are not well established. Another kind of boundary can be provided by branding: when Allstate purchased Esurance, it opted to run the direct-to-consumer business as an independent unit under a different brand.

Warfare Mentality

Both co-opetition and the search for leverage in value trains require leaders to look at competition as more than a zero-sum contest.

In organizations where the "competition is war" metaphor and mindset run deep, cooperating with rivals and competing with partners can pose a cultural challenge. When Doreen Lorenzo, former president of Frog Design, first took the helm of that company, a peer gave her a book: Sun Tzu's *The Art of War*. "I don't want to sound like a baby boomer," Doreen told me, "but sometimes, war is not the answer. Or not the only answer."

Sun Tzu is not alone. Among the many bellicose management guides published are books such as Wess Roberts's *Leadership Secrets of Attila the Hun*. That scorched-earth conqueror is famed for quotes such as "There, where I have passed, the grass will never grow again."

There are certainly times for fierce competition with rivals. But to succeed in the dynamic ecosystem of business today, leaders need to know when to fight and when to make peace. The creators of PayPal certainly learned this. They actually started out as the leaders of two bitterly competing start-ups, Confinity and X.com, with mirror-image products. "By late 1999, we were in all-out war," writes Peter Thiel, who goes on to describe 100-hour workweeks gripped by a mania of competition. "No doubt that was counterproductive, but the focus wasn't on objective productivity; the focus was defeating X.com. One of our engineers actually designed a bomb for this purpose. . . . Calmer heads prevailed." Finally, in 2000, faced with a rapidly deflating tech bubble, the founders of the two companies met on neutral ground and negotiated a 50–50 merger. "De-escalating the rivalry post-merger wasn't easy, but . . . as a unified team, we were able to ride out the dot-com crash and then build a successful business."[28]

Openness

One of the biggest challenges of a platform business model is letting go of some of the value creation process. By their nature, platforms grow by letting their distinct outside parties each bring their own value to the platform and interact with a substantial degree of independence. This requires a hands-off approach that may not be possible for some leaders or some company cultures.

The most valuable platform business in the world struggled mightily with this. Apple and its founder, Steve Jobs, had always distinguished themselves with an exacting focus on controlling every aspect of the customer experience for products like Macintosh computers, iPod music players, and the iTunes music store. Their seamless integration seemed to hinge on Apple's maintaining absolute and total control.

When the iPhone first launched, the company followed this same philosophy: everything was designed and built by Apple. In its first year, users immediately recognized the power of the computer sitting behind the iPhone's glowing touchscreen, and hackers began "jailbreaking" their phones so they could experiment and add new programs of their own design. Apple was faced with a decision: fight back against the hackers (who were, in fact, Apple's early adopters and avid customers) or shift course and provide tools for outside developers to program directly for the iPhone. Jobs's uncharacteristic reversal led to the release of the software development kit that launched the App Store. This move sparked incredible innovation, turned the iPhone into a platform business, and led Apple's growth into the most valuable public company in the world.

For leaders navigating today's shifting landscape of competition, knowing how open or closed to keep their business model is critical.

~

To operate successfully in the digital age, businesses must have a dynamic understanding of how firms compete and cooperate. Rather than a simplistic view of bitter enemies and unalloyed partnerships, businesses need to see all their interfirm relationships as a shifting mix of competition and cooperation. They must understand the value of cooperating with direct rivals, the threat of asymmetric competitors who look nothing like them, the importance of leverage within their relationships with partner businesses, and the power of digitally enabled platform business models to bring together different parties and drive new value creation.

Relationships with other firms, in short, have become just as networked and interconnected as relationships with customers. In both relationships, the increasing digitization of interactions is yielding another product as well: data. Every interaction with customers or with businesses is producing streams of information that can now be recorded, captured, and analyzed in ways that were impossible only a short while ago. Understanding how to utilize this data strategically, as a source of new value for businesses, is the next important domain of digital transformation.

4

Turn Data Into Assets

DATA

The role of data for businesses is changing dramatically today. Many companies that have used data as a specific part of their operations for years are now discovering a data revolution: data is coming from new sources, being applied to new problems, and becoming a key driver of innovation.

One innovator is The Weather Company (TWC). This media company started in 1980 with a television channel, The Weather Channel. Since then, it has branched out into third-party publishing platforms, websites, and mobile apps, including the one I use every morning to decide whether to pack an umbrella. Like most media companies, TWC is in the business of making content that draws an audience and selling ads that are placed in that content. Data has always been part of that business model: every day vast quantities of weather data need to be captured, analyzed, and turned into the colorful charts, animated graphics, and reliable forecasts that keep audiences tuning in.

But TWC has discovered that its data can be much more than just the raw material it uses to create programming for its viewers. The same data that the firm collects, manages, and analyzes constitutes a key strategic asset and, increasingly, a source of new innovation and value creation.

I learned about this in detail from Vikram Somaya, who was the general manager of WeatherFX (later renamed WSI), a new TWC division focused on thinking differently about weather data. Somaya was an art history major in college and is fond of quoting Shakespeare, but at TWC, he led the teams of data scientists who analyze the company's data to generate additional value for both business customers and end consumers.

Weather has a powerful impact on a wide range of businesses. By one estimate, up to one-third of the U.S. economy is shaped by variations in weather.[1] Walmart has said that local weather is one of the biggest factors in its predictive models for store sales. TWC's data scientists work with major retailers to identify when they should predict a spike or slump in their sales so they can adjust their advertising spend (to commit more resources or to hold them back) as well as their merchandising.

The company also works directly with brand advertisers—in categories like allergy medication, fleece jackets, and snow tires—to predict the best time for them to spend on ad placements. Even our snack food purchases on a given day (nacho chips or pretzels?) have been found to be shaped by whether the weather feels bright, sticky, or gloomy. With digital advertisements (inserted on websites or in apps like TWC's own), brands now have the opportunity to adjust and target their message on the fly, choosing which image to show specific viewers based on the weather where they are standing.[2]

TWC is even using its data to create new products and services for industries like the insurance sector. For instance, it has built an app called Hailzone for insurers like State Farm and Travelers to offer their auto insurance customers. Whenever a hailstorm is about to hit, Hailzone sends out a text message alert to those customers, warning them to move their cars inside. That saves a tremendous headache for the drivers and costly hail damage bills for the insurer.

The company is even collaborating with some of its most avid customers to grow and improve its data asset. Every day TWC crowdsources data from a community of 25,000 self-described "weather junkies" who pay to subscribe to a service called The Weather Underground. These avid hobbyists spend hundreds of dollars to buy their own weather-monitoring equipment, which they set up on their own property. Findings are shared and discussed among the network of fellow enthusiasts. With typical members uploading weather measurements at their own locations every

2.5 seconds, their input helps the company greatly improve the quality of its own data sets.

TWC has evolved from a media company that simply produces data as part of running its core operations to a company that is treating data as a source of innovation, new revenue, and strategic advantage.

Rethinking Data

The third domain of the digital transformation playbook is data. Growing a business in the digital age requires changing some fundamental assumptions about data's meaning and importance (see table 4.1). In the past, although data played a role in every business, it was mainly used for measuring and managing business processes and assisting in forecasting and long-term planning. Data was expensive to produce through structured research, surveys, and measurements. It was expensive to store in separate databases that mimicked silos of business operations. And it was used primarily to optimize existing operations.

Today, the role and possibilities for data are seemingly limitless. Generating data is often the easiest part, with great quantities continuously created by sources outside the firm. The greater challenge is harnessing this data and turning it into useful insights. Traditional analytics based on spreadsheets have given way to *big data*, where unstructured information joins with powerful new computational tools. But for data to become a real source of value, businesses need to change the way they think about data. They need to treat it as a key strategic asset.

Table 4.1
Data: Changes in Strategic Assumptions from the Analog to the Digital Age

From	To
Data is expensive to generate in firm	Data is continuously generated everywhere
Challenge of data is storing and managing it	Challenge of data is turning it into valuable information
Firms make use only of structured data	Unstructured data is increasingly usable and valuable
Data is managed in operational silos	Value of data is in connecting it across silos
Data is a tool for optimizing processes	Data is a key intangible asset for value creation

This chapter explores how the role of data is changing in business and what leadership challenges this poses. We will examine the value of data as an asset, the components of an effective data strategy, and the power and misconceptions of the big-data revolution. We will see where businesses are finding the data they need and how they are turning it into new sources of value. This chapter also presents a strategic ideation tool, the Data Value Generator. This tool allows businesses to use customer data to create new value in specific areas of their operations.

But, first, let's look at what it means to manage and invest in data as an intangible business asset.

Data as Intangible Asset

For many of the digital titans of today's business world, it seems clear that the data they capture regarding their customers is one of their most valuable assets. Much of Facebook's market capitalization is rooted in the value of the rich data it collects on users and in its ability to harness that data with innovative tools for advertisers, helping them understand and reach precisely the right audience.

But other kinds of data can be valuable as well. In building its Maps service, Google has invested heavily for years in developing a best-in-class set of cartographic data. This includes sending camera-equipped cars around the world to measure out every road and capture its photographic Street View (more recently, it has sent cameras by camelback to map the deserts of Arabia). The company is constantly updating and "hand-cleaning" its data with teams of human data wranglers. It tracks up to 400 data points per road segment (the stretch of asphalt between two intersections). Depending on the pace of economic development, that road data needs to be updated with daunting regularity.[3]

On the other hand, we saw Apple's failure to invest sufficiently in mapping data—which led to a famous competitive fumble in 2012. As part of its ongoing rivalry with search giant Google, Apple chose to remove Google Maps as the default mapping app on all iPhones. Instead, it gave iPhone customers its own new Maps app, running on data Apple had purchased from various third parties. True to form, the Cupertino company had designed a stunning user interface for its app. But it had underestimated the quality of Google's data asset. Millions of iPhone users who were forced to use the new maps flooded Apple with complaints. Cities were misspelled or erased, tourist attractions were misplaced, famous buildings disappeared, and roads literally vanished into thin air. The errors were so bad that they compelled the first letter of apology by an Apple CEO to customers. In it, Tim Cook went so far as to advise customers to download and use competitor apps from the App Store until Apple's own maps improved.

Data is valuable not just for companies like Google and Facebook. For any business today, data—like intellectual property, patents, or a brand—is a key intangible asset. The relative importance of that asset will vary somewhat based on the nature of the business (just as brands have greater importance to a fashion company than an industrial manufacturer). But data is an important asset to every business today—and neglected at our peril.

One of the most common ways that businesses can build an asset out of customer data is through loyalty programs. For years, retailers and airlines have offered loyalty miles, points, rewards, or a tenth sandwich free in hopes of increasing customer retention and total spending over time. But, today, much of the value of loyalty programs is in the accumulated customer data that they generate. When I sign up for your loyalty program, I am explicitly asking you to track my shopping behavior in order to earn rewards. That gives your business much more than an address for direct mail; your data about me grows over time to help you better understand my unique behaviors and interests as a customer.

By designing new customer experiences with data in mind, companies can extend this model of providing customer benefits in return for customer data gained. Take Walt Disney Parks and Resorts and its new MagicBand wristbands. Promoted as a way to bring the convenience of smartphones in to the traditional theme park experience, these colorful rubber bracelets (outfitted with RFID tags) allow guests to enter the park, unlock their hotel room, purchase meals and merchandise, and skip the wait on up to three rides per day. The MagicBand is the heart of a $1 billion initiative to bring digital interactivity to Disney theme parks, and it aims to earn that money back by increasing the "share of wallet" that visitors spend at Disney. But it is also designed to provide Disney with previously inaccessible data on the behaviors of its guests: Where do they go when? Which rides are popular with which types of guests? Which foods might be better moved to different areas of the sprawling park? The MagicBands even allow guests to opt to be identifiable to Disney staff so that a child can be greeted by name by costumed characters or offered a birthday wish by a talking animatronic animal on a ride. These and other types of personalized service experiences will become available as Disney builds more data around its visitors on both the large scale and the individual level. The trick is in crafting the right experience so that, just as with a loyalty program, customers willingly exchange their data for added value from the business.

You don't have to be a company as large as Disney or Google to start building your data asset. Even small businesses can now use Web-based customer relationship management tools to keep track of who opened which e-mails, tailor follow-up messages, analyze which offers are the best fit for which customers, and more. As we will see in our discussion of big data, the shift to cloud computing is putting ever more powerful data management tools into the hands of small and mid-sized businesses.

Every Business Needs a Data Strategy

Once you start to treat data as an asset, you need to develop a data strategy in your organization. That includes understanding what data you need as well as how you will apply it.

An explicit data strategy may seem obvious in industries like financial services and telecommunications, which are accustomed to copious amounts of customer data. But smaller firms and those in less data-rich industries must also develop forward-looking strategies for their data.

The following five principles should guide any organization in developing its data strategy.

- *Gather diverse data types*: Every business should look at its data asset holistically and include diverse types of data that serve different purposes (see table 4.2). Business process data—such as data on your supply chain, internal billing, and human resources management—is used to manage and optimize business operations, reduce risk, and comply with reporting requirements. Product or service data is data that is essential to the core value of your products or services. Examples include weather data for TWC, cartographic data for Google Maps, and the kind of business data that Bloomberg provides to business customers. Customer data ranges widely—from transaction data, to customer surveys, to reviews and comments in social media, to customer search behavior and browsing patterns on your website. Companies that do not sell directly to consumers (e.g., packaged goods companies) traditionally could gather customer data only through market research. As we will see later, even these businesses are discovering

Table 4.2
Key Data Types for Business Strategy

Data type	Examples	Utility
Business process data	Inventory and supply chain Sales Billing Human resources	Manage and optimize business operations, reduce risk, provide external reporting
Product or service data	Maps data (for Google) Business data (for Bloomberg) Weather data (for TWC)	Deliver the core value proposition of the business's product or service
Customer data	Purchases Behaviors and interactions Comments and reviews Demographics Survey responses	Provide a complete picture of the customer and allow for more relevant and valuable interactions

new opportunities to piece together data to get a much clearer picture of their customers than was possible before.

- *Use data as a predictive layer in decision making*: The worst thing that companies can do with data is gather it and not apply it when making decisions. You need to plan how your organization will utilize its data to make better-informed decisions in all aspects of its business. Operations data can be used in statistical modeling to plan for and optimize the use of your resources. Customer data can be used to predict which changes in your services or communications may yield improved results. With detailed data from its MagicBands, Disney can make better-informed decisions on which merchandise to feature near different rides and how to manage variable demand and foot traffic. Amazon uses your past browsing behavior to determine which products it should show you in your next visit.
- *Apply data to new product innovation*: Data can power your existing products or services, but it can also be used as a springboard for imagining and testing new product innovations. TWC's Hailzone mobile app is a perfect case of a company using its existing product data (for its TV shows and apps) to build a new service that added value for multiple customers (insurance companies and their insureds). It helped that TWC was able to step outside its normal perspective as a media company and think about different business models based on

things like utility and risk management rather than just viewer eyeballs and advertising. Netflix uses its vast amounts of data on viewer preferences—for genres, actors, directors, and more—to help it craft new television series like *House of Cards*. This practice lets Netflix circumvent the traditional network TV practice of investing in pilots for numerous new shows in hopes that one or more will pan out. That's using data to innovate more quickly and cheaply.

- *Watch what customers do, not what they say*: Behavioral data is anything that directly measures actions of your customers. It can include things like transactions, online searches (a powerful measure of your customers' intentions), clickstream data (which pages they visited, where they clicked, and what they left in their shopping carts), and direct measures of engagement data (which articles in your newsletter they clicked to read). Behavioral data is always the best customer data—it is much more valuable than reported opinions or anything customers tell a market researcher in a survey. That is not just because people lie in surveys but also because, as humans, we are extremely fallible at remembering our behavior, predicting our future actions, or considering our motivations. This is why Netflix shifted its recommendation system from customers' own rankings to behavioral data as soon as it moved customers from DVDs to streaming video, which made it possible to measure what we actually watch rather than the unopened red envelopes on our dresser. Netflix knows that there are big differences between the movies that we give a five-star ranking and those that we actually wind up watching while doing the dishes on a Wednesday night.

- *Combine data across silos*: Traditionally, businesses have allowed their data to be generated and reside in separate divisions or departments. One of the most important aspects of data strategy is to look for ways to combine your previously separate sets of data and see how they relate to each other. A memorable example of the benefits of combining data sets comes from municipal government here in New York City. Scott Stringer, the city's comptroller (CFO), was seeking to reduce the costs of lawsuits against the city. He launched an initiative to compare the data on lawsuits and damages paid with other city data sets, including the budgets of different departments over time. A surprising correlation was discovered: after the city's parks budget had been slashed a few years earlier and its seasonal tree pruning reduced, legal claims from citizens injured by falling tree limbs skyrocketed. The cost to the city from a single lawsuit was greater than the entire tree pruning budget for three years! Once this was discovered and the budget funding was restored, lawsuits dropped dramatically.[4] As your business environment becomes increasingly complex, your ability to find, combine, and learn from diverse sources of data will become more important than ever.

In putting together a data strategy, it is also important to understand that many of today's data sets are very different from the spreadsheets and relational databases that drove the best practices of data-intensive industries in the pre-digital era. The entire nature of available data, and how it can be applied and used by business, has undergone a revolution in recent years. That revolution is commonly termed *big data*.

The Impact of Big Data

The term *big data* first appeared in the mid-1990s, introduced in tech circles by John Mashey, chief scientist of Silicon Graphics, around the time of the birth of the World Wide Web.[5] But the phrase entered the broader business conversation around 2010 as businesses of all kinds began to grapple with the vast supply of data generated by digital technologies. At first, the term seemed a bit faddish, a marketing ploy used by data storage firms to get IT departments to increase their spending on data servers. But the real changes at work have been much more profound than the size of hard drives or server farms.

Make no mistake: the size of data sets is increasing rapidly. Every graph representing the amount of digital data stored worldwide each year shows the skyward leap of an exponential curve. These curves all recede exponentially into the past as well. The sheer amount of recorded data, in other words, has been growing for a long time—likely since the origin of computers, maybe since the origin of writing.

So what is new about big data if not the rapidly growing "bigness" of it?

The phenomenon of big data is best understood in terms of two interrelated trends: the rapid growth of new types of unstructured data and the rapid development of new capabilities for managing and making sense of this kind of data for the first time. The impact of these two is shaped by a third trend: the rise of cloud computing infrastructure, which makes the potential of big data increasingly accessible to more and more businesses.

Big Data Is Really Unstructured Data

Traditionally, a firm's data processes were based on analyzing *structured* data—the kind of data sets that fill a database with neatly organized rows and columns (e.g., with addresses of customers, inventories of products, or expenses and debits of various financial accounts).

But the big-data era has been marked by the profusion of new types of *unstructured* data—information that is recorded but doesn't fit easily into neat forms. A business may have access to the ungrammatical text posts of social media, the flood of smartphone-generated images, real-time mapping and location signals, or the data from sensors rapidly spreading over our bodies and our entire world; all these types of data are rich in meaning—but difficult to parse by familiar tools like spreadsheets.

One of the biggest sources of unstructured data is social media. As over a billion users worldwide participate in networks like Facebook, Twitter, and Weibo, they are constantly producing vast amounts of data in the form of their posts, comments, and updates. This social data is attitudinal (what people are saying can capture their opinions, likes, and dislikes) and can be used to measure affinity (whom they friend, follow, or link to reflects social ties and allows businesses to infer relationships between them and others in their network). And this data is real-time and continuous, allowing businesses to analyze shifts in opinion, sentiment, and conversation with precise longitudinal detail. Because of this, numerous organizations have sought to gain insight from the analysis of social data. Brands monitor their reputation over time based on what customers are saying, the Centers for Disease Control uses social media to help track the spread of flu and influenza, Hollywood predicts the opening weekend performance of new movies based on the social "chatter" after opening night, and economists have even used social media to effectively predict stock market performance.

Another new kind of unstructured data is location data. The data being generated by mobile devices like smartphones comes with geolocation markers, which provide a continuous record of where we are and where we're going in real time. The inclusion of location data with other kinds of behavioral data adds tremendous additional context. Increasingly, search engine results are shaped not just by the words we are using in our search but also by where we are when we search. (If we Google the word *pizza*, we are likely to be shown the closest establishments, with links to their phone numbers and addresses, instead of pizza history or recipes.) Research by my colleague Miklos Sarvary has shown that the patterns of where we go at various times of the week (as measured by our phones) reveal a great deal about who we are. By analyzing these "co-location" patterns, Sarvary and his coauthors were able to show that customers with similar location "footprints" were likely to buy similar products and could be effectively targeted for marketing based on that data alone.[6]

The biggest emerging source of unstructured data is the sensors that are becoming embedded in everything around us as we shift to a world of truly ubiquitous networks. By 2020, Cisco expects that over 50 billion devices will be connected and sharing information over the Internet—and the vast majority of these devices will not be computers, smartphones, or Web servers. This phenomenon, known as the Internet of Things, encompasses smart automobiles, factories and product supply chains, and lightbulbs and home appliances as well as sensors embedded in the watches and clothing we wear and in the medicines we ingest. Together, all of these applications will soon result in billions of devices transmitting and generating new sets of data that can be put to business use. For example, GE has installed sensors on its jet engines that allow the engines to continuously post updates on their status and operating details. (GE calls the system "Facebook for jet engines.") This real-time data lets airline mechanics monitor the status of critical aircraft equipment so they can make repairs when they actually are needed rather than on a schedule of estimated need. This makes fleet maintenance more efficient and makes air travel cheaper and more convenient.

New Tools to Wrestle Unstructured Data

The second trend shaping big data is the rise of new technological capabilities for handling and making sense of all this unstructured data. If not for this, big data would be simply a giant haystack in which the needle of business insight might well be invisible. Fortunately, a range of technological developments is expanding our abilities to use the unstructured data that technology is producing.

The continuing exponential growth of computer processing power is a big factor in our improved ability to use data. Moore's law, coined by Intel cofounder Gordon Moore in 1965, predicts a doubling in the performance of computer chips roughly every eighteen months as transistors become faster and smaller. For fifty years, the prediction has held, and the results have transformed the world. ENIAC, the first modern computer, was built in 1946 and filled a room the size of a small gymnasium. But by 1983, when I first studied computing, my student-grade Texas Instruments pocket calculator had more processing power than ENIAC. Moore's law tells us that this decade's supercomputer is the next decade's pocket device.

Recent technologies have further enabled data processing on a large scale with acceptable costs. In-memory computing can accelerate analytics to the kind of real-time computing that allows digital advertising to select the ad seen by each visitor to a webpage, based on the weather where they are, the sites they have visited recently, or any other critical determinants that can be mined through data. Hadoop is an open-source software framework that enables distributed parallel processing of huge amounts of data across multiple servers in different locations. With Hadoop, even the biggest data sets can be managed affordably.

Other tools focus less on increasing power and more on making sense out of the chaos of unstructured data. New data-mining tools allow programs to sift through the raw stuff of social media and pick out patterns that human managers then can examine to recognize trends and key words.

Perhaps the biggest advances in managing unstructured data have come from new developments in "cognitive" computing. Natural language processing, for example, can interpret normal human language, whether from spoken commands, social media conversations, or books or articles, without adaptation. It is critical to the development of systems that can identify patterns in big-data sets of human language, such as recordings of customer phone calls to call centers. Another key development is machine learning—resulting in computing systems that can recognize patterns and improve their own capability over time, based on experience and feedback. As computers are modeled around neural networks, they go beyond just spotting patterns in unstructured data: they receive feedback from their environment or human trainers (indicating which conclusions were wrong and which were correct) and reprogram themselves over time.

Natural language processing and machine learning are combined in a system like IBM's Watson, which can read vast amounts of written language and develop ever more accurate inferences by using feedback and coaching from human experts. Watson famously debuted on the world stage by playing the quiz show *Jeopardy!*—where it bested the top human champions by combining encyclopedic recall with a human-like ability to have educated "hunches" (e.g., estimating that its best guess to a question had a 42 percent likelihood of being correct). Since then, Watson has moved to the real world. Physicians have trained Watson, using a library of millions of patient case histories, to the point where Watson is more accurate than many doctors in making an initial diagnosis of a new cancer patient. Watson and similar technologies will be at the forefront of the next wave of big-data analytics—informing everything from customer service, to fraud detection, to advertising media planning.

Big Data on Tap from the Cloud

An additional trend is shaping the impact of big data: a revolution in the storage and accessibility of both data and data processing. In the old data paradigm, for a business to manage data, it needed to invest in owned infrastructure to collect and hold all of the data as well as any tools to analyze it. This significant capital requirement led to disparities among companies, with many unable to afford the sophisticated use of data. Today, businesses no longer need to store their own data, and even small businesses are increasingly able to access the leading tools for using unstructured data. The reason is the rise of cloud computing.

Think of voice-recognition systems like Siri or Google Now on our smartphones. There is a reason Siri doesn't work when our iPhones are offline: the computations required to understand spoken language and respond to it are too intensive to be managed with the processors on a current smartphone. Yet Siri works perfectly fine when able to access the cloud. All our device needs is a steady connection so that it can send our voice to a remote server with all the power necessary to process that unstructured data and respond in real time.

Increasingly, more and more computing applications and services are delivered seamlessly over the Internet, with the real processing power residing in the cloud rather than on our devices and computers. Amazon Web Services (the company's huge B2B computer services division), Microsoft, Google, and others are all driving a shift to a computing environment where businesses increasingly meet their needs through subscription and SaaS offerings rather than by buying and installing the most powerful computers on their own premises.

Cloud computing has profound implications for scalability and small business. Services like Watson are available "on tap" to businesses, just like cloud-based storage and customer databases are for small businesses. This means that big data is not the exclusive terrain of the world-class companies with huge IT departments. Any business can tap into best-in-class analytics tools today—from cloud providers like SAP and IBM—paying only for the data and the processing it uses. Big data doesn't have to have a big price tag.

Three Myths of Big Data

Although the rise of big data—the new unstructured data sets and the tools to make sense of them—is influencing every industry, there are some myths and misconceptions about what exactly has changed for businesses.

Myth 1: The Algorithm Will Figure It Out

I also call this the myth of the magic algorithm. Early reporting about big data created a false impression that to build the smart cities and businesses of the future, we would just put the best supercomputers together, let them compare all our unstructured data sets and unearth unexpected patterns, and voila! Your insights would appear on screen. In reality, this is not how data analytics is done.

Making sense of big data still requires a lot of involvement by skilled human analysts. There are several reasons for this. The quality and accuracy of the data are critical. How was the data collected? Is there a margin of error? Is it truly a representative sample? Are different data sets in the same format so they can be accurately compared? Much data wrangling is still done by human analysts, as these issues are not yet fully automated by software.

Biases can also exist in the algorithms used to look at the data, based on the assumptions of those who program them. An algorithm can be designed to filter applicant resumes to find the ones that most closely fit the profile of employees at your company. But past hiring may not reflect the diversity or skills you are seeking from future employees.

Most importantly, you need managers to ask the right questions of your data. What outcomes is your business most concerned about? Which kind of data patterns could you even act on? Algorithms are increasingly good at finding answers, but they still need humans to pose the right questions. Tariq Shaukat, chief commercial officer of Caesar's Entertainment, puts it this way: "If you start with the data, you will end with the data. The question that I ask my teams all the time is, 'What question are we trying to answer?'"[7]

Myth 2: Correlation Is All That Matters

Spotting a pattern is not (always) enough. Some commenters on big data have reported that data science is no longer concerned with causation, just correlation. The belief is that underlying patterns across data sets are a truth unto themselves that does not need to rely on foggy human ideas of cause and effect.

This is simply not true. It is critically important that managers understand the difference between simple correlation and causation—and know when this difference matters and when it doesn't. A simple rule of thumb: if you are only making predictions, data *correlation* is sufficient. But if you are looking to change the precondition, you need to know there is *causation* as well.

Think of Stringer, the city comptroller who discovered the data correlation between declining budgets for tree pruning and rising lawsuits against the city. If the tree-pruning budgets weren't actually *causing* the accidents that led to lawsuits, his decision to restore the pruning budget would not have helped. In Stringer's case, causality mattered a great deal.

On the other hand, imagine your ad agency has determined that married women in Ohio are more responsive to advertisements for your new hair care product. You are not going to try to grow your shampoo sales by encouraging Ohioans to get married (that would be influencing the precondition). You are just going to use this information to target more of your ads to married Ohioans instead of single ones. In a case like this, simply knowing a data correlation is fine.

Myth 3: All the Good Data Is Big Data

It would be a mistake to conflate big data with data strategy. In many cases, companies can build valuable data assets and apply them to strategic ends without delving into the messy world of big data.

Data does not always need to be "big" (i.e., unstructured) in order to be useful to a business. Powerful insights can be derived from the analysis and application of traditional, more structured data such as customer clickstream behavior (Where do customers click on a website, scroll down the page, spend more or less time, put things in shopping carts, etc.?). Even at a big-data powerhouse like Facebook, home to some of the biggest server clusters in the world, most queries run by engineers on a given day are of a scale that could be processed on a good laptop.[8] The point of your data strategy should be to generate value for your customers and business. Sometimes that will involve big data, and sometimes it won't.

Where to Find the Data You Need

As you begin to put together a data strategy, you will start with the data you are generating in your own business processes. However, you will likely identify gaps in the data you need for some of your goals. Finding the right additional sources of data is critical to filling in gaps and building your data asset over time. Important sources of data from outside your organization include customer data exchanges, lead users, supply chain partners, public data sets, and purchase or exchange agreements.

Customer Value Data Exchange

One of the best ways to generate additional data is to invite customers to contribute data as part of interacting with your business or in direct exchange for value you offer them. As mentioned in chapter 2, the navigation app Waze built both its map data and its real-time traffic data through user contributions. Waze was designed from the beginning around generating data. Whenever a customer has the app turned on, it is pinging their phone's GPS once a second. In densely populated areas, this approach provides exceptional real-time awareness of traffic conditions and allows for superior rerouting compared to competitors' apps. (After it reached 30 million users, Waze was bought by Google for $1.3 billion.) Because it does not sell directly to consumers, Coca-Cola historically has had little consumer data. But with the help of its MyCokeRewards loyalty program, the company has built up a data view on 20 million of its customers, the linchpin of its data asset. The Metropolitan Museum of Art was able to gather 100,000 new, valid e-mail addresses simply by asking visitors for their e-mail addresses in exchange for access to the Met's free Wi-Fi. What makes consumers willing to share their information with businesses? In a global research study that I conducted at Columbia University with Matt Quint, we observed four key factors: the type of value or rewards offered, the presence of a trusted relationship with the business, the type of data being requested, and the industry of the business.[9]

Lead User Participation

Lead users (a term coined by Eric von Hippel[10]) are your most active, avid, or involved customers. Their greater needs lead them to have greater interest in interacting with your products or business, and they can often be a unique and powerful source of data. We saw one example in The Weather Underground: the volunteer army of meteorological enthusiasts who happily contribute real-time feeds of additional weather data to TWC as part of participating in that community. Other companies use exclusivity to identify and leverage their lead users. Alexandre Choueiri, L'Oréal's president of international designer collections, explained to me that the cosmetics firm creates and engages confidential customer communities for designer brands such as Viktor & Rolf. The allure of joining a special club (literally called the "secret service") appeals to consumers, and the exclusivity helps the brand learn more about loyal users—not just casual one-time purchasers. "You get fewer people," Choueiri told me. "But they're really engaged. We sell this brand through the retailers, so this engagement tool is how we get data."[11] By engaging lead users, brands can solicit input and feedback from much more selective and important communities.

Supply Chain Partners

Business partners can be crucial sources of additional data for building your data asset. Companies producing consumer packaged goods now work closely with large retailers and with retail data services like Dunhumby. Power, leverage, and levels of trust can greatly influence who shares data with whom in many industries. In the travel industry, large airlines (such as Delta) can have nearly 100 million customers enrolled in their loyalty programs. But airlines and the online travel agencies (such as Travelocity or Orbitz) share only limited data. As a result, neither the agencies nor the airlines have access to the full picture of customers' travel behaviors when they want to customize pricing and offers at the point of sale. Increasingly, data partnerships will be a key element of how businesses negotiate terms of working together.

Public Data Sets

Another important source of new data is publicly accessible data sets. Some of these are in online public forums. The car reviews website Edmunds. com, for example, contains many years' worth of discussion forums—providing huge amounts of unstructured data in customers' conversations about car models, makes, preferences, and experiences. Many social media platforms, like Twitter, are easily searchable for real-time data. In addition, governments are increasingly providing public access to large data sets in machine-readable format. The U.S. government's census data, for example, has been in huge demand since being made available. In addition, more and more city governments are opening up APIs to let innovative businesses make use of government data and to spur new business opportunities.

Purchase or Exchange Agreements

Lastly, there are many opportunities for businesses to purchase or swap legitimate, valuable data with other firms. Businesses should avoid companies that offer shady sets of customer records collected through questionable means. Instead, firms should seek out the many reputable services that enable anonymized data comparisons. Anonymized data lets a company learn things like the conversion rate of offers (the portion of customers accepting the offer sent). The company's data shows which customers got the offer, the retailer's data shows who made a purchase, and the third-party service measures the conversion rate without revealing customer identities (which could be a violation of privacy terms).

Sometimes data can be received through an exchange or donation. During the 2014 World Cup, Waze shared anonymous driver data with city governments in Brazil to help them identify and respond more quickly to traffic buildups and road hazards. In Rio de Janeiro alone, up to 110,000 drivers a day were providing traffic data through Waze's API. Since then, Waze has been developing partnerships with other governments, such as the State of Florida. The company is not asking for payment but rather is seeking an exchange of more data. By receiving real-time data from highway sensors and information on construction projects and city events, Waze is improving its own data asset.

There are many more sources of data available today. The challenge for your business is often simply choosing which ones will best fit your needs. A recent forecast published by the *Journal of Advertising Research* summarized the changes anticipated in market research: as businesses are faced with a "river" of continuously generated data, the goal of research is not to expensively manufacture data, but to find the right tools to "fish" in that river in order to draw forth the insights and intelligence needed.[12]

Turning Customer Data into Business Value: Four Templates

As organizations gather more data and develop it into powerful assets, the next challenge is to continuously apply these assets to create new value for themselves.

We've seen examples of how product or service data provides value by enabling a business's core service to customers: think of TWC's use of weather data and Google's use of mapping data. We've also seen that business process data can yield value by optimizing and improving decision making, even in surprising ways—like Stringer's use of budgetary data.

If we look at customer data, we can find recurring patterns of best practices used to add value across differing industries and organizations. We can think of these practices as four templates for creating value from customer data: insights: revealing the invisible; targeting: narrowing the field; personalization: tailoring to fit; and context: providing a reference frame.

Let's take a look at each of these four data value templates and see how they are applied in different industries to create new value.

Insights: Revealing the Invisible

The first template for value creation is *insights*. By revealing previously invisible relationships, patterns, and influences, customer data can provide immense value to businesses. Data can provide insights into customer psychology (How are my brands or products perceived in the marketplace? What motivates and influences customer decisions? Can I predict and measure customer word of mouth?). Data can reveal patterns in customer behavior (How are buying habits shifting? How are customers using my product? Where is fraud or abuse taking place?). Data can also be used to measure the impact of specific actions on customers' psychology and behavior (What is the result of my change in messaging, marketing spending, product mix, or distribution channels?).

Today, many businesses have access to large quantities of customer data in the form of online conversations about their products and brands. A good example is automobile manufacturers. My colleague Oded Netzer of Columbia Business School, along with three research coauthors,[13] has dug into the data created by discussion forums to explore what it reveals about the automotive market structure and consumer behavior. Netzer's team applied a variety of text-mining tools—algorithms that are trained on human language and apply formulas to detect patterns in huge quantities of unstructured text from online conversations. One area of their research looked at how customers perceive brands. By examining patterns of statistical "lift," they could identify which specific attributes are more frequently associated with one auto brand versus its closest competitors. The patterns revealed opportunities in terms of audiences to target, content for messaging, and ideas for product development.

Netzer's team also used the data to investigate the impact of long-term advertising efforts. They focused on a period when Cadillac had spent millions on brand advertising to shift customers' perception of Cadillac from "classic American car" (like Lincoln) to "luxury brand" (like Lexus and Mercedes). A textual analysis of the conversations over several years showed that, consistent with the campaign objective, the Cadillac brand was gradually moving—in customers' associative perceptions—from the first group (classic American brands) to the second (luxury brands). When the researchers compared this with public data on dealer trade-ins, they confirmed that the shift in perception was also a leading indicator of purchase behaviors. Rather than trading between Lincolns and Cadillacs, more and more customers were exchanging their luxury cars for Cadillacs.

In another case, Gaylord Hotels used insights from customer data to sharpen its referral strategy. The business has a few large hotel properties that are well suited for major events as well as personal stays. With a limited advertising budget, it knew that referrals (word of mouth from happy guests) were the biggest source of new customers. So management set a priority to increase that word of mouth by improving the already good guest experience. The first step was an internal review of operations that identified eighty areas of focus that might help inspire customers not only to be pleased but also to actually mention Gaylord to others. The obvious next challenge was prioritization: Which items on this long list were most important? To help, the company undertook an analysis of social media data, looking at every instance where the hotel's name was mentioned by customers in public platforms like Twitter. Customer recommendations and praise were examined for any clues as to what had spurred them and at what point in the customer's stay. The results were illuminating. A short list of just five elements of the guest experience seemed to have the greatest influence in sparking word of mouth, and all of them took place in the first twenty minutes after arrival.[14]

Targeting: Narrowing the Field

The second template for data value creation is *targeting*. By narrowing the field of possible audiences and identifying who is most relevant to a business, customer data can help drive greater results from every inter-action with customers. In the past, customers were often divided into a few broad segments for targeting based on factors like age, zip code, and product use. Today, advanced segmentation schemes can be based on much more diverse customer data and can produce dozens or even hundreds of micro-categories. How a customer is targeted can change in real time as well, as they are assigned to one segment or another based on behavioral data such as which e-mails they clicked on, rewards they redeemed, or con-tent they shared. Ideally, customer lifetime value (as discussed in chapter 2) should be included as one metric for targeting customers based on their long-term value to the business.

Custora is a data analytics company that helps e-commerce busi-nesses determine the likely customer lifetime value (CLV) of their website visitors—that is, not just their likelihood to buy in this visit but their likely profit potential in the future. This is done by analyzing historical customer data and applying both a CLV model and Bayesian probabilistic models. For example, when a new customer makes just one purchase on a web-site, Custora can predict that they are likely to make six purchases in the upcoming year, totaling $275 and placing them among the top 5 percent of the company's customers. Other predictions based on historical data include the category the customer's next purchase will likely come from (e.g., home furnishings vs. lawn care). The model can even provide warn-ing signs—such as predicting that if this customer doesn't place an order for three consecutive months, the business can assume they have only a 10 percent chance of returning.[15]

InterContinental Hotels Group carefully uses data on the 71 million members of its Priority Club loyalty program to understand and target them more effectively. This data includes much more than zip code and hotel room preferences. Up to 4,000 different data attributes—such as their income level, their preferred booking channel, their use of rewards points, and whether they tend to stay over weekends—are used to assign each member to a customer group. This level of segmentation has allowed the hotel to shift from sending out a dozen varieties of an e-mail mar-keting message to sending out 1,552 different variations, targeted around past behaviors and special offers such as local events. These new market-ing campaigns have generated a conversion rate (the portion of customers accepting the offer sent) that is 35 percent higher than that of less targeted campaigns the year before.[16]

Using data for targeting can even have a powerful impact in a field like nonprofit health care, thanks to a practice known as "hot spotting." Dr. Jeffrey Brenner, a family physician in Camden, New Jersey, studied medical billing records from hospitals in his hometown and discovered that 1 percent of the town's population was responsible for 30 percent of its health-care costs. "A small sliver of patients are responsible for much of the costs, but we really ignore them," said Brenner.[17] He used that data, and small grants from philanthropies, to start the Camden Coalition of Healthcare Providers and focus on "spotting" these patients and improving their care. Over three years, the organization was able to reduce emergency room visits by 40 percent among the initial group of the "worst of the worst" patients and to reduce that group's hospital bills by 56 percent.[18]

Personalization: Tailoring to Fit

Once businesses are targeting micro-segments of customers, the next opportunity is to treat them each differently, in ways that are most relevant and valuable to them. This is the third template for creating value: *personalization*. By tailoring their messaging, offers, pricing, services, and products to fit the needs of each customer, businesses can increase the value they deliver.

Kimberly-Clark, which sells some of the biggest brands in diapers (among other personal care products), uses an audience management platform that integrates data from sales and media channels to build an integrated view of the "customer journey" of each customer. For the company's business, that means tracking a family's progression through various products—from Huggies newborn, to full-size diapers, to transitional pull-ups during toilet training and "Little Swimmers" (for kids just starting out in the pool). Keeping track of each customer allows it to advertise the right product to the right family.[19]

British Airways has launched a service personalization program known internally as Know Me. Its goal is to bring together diverse data to create a "single customer view" that will help airline staff to make a more personal connection with each customer. Know Me started with a two-year project to link data from commercial, operational, and engineering systems and put it at the fingertips of customer service directors. But the program works only because the data analytics are linked to the judgment and "emotional intelligence" of the British Airways service staff. Know Me data is used to deepen staff awareness of fliers' personal needs and preferences, and staff are empowered to make their own observations and record data that helps personalize future trips. This feedback loop helps the airline deliver more-relevant offers to each customer and provide personalized recognition and service during a trip. That can include recognizing a VIP business traveler—even when traveling in coach class with family—so that service staff can welcome and thank them and offer a glass of champagne. It could also mean providing discreet assurances to a customer who has previously indicated they have a fear of flying. With urgent updates entered in the system in minutes, one flight crew spotted a passenger's iPad, forgotten on board, and passed word to the connecting flight crew to notify the passenger. One of the most popular service touches has been that of welcoming customers mid-journey when they have reached Silver Tier status, the first level that offers access to lounges. The airline has seen extremely positive response from customers, both one-on-one and in long-term tracking of their satisfaction and their likelihood of recommending British Airways to others. In addition, Know Me has allowed the airline to broaden its view of customers far beyond its loyalty-program members, with a goal of knowing the needs of all of its 50 million fliers.[20]

One challenge of personalization has been the proliferation of different devices and platforms where customers interact with a business. How does a business know it is communicating with the same individual on a phone, tablet, and PC, let alone through Facebook, its own shopping portal, or a display ad being served up by Google on pages all over the Internet? The good news is that this challenge is diminishing rapidly, allowing for "addressability" of the same customer across numerous platforms. As David Williams, CEO of database powerhouse Merkle, explained, we are quickly becoming able to communicate to individual consumers with "addressability at scale" across Google, Facebook, Amazon, and all the dominant platforms of the Web.[21]

Context: Providing a Reference Frame

The final template for data value creation is *context*. By providing a frame of reference—and illustrating how one customer's actions or outcomes stack up against those of a broader population—context can create new value for businesses and customers alike.

Putting data in context is at the heart of the "quantified self" movement—evidenced by customers' rising interest in measuring their diet, exercise, heart rates, sleep patterns, and other biological markers. Nike was one of the first companies to tap into this trend with its Nike+ platform, which originally used in-shoe sensors, then the Nike Fuel wristband, and later mobile software apps. At each stage of its development, Nike+ has been designed to let customers capture their data and share it with their online communities. Nike customers who track their running data don't just want to know how they did today; they also want to know how today's performance compares to their own performance over the last week or month, to the goals they have set, and to the activity of friends in their social network. Context is king.

Comparing their own data with the data of others can also add value by helping customers understand the probabilities of different outcomes. Naviance is a popular platform for U.S. high school students preparing for the college search and application process. One of its primary services is a tool that lets students upload their transcript data (test scores, class grades, high school attended) and compare it against a huge database of students who have applied to college while using Naviance. Based on the past results of similar applicants, the platform can show students their likely odds for admission to different colleges they are considering. Rather than applying in the dark (as we did in my day), students can use Naviance to find out which college on their list is a long shot, which one is a sure thing, and which schools fall in between.

Sharing and comparing customer data can be a powerful way to identify hazards. BillGuard is a popular financial protection app that tracks its customers' credit card statements and helps identify both fraudulent billing (e.g., if the card was one of 50 million hacked in the latest cyberscandal) and "grey" charges (hidden fees customers likely didn't realize a company was charging them). BillGuard's algorithms are effective precisely because they compare a customer's bills against the anonymized bills of peers and against whatever charges were flagged as questionable by any other customers in its community.

Other examples of businesses using data for context include Glassdoor, which lets job seekers compare their salaries with averages for others in their industry and role, and Pricing Engine, which helps small businesses improve their digital advertising spending (on platforms like Google AdWords) by comparing their own success rates with those of their peers.

Tool: The Data Value Generator

We've looked now at the different types of data being used in business today. We've examined the sources where businesses can find more data to fill in their own gaps. And we've seen four templates for generating new value using customer data. Let's look now at how to apply these concepts to generate new strategic options for data initiatives in your own organization. That is the focus of our next tool, the Data Value Generator.

The tool follows a five-step process for generating new strategic ideas for data (see figure 4.1). Let's look at each of the steps in detail.

Step 1: Area of Impact and Key Performance Indicators

The first step is to define the area of your business you are seeking to impact or improve through a new data initiative. You might define it as a specific business unit (e.g., product line), a division (e.g., marketing), or a new venture. You might decide that you are looking to apply data to improve customer service at a resort, to develop better product

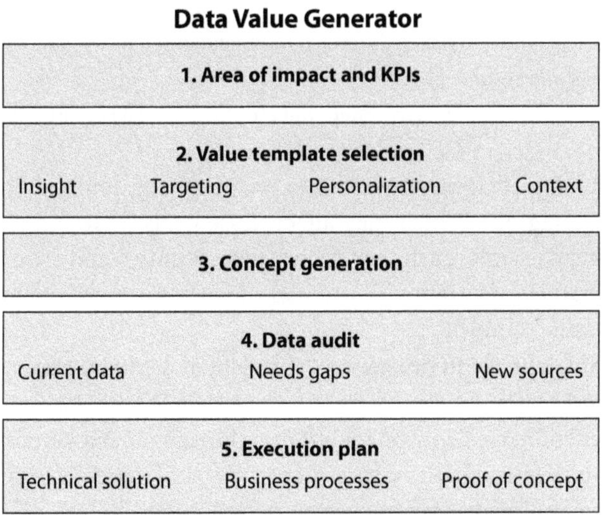

Data Value Generator

1. Area of impact and KPIs		

2. Value template selection			
Insight	Targeting	Personalization	Context

3. Concept generation		

4. Data audit		
Current data	Needs gaps	New sources

5. Execution plan		
Technical solution	Business processes	Proof of concept

Figure 4.1
The Data Value Generator.

recommendations, to improve outbound communications to existing customers, to improve the customer call center, or to develop a new app to drive customer engagement.

Once you have defined the area of impact, you should identify your primary business objectives in that area. What goals are you hoping to support? In addition to broad goals, what are your established key performance indicators (KPIs) that are being used to measure performance? Because this is a data-driven project, you will want to think about highly measurable outcomes, those where you may be able to clearly measure impact. It is alright if you identify multiple objectives and KPIs at this step; you may end up seeking to influence one or more as you generate your strategic ideas.

Step 2: Value Template Selection

Now that you know the domain you are focused on, look back at the four templates for value creation, and identify one or more that may be most relevant to your objectives:

- *Insight*: Understanding customers' psychology, their behaviors, and the impact of business actions
- *Targeting*: Narrowing your audience, knowing who to reach, and using advanced segmentation
- *Personalization*: Treating different customers differently to increase relevance and results
- *Context*: Relating one customer's data to the data of a larger population

Which template is most relevant to your business domain? To the KPIs you are focusing on? Which may affect those goals more indirectly? (For example, insights into customer brand perceptions could help influence a goal of market penetration if you can identify the right opportunity to reposition your product.)

You could choose to pursue one template or a combination. Note that targeting and personalization often work together. Whereas targeting efforts are sometimes focused only on identifying the right audience, effective personalization requires that you have some system of targeted segmenting in place. You may already have one template or another more developed (e.g., you are strong on segmentation but weak on consumer insights). The question is, What area of value creation is the next focus for your data strategy?

Step 3: Concept Generation

Now that you have selected a value template (or more than one), you will want to use it to ideate specific ways that data could deliver more value to your customers and your business.

For example, if you select context, how can you best use contextual information to influence desired behaviors? Behavioral economics has revealed that seeing our data in context can be an extremely powerful motivator. Voters are more likely to be persuaded to make it to the polls when reminded of their own past voting history and that of their neighbors. Using this insight, Opower has developed a data-driven service to influence home power consumption. The company, which works with local utilities, shows consumers data on how their own energy usage compares with that of their neighbors. The result: consumers are much more likely to reduce their energy consumption when shown comparative data.

Concept generation should aim for this level of concrete application so you can really define the possible data strategy. For a personalization strategy, what are the specific moments of customer interaction that you are trying to personalize? For example, hotel and casino company Caesar's Entertainment has pursued a strategy similar to that of British Airways— using data for the personalization of service, starting from a loyalty program and aiming to increase repeat business. But Caesar's focuses on a different set of moments. For example, Caesar's can determine when a repeat visitor is having a bad night on the gambling floor and will send service staff to offer an unexpected gift—a steak dinner, tickets to a show—so the customer won't leave feeling they had "bad luck" at Caesar's and should try another casino.

At the concept generation stage, you want to produce specific ideas for putting the data to work in your business.

Step 4: Data Audit

Now that you have a strategy in mind, you need to assemble the data that it will require. That starts with surveying what data you already have that could be used to enable or power your strategy. You may have a large, established data set based on your core product or service (like TWC). You may be starting with a data set on website visitors, or you may have access to loyalty-program data. For some businesses, the only data may be an incomplete list of customer e-mail addresses.

Next you should identify what data you still need. For the purpose of the strategy you have sketched out, what data is still lacking? What will it take to provide the full view of the customer needed by your new initiative? You may need to increase your data in terms of

- more records or rows (e.g., expanding from a limited sample of your customers to a much broader list),
- more types of data (e.g., adding preference data and transaction data to your customer contact data), or
- more historical data (e.g., going back many months in time in order to develop an effective analytics tool that can model and predict future outcomes).

Lastly, now that you've identified the gaps, you need to determine ways to fill them. This is where you can apply the options discussed earlier: customer value exchange, lead users, supply chain partners, public data sets, and purchase or exchange agreements.

Step 5: Execution Plan

For your data strategy to be effective, you must do more than assemble the right bits of data (the zeroes and ones). You must put that strategy to use in the work of your organization. The last step is to plan for the execution of the key pieces of your data plan.

What technical issues need to be worked out? This may include data warehousing, latency, or how quickly the data needs to be updated. Your IT people will need to weigh in here.

What business processes will need to change? Most data initiatives assume employees of your firm will make different decisions and take different actions based on your data. You will need to identify those changes in advance of rolling out any technical solution.

How can you test out your strategy and build internal support? One of the best ways is to integrate the new data strategy into an existing initiative at your company. Jo Boswell, the program lead for Know Me at British Airways, knew that it would be difficult to enlist in-flight service staff if her initiative was seen as one more competing priority in their work. Instead, she integrated Know Me with their existing customer service program, showing how its data would help staff to deliver on the same four "customer service hallmarks" that anchored all their training.[22] Data-driven strategies should be in line with everything your business is doing and help people to do their jobs better.

~

The Data Value Generator outlined in the previous five steps in an ideation tool; its goal is to enable you to generate multiple ideas for possible data initiatives in an area of your business. After developing these strategic ideas, you will need to test the assumptions behind each. Can you, in fact, get the data? Can you get buy-in from the business units in your organization to act on your findings? Will the results really matter to customers? Can you develop an initial pilot to test your data strategy for proof of concept? We will look in depth at the issue of how to iteratively develop new innovations like this in chapter 5.

Before we leave the discussion of data, though, let's consider some of the challenges that a traditional, pre-digital-era enterprise may face in reorganizing around data capabilities today.

Organizational Challenges of Data

When Mike Weaver was brought in as director of data strategy for the Coca-Cola Company, his mission was clear. "We must understand consumers' passions, preferences, and behaviors so we can market to them as individuals," he told me. As an expert in the area of applied analytics, Weaver saw that this required building a data asset in an industry that is not traditionally rich in consumer data. By combining its MyCokeRewards loyalty program with a variety of other data sets—observed behaviors on its websites, social log-ins via Facebook, cookie stitching, and data from various partners—the company was able to advance rapidly toward its goal of becoming a more data-driven marketer.

But the biggest challenges, Weaver told me, were organizational, not technical. He compared the process of shifting business practices at "the world's greatest brand/mass media company" to turning an aircraft carrier at sea. He knew that the right data models could be used to develop advanced segmentation schemes for Coca-Cola's customers, to understand customers' different needs and wants, and to allow the firm to better serve and communicate with them. But before installing all the data centers and analytics models that would allow for real-time targeting of customers, the company first had to plan out the changes to its business processes. Before a brand can take advantage of its ability to differentiate customer segments in real time and deliver targeted messaging to them, it first needs to learn how to create messages in a very different way. This kind of targeting doesn't require Coke to create a single, blockbuster Super Bowl ad; rather, it has to create dozens of versions of the same message and test them to see which ones drive response among different customer segments. The first step of the journey, Weaver reiterated, is to plan the changes in your business process—before you start buying all the latest hardware or cloud services.[23]

In my speaking, teaching, and work with a wide range of companies, I've observed a number of common organizational challenges that businesses face as they shift to a more data-driven strategy. Each of them is worth considering when developing a data strategy.

Embedding Data Skill Sets

The first challenge in the transition to a more data-driven organization is finding people with the right skill sets.

This starts with data scientists—the folks who can do the technical work of data analysis, be it hand-cleaning the raw data, programming algorithms to apply real-time data in an automated fashion, or designing and running rigorous data experiments. Depending on the organization, it may be using an outside partner for analytics, hiring a single analyst, or building an entire team. Good data scientists have strong statistical and programming skills and often come from an academic or scientific background. They also serve as truth-tellers within the organization. These are the folks who know that data can lie very easily, and they will keep a company honest about things like sample size, significance testing, and data quality (the old "garbage in/garbage out" rule).

But the data experts cannot be the only people in an organization who understand or think about data. In order to truly build data into a strategic asset, everyone in the business has to adopt a mindset that includes using data, and the questions they pose to it, as a part of their daily process. Part of this is educating the workforce about the ways data can be applied in their business. Another part must be developing a company culture that embraces data and analytical thinking. For a consumer goods company like Coke or Frito-Lay, that involves a shift from thinking about marketing as an art to thinking about it as a discipline that includes both art and science.

Lastly, the company may need someone who can bridge two worlds: the world of quantitative analysts and that of business decision makers. This person will be the one who can connect the work of data science with that of the senior managers or the creative types in the marketing department. Think of Somaya, the former art history major who learned to speak the language of both the data scientists at TWC and the advertisers and brand managers who were his clients.

Bridging Silos

Sometimes the biggest challenges to sharing data are within the organization. At Coca-Cola, Weaver found that website analytics data was sitting in one database while data on consumer purchase behavior from loyalty programs was being kept somewhere else entirely. In order to create a complete picture of the customer, he first had to bring all the data together in a unified way.

In many organizations, these divisions are reinforced by departmental silos and each department's desire for "ownership" of its data (sales data vs. marketing data, etc.). In a research study that I coauthored with my colleague Don Sexton, we spoke with hundreds of senior marketers at businesses across a wide range of B2B and B2C industries. The most commonly cited obstacle to using data effectively was internal sharing, with 51 percent of respondents reporting that "the lack of sharing data across our organization is an obstacle to measuring the ROI of our marketing."[24]

In large organizations operating in different locations, another important question is whether or not to centralize data analytics. This is partly a matter of where the data is warehoused but also where the data scientists are. Should each business unit have its own analytics team so it is closer to local decision making? Or should one central analytics unit service the key data needs of every part of the business? As large organizations mature in terms of their data capability, they seem to be centralizing analytics while striving to raise the data savvy of managers in each business unit.

Sharing Data With Partners

Data sharing is critical not only within an organization; it is becoming a key element of negotiations with business partners. Contracts and deals of all kinds are no longer just about who pays what to whom but what data will be shared as well. This sharing is particularly important for businesses that don't own the ultimate point of sale for their products.

Industrial equipment manufacturer Caterpillar now requires its 189 dealers to enter into data-sharing agreements; in return, it provides them with benchmarks and tools to improve their own sales efficiency and with customer leads generated from Caterpillar's Web analytics.[25]

Ann Mukherjee, chief marketing officer of Frito-Lay, is able to measure the impact of all kinds of innovative digital marketing for popular brands like Doritos and Lay's, but this measurement is possible only due to partnerships with key retailers. "Retailers are unbelievable sources of analytical understanding," and the ability to partner with them around data and measurement is critical to building store traffic and product sales.[26]

As data becomes more essential to business strategy, data sharing will become a key element of every important business partnership with suppliers, distributors, media channels, and more.

Cybersecurity, Privacy, and Consumer Attitudes

As businesses gather and utilize more and more data, particularly customer data, they also bring on additional security risks. Cyberthreats that used to be the concern of CIOs are going to be front and center for senior leadership now. When Target suffered a huge data breach in 2013, with 40 million customer credit cards stolen, it was not just an IT problem but also a brand reputation issue. Sales at the retailer slumped as consumers stayed away during the holiday shopping season, and the CEO was forced to step down a few months later. Since then, we have seen subsequent massive consumer data theft (Anthem), data attacks as a means of corporate warfare (Sony Pictures and Ashley Madison), and data hacks as government espionage (the U.S. Office of Personnel Management). Sony Pictures CEO Michael Lynton said in the aftermath of its own high-profile hack, "If there's a silver lining, it's that this was a call for America to wake up and pay attention. This is going to happen—in fact, it already is happening, on a regular basis."[27]

Part of data strategy is developing a legal, risk management, and security plan. Rather than letting fear of risk postpone action (and likely not really reduce risks), leaders need to establish assessment, responsibility, and planning, with appropriate outside partners to support them. The risks of data theft are unavoidable, but they can be reduced if risk reduction is a leadership priority.

Consumer attitudes are also crucial to data strategy. Beyond the threats of identity theft and cybercriminals, many consumers are more generally concerned about privacy and the increasing amount of information businesses gather about them. Much of the data about customers is collected in ways that the public is only vaguely aware of, at best. Advocacy around consumer data privacy has raised the possibility of government regulation in many markets. Start-ups like Datacoup, Handshake, and Meeco have argued that individuals should own their personal data and be paid for access to it. They hope to create tools that allow customers to store their interests, preferences, social data, and credit card transactions and choose how much of this information to sell to companies for a fixed price.

With rising concerns about ownership of personal data, it is increasingly important that any data strategy be based on a transparent value exchange with the customer: an exchange in which the customer knows that data is being collected and sees the benefits they are receiving in return. This is the foundation of loyalty programs with points and rewards. It is also the reason customers willingly provide personal ratings on a service like Netflix and are not alarmed when Amazon suggests products based on their recent browsing history. When customers can easily see both the ways that companies are gathering data and the benefits they are gaining as a result, they will be more likely to allow sustainable access to businesses.

As sensors, networks, and computing become embedded in every part of our lives, the data that is available to business continues to grow exponentially. For some managers, this data deluge will seem overwhelming. Other managers may tell themselves that "I don't operate in a very data-intensive industry" simply because that was the case a few short years ago. But the world has changed. Every business now has access to data.

The strategic challenge for business is to develop the clear vision and the growing capability needed to put data to work in the service of innovation and value creation. By treating data as a key intangible asset to build over time, every business can develop a data strategy that informs critical decision making and generates new value for business and customer alike.

Data allows us to continually experiment, learn, and test our ideas. This means data can do more than power products, optimize processes, and deliver more-relevant customer interactions; it can also help change the way organizations learn and innovate. This different kind of learning—through constant experimentation—is at the heart of a profoundly different approach to innovation. That new approach to innovation is the subject of the next chapter.

5

Innovate by Rapid Experimentation

INNOVATION

Think of the last time you used a search engine. Every time you type a query into Google or a similar service, you are the subject of a human experiment. Google presents you with search results and measures which ones you click on, in what order, and how quickly. And in subtle ways, those search results that you see are constantly changing. Changes occur in the primary listings, in the search ads you are shown, and in the auto-complete guesses that start to appear after you type your first letter. Google is constantly trying to learn more about how to innovate and improve its search service for users. Which links are you most likely to be looking for? How should it group them? (Local services vs. global ones? Recent news stories vs. company webpages? Links to subsections of a website? Biographical tidbits about the politician whose name you just entered?) To improve its products, Google doesn't sit down with customer focus groups to discuss their search engine experiences. Nor does it convene a committee to vote on which new features to implement. Instead, the company is constantly experimenting, testing each of its new ideas, measuring customer response, and iterating on what it learns.

We can define innovation as any change to a business product, service, or process that adds value. This change can range from an incremental improvement to the creation of something totally new and unprecedented. For Google, an innovation may be launching a completely new product such as Gmail, Android phones, Google Maps, or its Chromebook laptop line. But innovation at Google also includes the continuous process of refining, adding and subtracting features, and evolving the user interface and experience. As Scott Anthony says, innovation is not just about "big bangs"; it is about anything new that has impact.[1]

The fourth domain of digital transformation is innovation—the process by which new ideas are developed, tested, and brought to the market by businesses. Traditionally, innovation was singularly focused on the finished product. Testing ideas was relatively difficult and expensive, so decisions and early ideas were based on the analysis, intuition, and seniority of managers involved in the project. Actual market feedback tended to come very late in the process (sometimes after public release), so avoiding a marked failure was an overriding concern.

In the digital age, enterprises need to innovate in a radically different fashion, based on rapid experimentation and continuous learning. Rather than concentrating primarily on a finished product, this approach focuses on identifying the right problem and then developing, testing, and learning from multiple possible solutions. Like the lean start-ups of Silicon Valley, this approach focuses on developing minimum viable prototypes and iterating them repeatedly—before, during, and even after launch. At every stage, assumptions are tested and decisions are made based on validation by customer and market responses. Leaders are those who know how to pose the right questions, not claim the right answers. As digital technologies make it easier and faster than ever to test ideas, this new approach to innovation is essential to bringing new ideas to market faster and with less cost, less risk, and greater organizational learning. (See table 5.1.)

This chapter explores how rapid experimentation is transforming the way innovation happens and how digital technologies are making experimentation both more possible and more necessary. We will consider two complementary methods of experimentation for innovators. We will also examine how organizations must change to become effective experimenters and what the real financial benefits are of learning to take an experimental approach to innovation. The chapter presents two strategic planning tools, each one offering a method for designing, running, and capturing value from innovation experiments. It also explores the four paths to scaling

Table 5.1
Innovation: Changes in Strategic Assumptions from the Analog to the Digital Age

From	To
Decisions made based on intuition and seniority	Decisions made based on testing and validating
Testing ideas is expensive, slow, and difficult	Testing ideas is cheap, fast, and easy
Experiments conducted infrequently, by experts	Experiments conducted constantly, by everyone
Challenge of innovation is to find the right solution	Challenge of innovation is to solve the right problem
Failure is avoided at all cost	Failures are learned from, early and cheaply
Focus is on the "finished" product	Focus is on minimum viable prototypes and iteration after launch

up an innovation and offers guidance on choosing the appropriate one. By applying these frameworks and tools, businesses can learn faster, fail cheaper and smarter, and shorten the time to successful innovation.

But, first, let's look at a case study of a company using experimentation to rethink how it innovates for customers.

How to Grow the Innovation Premium: Intuit's Story

Since its founding in 1983, Intuit has focused on designing and selling great accounting and finance tools for individuals and small businesses. With a track record of innovative products, the company grew from a start-up to a company worth billions. But after twenty-four years, founder Scott Cook realized the firm needed to change its model of product innovation if it was going to continue to grow. He started a new initiative with Kaaren Hanson that focused on rapid experimentation. When I met Hanson in 2013, she was chief innovation officer, and Intuit had run over 1,300 experiments in the previous six months. To provide a sense of how this new model for innovation worked, she described a project in India.[2]

Deepa Bachu was the head of Intuit's emerging markets team. The team had been tasked with developing a product for India's farmers, who make up the bulk of the economy. After spending time immersed with small farmers to discover their pain points and customer needs, the team found a pressing problem for those who were selling perishable goods, such as produce. These farmers, they learned, could afford to travel to only one market (or *mandi*) when it was time to find a merchant to buy their crop. When they did, they negotiated prices with a *mandi* agent, but there was a complete lack of market transparency. The *mandi* agents would actually put a cloth over their hand when indicating to one farmer the price they would pay for goods so that the next farmer in line could not see the price. Without access to refrigeration, the farmers had limited time to sell their perishables and no way to find the best buyer based on local supply and demand. In many cases, the farmers were forced to unload their produce for deeply discounted prices just to bring some income home. Bachu's team set a goal: develop a product that could help farmers raise their income from crop sales by 10 percent. Then they set to work generating ideas.[3]

The team's first solution was to create an eBay-like marketplace where buyers and sellers could find each other and negotiate prices before sellers loaded their produce and traveled to market. But when they presented mock-ups of the product to *mandi* agents, they discovered the agents would be unwilling to offer a price for produce without inspecting it first in person. The team's second solution was to create a service that would let farmers alert each other to what crops they were growing so that each farmer could make a better guess as to what crops would be in higher demand. But when the Intuit team tested this idea, they found that farmers were unclear how to act on the information. The team's third solution was to provide an SMS notification service that would inform farmers of the prices being offered at various markets before they left their farms. Bachu realized there were several assumptions behind this product idea: Could the farmers read the text messages? Would the *mandi* agents provide prices to Intuit to share? Would they honor those prices when the farmers arrived at the market? The team decided to run an experiment and recruited fifty farmers and five *mandi* agents willing to try out the notification service. For six weeks, two Intuit team members went into the markets to gather pricing information, while a third team member sat in a back office texting each farmer the prices of produce in various locations. This bare-bones operation would never scale, but it allowed the team to find out if the premise of an eventual mobile technology solution would actually work. At the end of the test, they found that both farmers and *mandi* agents had adopted it and that the farmers' incomes were raised by 20 percent—twice the original goal. That impact continued as the final product, now called Fasal, was developed and rolled out as an automated service providing customized text messages to the more than 1 million participating farmers.[4]

The experiment-driven approach to innovation was not isolated to emerging markets but became the hallmark of Intuit's company-wide efforts to rethink innovation. "We have gone from a company of 8,000 employees to 8,000 innovators," Hanson told me.[5] Over the five years the company had been using this new approach, its innovation premium—the portion of its market capitalization attributable to future innovation—grew from 20 to 29 percent, adding $1.8 billion in value.[6] In shifting to a culture of rapid experimentation, the company had made a bet on running a large enterprise as a lab for continuous learning. That bet paid off big.

Experimentation Is Learning

Experimentation can be defined as an iterative process of learning what does and does not work. The goal of a business experiment is actually not a product or solution; it is learning—the kind of learning about customers, markets, and possible options that will lead you to the right solution.

When you innovate through experimentation, you don't try to avoid wrong ideas; rather, you aim to quickly and cheaply test as many promising ideas as possible in order to learn which ones will work. This is very different than a traditional innovation process: analyze the market, generate ideas, debate internally, pick a solution, and then develop it through many stages of quality testing before launching it and getting feedback from actual customers. In developing Fasal for the Indian market, the Intuit team didn't convene meetings to debate which of their three proposed solutions was the optimal one. To test their assumptions, they put their ideas, in rough form, in front of the actual farmers and merchants who would have to use the final product. This approach requires a paradigm shift from innovation based on analysis and expertise to innovation based on ideation and experimentation for constant learning.

This shift toward a more iterative, learning-based model for innovation has been growing for several years and in many quarters. It is at the heart of Steve Blank's customer validation model and Eric Ries's writing on "lean start-up" methods. It is integral to the model of design thinking that product development firms like IDEO and frog have been using with clients like Apple, JetBlue, Target, Disney, Intel, and SAP. With the rise of digital A/B testing, constant experimentation has become the norm for more and more products, services, and communication channels. It has become fashionable to take the stance of a Silicon Valley start-up and assert that the product is never finished and that every new innovation should be released as a beta ready for continuous evolution.

But innovation in an enterprise (seeking to launch a new venture or offering or to improve an existing one) is not exactly the same as innovation in a three-person start-up (whose new app may be the entire focus of the organization). And not every product can be launched to the full public in beta (e.g., think of a car). Some of the principles of experimentation therefore need to be adapted or translated to the context of an existing enterprise. And, in fact, not everything called an experiment is the same. Different types of business experiments may not be designed or run in the same manner or be used to answer the same kinds of questions. But all business experiments do have this in common: they seek to increase learning by testing ideas and seeing what works and what doesn't.

Two Types of Experiments

Think back to the two examples we have seen so far: Intuit's experimentation to develop Fasal and Google's experimentation to continuously improve its search engine. Both companies are experimenting, but there are many differences. Google is testing on the actual product: the real search engine used by its customers. With Fasal, Intuit intentionally tested simple mock-ups and a rough prototype of what an actual product might eventually be. Google's testing is in real time, with thousands or millions of subjects whose behaviors can be compared scientifically to identify meaningful statistical differences. With Fasal, the experiments were conducted with small groups of customers, and the results would not appear to pass muster with anyone's statistics teacher ("What's the standard deviation among five *mandi* agents?"). For Google, the goal of innovation is to improve something known. For Fasal, the goal was to develop something completely novel.

In fact, a wide range of practices can be called business experiments. The most fundamental difference is between more formal (scientific) experiments and the kind of informal experimentation that is common to new product development. This is not due just to the organizational culture of the business that is doing the experimenting (i.e., experimental "style"), nor is it due to the ready availability of a large sample size (even if Intuit had access to 1,000 farmers, it wouldn't have made sense to use a formal scientific experiment). Rather, we can see two types of business experimentation that are suited for two types of learning.

I will call these two types convergent and divergent because I prefer to name them by their function rather than their form (e.g., formal vs. informal). *Convergent* experiments are best suited for learning that eliminates options and converges on a specific answer to a clearly defined question (e.g., Which of these three designs is preferred by the customer?). *Divergent* experiments are best suited for learning that explores options, generates insights, asks multiple questions at the same time, and, when done right, generates new questions to explore in the next iterative stage. (See table 5.2.)

Both types of experiments increase our knowledge and test our assumptions. Both involve looking outside the organization for answers, and both require willingness to learn versus just planning and deciding. But the approach of each type is quite different. Let's look at them in detail.

Table 5.2
Two Types of Experiments

Convergent Experiments	Divergent Experiments
Example: A/B feature testing or a pricing test	Example: putting a prototype in the hands of customers
Formal (scientific) experimental design	Informal experimental design
Asks a precise question or finite set of questions	Poses an unknown set of questions
Seeks to provide an answer	May provide an answer or raise more questions
Needs a representative customer sample (test and control groups)	Needs the right customers (who might not be average customers)
Needs a statistically valid sample	Sample size may vary
Focused on direct causality	Focused on gestalt effects and meaning
Goal is to test the thing itself	Goal is to test as rough a prototype as possible for the question ("good enough")
Confirmatory	Exploratory
Useful for optimization	Useful for idea generation
Common in late stages of an innovation	Common in early stages of an innovation

IN COMMON

Increases knowledge
Tests assumptions
Looks outside for answers
Requires willingness to learn versus decide

Convergent Experiments

The key element of every convergent experiment is the initial causal hypothesis: "If I add this feature, customers will spend more time on my site." Or "If I change this interaction, customers will spend more money in my store." Convergent experiments are critical for cases where it is not enough to know the correlation between two events; you also need to verify which event is causing the other.

Convergent experimentation is applicable in a variety of contexts. It can be used with any digital product or service (website, mobile app, software, etc.) to test and improve any element of the customer experience. This is why not only Google but also every major Internet service, such as Amazon or Facebook, is constantly running A/B tests, in which two sets of customers see the same webpage (or the same e-mail) with one difference in design and the company measures any difference in customer behavior or response. Facebook is famous for experimenting with the News Feed of its users to find the right balance of photos versus text posts versus videos, the friends a user is more interested in hearing from, and the kind of content that is interesting only in the short term or meaningful to a friend who only logs in to Facebook several days later.

However, convergent experimentation can be applied in nondigital environments as well. These kinds of experiments are at the heart of data-driven strategies to optimize the guest experience and loyalty rewards given to customers of hotels, airlines, and resorts. When convenience store chain Wawa is planning changes to the food menu, it will run experiments to measure not just if customers buy the new item but also if there's an impact on the overall profitability of customer visits.[7]

Convergent experimentation is often used in communications and direct marketing. In both presidential campaigns of Barack Obama, continuous, rapid experiments on e-mail subject lines and website page designs helped to dramatically increase their effectiveness in signing up new supporters and garnering more donation dollars. Starting in the pre-Internet era, Capital One bank used convergent experiments to test the right promotional offer, the right target audience, and even the right color of envelopes as it mailed out credit card invitations. By running tens of thousands of experiments each year that focused on customer acquisition and lifetime value, it grew from a small division of another bank into an independent company worth $42 billion.[8]

A convergent experiment can be as expensive as testing two different store layouts for a retail chain or as cheap as sending two versions of an e-mail promotion, each to a different group of randomly selected customers, and comparing the responses.

Because convergent experimentation needs to measure causality, it needs to adhere to the key principles of formal scientific experiments:

- *Causal hypothesis*—so that you have an independent variable (the cause) and one or more dependent variables (the effect)
- *Test and control groups*—so that you can see the difference between those who are exposed to your stimulus and those who aren't
- *Randomly assigned participants*—so that an external factor doesn't influence the outcome of your test group
- *Statistically valid sample size*—so that the differences you measure can rise above the noise of random fluctuations
- *Blind testing*—so that you avoid the Hawthorne effect, where those involved in the experiment unintentionally influence its outcome

Common mistakes in convergent testing mostly center on improperly assigning participants to the test and control groups. For example, a retailer might select a set of participants (its top customers or its better-performing stores) for a new treatment and erroneously assume that "everyone else" (all its other customers or stores) can serve as an equivalent control group.

Some of the key writers on convergent experimentation for business include Stefan Thomke, Thomas Manzi, Eric T. Anderson, and Duncan Simester.[9]

Divergent Experiments

Divergent experiments are generally not built around a causal question. Looking back at Intuit's development of Fasal, at the beginning of its experimentation the question was quite broad: "How can we increase the revenue of rural Indian famers?" It was far too early to form any specific hypotheses about a choice between two product features or marketing messages or design layouts.

Once the Intuit team had some initial solutions in mind and began to prototype and present them to possible customers, they were not looking to measure customer response in terms of a single number. They were looking for a range of qualitative feedback: "It was confusing." "I would use this only if others were already using it." "I don't know what to do with the information I am seeing." "I like this, but I need it more quickly." And so on.

The process of divergent experimentation is therefore more informal than that of convergent experimentation. But that does not mean divergent experimentation is simply ad hoc. It is still structured and benefits greatly from a clear process for conceiving of options or ideas, creating meaningful prototypes, testing these to gather real-world feedback on critical assumptions, and using that information to make decisions about whether to proceed and how to launch an eventual solution.

Common mistakes in divergent testing mostly center on testing too late, as when "product testing" of a new innovation occurs after development is nearly complete. In these cases, because of resources already committed and organizational momentum, the testing serves merely as "validation" for a course of action that has already been committed to.

Some of the key writers on divergent experimentation include Nathan Furr and Jeff Dyer (for established businesses) and Eric Ries and Steve Blank (for start-ups).[10]

Why You Need Both

To innovate successfully, you will need both convergent and divergent experiments at different stages and in different parts of your business. Successful innovation must balance both exploratory learning (to generate and develop new ideas) and confirmatory learning (to verify and refine ideas). A/B testing alone will never tell Wawa what new food product it should try in its stores, nor will it write the e-mail subject lines to be tested by a political campaign. Likewise, showing iterative design prototypes to customers in a lab will never tell you what the final pricing should be, what the optimal marketing mix is, or how customers will behave with your product once they are using it in the real world.

To some degree, the type of experiment you use may be shaped by the area of your business in which you are innovating. For innovations intending to improve your existing core business, you are more likely to rely on convergent experiments. For innovations intending to develop new business areas and generate substantially new products, services, or processes, you are more likely to rely on divergent experiments.

The two types of experimentation may also happen at different stages within the same innovation project. Imagine you are a financial services company planning to offer a new mobile app to assist customers in their financial planning. You might start with an iterative divergent process to test out broad ideas, learn what does and doesn't work, and develop the core value proposition and focus of the new innovation. Then, as you finalize the design, you might shift to a convergent process to test and optimize key elements (features, design, pricing, marketing messages for the launch). Once your app is in the market and you have established a large user base, you can apply more convergent experiments to determine what features are adding the most value for the customer, driving repeat customer engagement, and increasing customer retention or lifetime value.

Why Digital Is Impacting Both

Digital technologies are making rapid experimentation both more possible and more necessary than ever before. They are offering new tools for experimentation and increasing the speed at which companies must innovate to keep up with a rapidly changing environment.

Convergent experimentation is becoming increasingly powerful and affordable due to new technologies. As companies in every industry develop digital products and services for customers (and processes for employees and partners), these digital innovations are inherently much easier to test in real time and at low cost. (Think of how much easier it is for a bank to test the design of its mobile app than to test the design of its retail branches.) At the same time, new software tools are becoming available that allow even small firms with limited budgets to easily conduct A/B tests, run multivariable analyses on the results, and determine the optimal sample size for an experiment. Optimizely, a start-up cofounded by one of the early experimenters for the original Obama campaign, allows small businesses to start running A/B tests on their websites and mobile apps for free. The increasing focus on data analytics in companies of all sizes is making convergent experimentation widespread across industries.

As digital computing becomes more ubiquitous with mobile computing and the Internet of Things, the possibilities for convergent experiments will only increase. Imagine a grocery store wanting to test four possible promotions for its store-brand barbecue sauce. In the analog age, it would have needed four sets of stores, each running a different promotion. But, today, if it can use mobile or wearable devices to push the promotion digitally to consumers, even a single store could test four versions with random selections of customers in that store.

Divergent experimentation is gaining new tools from digital technology as well, particularly in the form of new ways to prototype ideas cheaply and rapidly to show customers. For new physical product offerings, both 3D printing and computer simulations decrease the time and cost involved in creating prototypes. For digital products and services, newer programming languages and repurposable code make it easier to develop "good enough" prototypes to test with customers. Even in industries like pharmaceuticals, as robotic systems take over the purely manual tasks previously done by junior lab technicians, the ability to rapidly and cheaply test new molecular and genetic combinations is increasing dramatically.

In the digital age, even the biggest companies are striving to innovate faster and become more "agile" and "lean" like start-ups. Fortunately, thanks to digital tools, all companies are able to run more experiments—both convergent and divergent—cheaply and quickly and accelerate the pace of innovation. As technological change continues to impact every industry, experimentation will become more important than ever as a means of reducing uncertainty and accelerating innovation.

Seven Principles of Experimentation

Applying experimentation to a business is not easy. To create the most value for your innovation efforts, a few principles are critical. These have been identified by observing innovative companies in a range of industries and by surveying the leading research on innovation from the past decade. These seven principles apply for any business experiment, whether convergent or divergent:

- Learn Early
- Be Fast and Iterate
- Fall in Love with the Problem, Not the Solution
- Get Credible Feedback
- Measure What Matters Now
- Test Your Assumptions
- Fail Smart

Let's take a look at each.

Learn Early

The first principle is to start experimenting from the very beginning of your innovation efforts so that you can learn as early as possible in the process. The same lesson that would trigger heavy financial loss at the end of a product development process ("our customer didn't need this solution or wouldn't pay for it") can come fairly cheaply if it is learned in the early stages of your project. You can think of this effect as "the value of early learning" or, conversely, "the cost of late learning." (See figure 5.1.)

Hanson described this phenomenon in terms of the shift at Intuit from a traditional innovation process—in which customers are exposed to a product only after a long design and development stage—to a process of rapid experimentation—in which customers are brought in much earlier to provide the feedback that helps the company decide which ideas are even worth pursuing. With much earlier learning, the failure rate for the company's product ideas did not decrease, but the cost of failure dropped dramatically. "We can run 50 different ideas through our rapid experimentation process in the time and resources it takes to run 3 ideas through our old process."[11]

Traditional innovation cycle

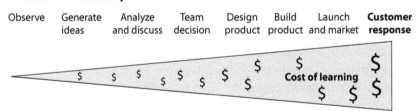

Innovation by rapid experimentation

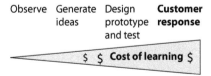

Figure 5.1
Financial Impact of Rapid Experimentation.

This distinction is important. In any innovation effort, you are dealing with uncertainty and inevitably will face a significant failure rate among your new ideas. (If you don't, then the ideas you are testing are not genuinely new, and the potential gains will be limited.) With experimentation, the ideas that don't work should fail *early* in the development process, long before your product gets to the public and while the cost of changing course is much lower. Waiting too late in your innovation process to show your idea to customers has the inverse effect: it increases the costs of error, reduces the likelihood that you can muster the organizational will to change course, and discourages you from testing other options.

Many firms measure the costs of running experiments (which in some industries can still be expensive), but very few attempt to measure their cost *savings* when learning from experiments—whether from early cancellation of what would have been an expensive flop or from course correction that turns a struggling project into a successful one.

Be Fast and Iterate

The second key principle of experimentation is speed. John Hayes, American Express's global chief marketing officer, spoke to me about his company's focus on learning through experimentation. He explained that one of his primary goals as a leader is to get his teams to learn faster—in iterative cycles of days rather than weeks or months.[12] For a nimble organization like American Express, institutionalizing that kind of faster learning can be a real source of competitive advantage.

Hayes's insight echoes that of an earlier famous experimenter, Thomas Edison, who proclaimed that "the real measure of success is the number of experiments that can be crowded into 24 hours."[13]

When John Mayo-Smith was chief technology officer for R/GA, he worked on numerous innovation projects with brands like Nike, including Nike+, FuelBand, and other early wearable technology successes. "Our goal at R/GA was always about building something quick. If you were our client, we didn't spend four months scoping out a project. We aimed to have something built in two weeks, to start showing to real athletes, and getting their feedback."[14] Mayo-Smith's approach to building technology as successive stages of workable iterations has been adopted by teams from Caltech to NASA.[15]

Increasing the speed of experimentation may require infrastructure, too. When Edison built his lab in West Orange, New Jersey, the physical layout was designed to facilitate speed in moving from any insight or hypothesis to a quick working test of it. Supplies of all kinds—tools, chemicals, ores, minerals, filaments—were stored in stockpiles in close proximity to every experimental lab so that delays in procuring equipment would not slow down the exploration of any new idea.[16]

To speed up its own innovation experiments, global snack maker Mondelez (formerly Kraft) uses a "garage" that is designed to get any new idea from concept to prototype and into the hands of visiting customers within two days' time.[17] Design firm IDEO places its prototyping shops in close proximity to its development teams so that physical product ideas can be fabricated in days or even hours.

Fall in Love with the Problem, Not the Solution

This phrase is a mantra at many innovative companies, cited by Waze cofounder Uri Levine as well as Intuit CEO Brad Smith. Why should innovators fall in love with problems and not solutions?

First, this keeps you focused on the customer and their needs. By forcing yourself to describe the customer's problem first (rather than the ingenious solution you are developing), you take an important step to ensure the innovation process is focused on customer value.

Second, focusing on the problem prods you to consider more than one possible solution. If your goal is the solution itself, there's a temptation to stop generating new ideas when you hit on one idea that appears promising to your team and to move on prematurely to building it.

The third reason to fall in love with the problem is that you inevitably become attached emotionally to a creative solution. It is hard to let it go. When Intuit's Fasal team was focused on solving the problem of Indian farmers' poor bargaining position, it was critical that they not stop after coming up with their first solution. As Hanson explained, "When you think you only have one idea, you're unwilling to give it up. If you've got many ideas, you're willing to see the evidence that they don't work, and move onto the next. With the Fasal team—they quickly learned that the eBay-type marketplace wasn't going to work; they quickly learned that their notion of helping farmers to plant more profitable crops wasn't going to work. If they'd only had one idea? Frankly, they might still be working on it today."[18]

Get Credible Feedback

Once you have solutions in mind, it is essential that you gather credible feedback on your ideas. That credibility starts with the people you speak to. They need to be real customers or potential customers—not yourself, your colleagues, or your executive sponsor.

The stimulus for credible feedback is what you show those customers. It needs to be something real enough to generate meaningful results. In a convergent experiment, as we've seen, the feedback is based on the actual product, service, or experience you would ultimately provide. For an A/B test on its new menu items, Wawa tested the actual food with customers in real stores.

In a divergent experiment, the goal is to use prototypes. This allows you to save the expense of building an offering you have not yet designed but gives the customer enough stimulus to respond to. Prototypes can be made with simple materials, like paper or cardboard or clay, or with more sophisticated ones. GE has given out desktop 3D printers to employee teams across various functions to help them rapidly prototype new design ideas without having to leave their offices.

A common innovation mistake is to ask a focus group of customers to speculate on a product or service they've never seen, with no prototype with which to interact. Joe Ricketts is the founder of TD Ameritrade, now one of the largest online stock brokerages in the world. In the 1970s, he was rapidly growing his new business as a phone-based service for stock trading. At the same time, he realized he needed to cut costs. Touchtone phone systems were just coming out, and he wanted to use them to offer self-service to his customers. When he asked focus groups if they would use a self-service option, they said, "No! Why would we want that when we could talk to a live broker?" Ricketts was nervous, so he decided to offer both options, with a big discount for the touchtone service. He didn't install a backup for the touchtone system, figuring that if it failed temporarily, the customers could simply be offered the live brokers instead. He was surprised, then, when the touchtone system did go down and the customers who had been using it complained about having to go back to live operators! As Ricketts stressed to me, you simply can't use focus groups to get credible feedback on a product or service that has never been in the market.[19]

Measure What Matters Now

It is important to take measurements in any experiment. But what do you measure? As interactions become more digitized, the number of things that can be measured is growing, and it is easy to get distracted by all the numbers you could be tracking—particularly in a real-world experiment with a large customer sample.

One solution is to try to identify the most important single metric for the success of your innovation. Alistair Croll and Ben Yoskovitz call this the "One Metric That Matters."[20] They stress how that one metric that matters most will change over time as a start-up moves from the early stages of customer definition to solution testing and eventually to revenue and scaling a business. The same is true when innovating within an existing enterprise: the one metric that matters most will change over time.

In the case of Intuit's Fasal, the ultimate goal was 10 percent more revenue for farmers. And, eventually, that would become a key metric to measure (as well as metrics like advertising revenue, once that became part of the business model). But at earlier stages of the product design, the company may have wanted to focus on different measures, such as "How many of our initial test farmers are able to receive and utilize the pricing information?" and later "How many new subscribers are we getting each week as we begin to roll out the public product?"

Although it is important to know the most critical metric for the current stage of your innovation, you should gather data on other metrics as well. This data may help explain the changes you see in your key metric. When Wawa introduced a flatbread sandwich to its menu in a number of test stores, the chain measured customer adoption and found the product was a big popular success. But it also measured the change in overall profitability at the stores. It turned out that customers were spending less on other, higher-margin items, so Wawa was actually losing money thanks to the popular new sandwich. Rather than rolling it out to more stores, the chain pulled it from the menu entirely.[21]

Test Your Assumptions

Another key principle of experimentation is to test your assumptions. Although this is essential to eliminating risk in any new venture, it is especially important for innovations that take your business into unknown territory.

When Jenn Hyman was still an MBA student, she developed an idea for a new company. Seeing her sister agonizing over whether to spend $1,500 on a Marchesa dress to wear to a friend's wedding, she saw a great business opportunity: Why not offer to rent designer dresses for special occasions? Joined by classmate Jenny Fleiss, Hyman decided to try to launch a new business: Rent The Runway. But rather than spending time writing up a business plan with detailed projections on pricing, costs, market size, and revenue, the two decided to start running experiments to see if their basic idea would even work.[22]

The business seemed promising to Hyman and Fleiss, but they realized that their idea was based on assumptions about customers, their interests, and their willingness to pay for such a service, not to mention product selection, the durability of dresses during repeated rentals, and the right channel to market their service. So they made a plan and methodically tested their assumptions in a series of experiments. Their first two market tests were run on college campuses (Harvard and Yale); at each, they sent out invitations to students, rented a room, and brought a large selection of designer dresses for rent. They quickly validated the assumption that middle- and upper-income women would pay one-tenth the price of a designer dress to be able to rent it for one occasion. They also tested what the impact of selection size was (increasing the number of styles raised the rate of rentals) and whether the dresses would be returned in good shape (only 4 percent came back with stains, which were easily removed). In their third experiment, they tested whether customers would still rent the dresses if they could not try them on in person (their plan for the business was to offer rentals online). Rather than hiring a Web designer to build a website, they sent e-mails with photos of rental dresses to 1,000 women in New York City. Although the rental rate dropped from 35 to 5 percent of those invited, it was still high enough to proceed with a plan for an online business. In their fourth experiment, they reached out to the fashion designers themselves. Their hope was to convince designers to promote the rental service on their own websites, so that visitors looking at a dress on Diane von Furstenberg's website would see that they could rent it rather than having to go to Neiman Marcus to buy it. They met with twenty designers, and the response from most was quite negative. Fearing cannibalization of dress sales, most replied that they would help the new business "over my dead body." Hyman and Fleiss knew they had to revise their marketing plan. Rather than focusing on order fulfillment and letting the designers lead the marketing of their service, they would purchase an ample inventory of dresses, build an e-commerce website, and drive traffic there themselves.[23]

When Hyman and Fleiss went looking for investors, Bain Capital was impressed with the speed with which they had tested the parameters of their new business model and signed on board with the first round of financing. Rent The Runway launched less than a year after Hyman's first flash of insight while watching her sister's dress dilemma. Two years later, Rent The Runway provided dresses for 85 percent of the women attending the 2013 U.S. presidential inauguration.[24]

Rent The Runway was a new start-up, and it is sometimes easier to recognize all the things you don't know about your business when you are just starting. For an established company, used to operating in its known territory, it is easy to overlook the step of testing your assumptions when you are planning an innovation. In their book *Discovery-Driven Growth*, Rita McGrath and Ian MacMillan explain how successful firms take on undue risk by not identifying the underlying assumptions of their new ventures. The authors suggest methods to identify such assumptions and test them, and they tie this process to development milestones on any new project.[25] This mindset is essential to good experiment-driven innovation.

Fail Smart

Failure is inevitable. We can define failure as trying something that doesn't work. Obviously, that is not the ultimate *goal* of innovation, but it is an inevitable part of the *process* of innovation. Intuit's cofounder Scott Cook has said that in their entry to the Indian market they ran thirteen early experiments; two of their ideas proved successful, one had to pivot (undergo a dramatic shift in the business model), and the other ten failed.[26] What if Intuit had been unwilling to tolerate failure in new innovations? If you try to avoid any failures, you will retreat into whatever seems most safe and never innovate.

The challenge of failure is to fail *smart*. We can think of a smart failure as one that passes these four tests:

- Did you learn from the failed test?
- Did you apply that learning to change your strategy?
- Did you fail as early and as cheaply as possible? (For example, you didn't waste a lot of resources developing a very advanced prototype before you discovered that the customer doesn't want the product.)
- Did you share your learning (so that others in your organization won't make the same mistake)?

Defined this way, *smart* failure is actually an essential part of experimentation. It is needed to eliminate bad options quickly and to build on the learning that testing generates (like Hyman and Fleiss's early lesson that they would be shunned by fashion designers and needed to market directly to consumers). Smart failure is simply a series of cheap, effective tests that show you the gaps between where you are and where you need to get. As baseball legend Babe Ruth said, "Every strike brings me closer to the next home run."

Stefan Thomke makes a distinction between what he calls a "failure" and a "mistake." For him, a mistake involves not learning from a failed test, repeating the error, and spending more resources without generating new learning.[27] We could also call that failing dumb.

Now that we've seen the seven overarching principles of good experimentation, let's take a look at the process for each type of experiment. We will do this with two step-by-step planning tools: the Convergent Experimental Method and the Divergent Experimental Method.

Tool: The Convergent Experimental Method

This experimental method is particularly useful for innovating on existing products, services, and processes; for optimizing and continually improving them; and for comparing versions in the later stages of an innovation process. Convergent experiments can sometimes be run very quickly—in a matter of hours or even minutes (e.g., testing e-mails or Web designs). Others (e.g., testing a retail concept) will take longer. You can see the seven-step Convergent Experimental Method in figure 5.2.

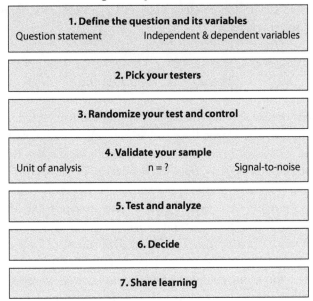

Convergent Experimental Method

1. Define the question and its variables
Question statement   Independent & dependent variables

2. Pick your testers

3. Randomize your test and control

4. Validate your sample
Unit of analysis   n = ?   Signal-to-noise

5. Test and analyze

6. Decide

7. Share learning

Figure 5.2
The Convergent Experimental Method.

Step 1: Define the Question and Its Variables

The first step of any convergent experiment is to define the question you are seeking to answer. This could be "How will our new service offering affect customer retention?" or "Which of these two pricing tiers will yield the highest total revenue for our new product line?" or "How will the planned redesign of our customer service portal affect customer satisfaction?"

In a convergent experiment, the question needs to be as specific as possible. It should also be framed, if possible, as a causal question: "If we do X, then what will happen to Y?"

Once you have stated the question, you need to translate it into two kinds of variables:

- *Independent variable (or cause)*: This is the factor that you will be testing in your experiment. Typically, it is a variation on current business practice. The aim of the experiment is to understand the effect of introducing this innovation.

- *Dependent variable (or effect)*: This is the factor that you expect may be influenced by your new innovation. It is a measure of the impact of what you are changing.

Step 2: Pick Your Testers

The next step is to select who will conduct the experiment. This could be the managers who have developed the possible innovation or an impartial party.

Because it follows formal experimental practices, the test will require some statistical knowledge or tools. Many tests can be automated with software tools. Services like Optimizely provide self-service tools to run A/B tests on webpages' content or design. E-mail service providers like MailChimp include tools for running A/B tests on e-mail content or subject lines. (These services are inexpensive or even free for small businesses.) Your employees can be easily trained to run and record these kinds of experiments.

However, for more complex phenomena, such as competing retail designs, testing will be less automated, and more statistical knowledge is required. For this reason, an organization may want to designate a testing team to run valid experiments for innovation projects. Such an internal team can be called on to ensure the experiment is set up properly and to assist in analyzing the data afterward.

Step 3: Randomize Your Test and Control

Before running a convergent experiment, you must identify a population whose responses you want to test (frequently your customers or a particular subset of your customers).

Next you randomly assign members of that population to one of two groups:

- The test group (or treatment group), which receives the experience or offer you are testing
- The control group, which does not

Randomizing the test and control groups is the step where most mistakes happen in convergent experiments. A business will identify its question and then carefully choose who will go into the test group versus the control group. When it first ran experiments on retail innovations in its stores, Petco made this mistake consistently. Seeking to test innovations in the "optimal" conditions, the firm would roll them out in its thirty highest-performing stores nationwide. It would then compare results from this group and results from its thirty lowest-performing stores. Not surprisingly, innovations that tested as "beneficial" among the superstar group would sometimes disappoint when rolled out nationally across all locations. Petco has since learned to avoid this mistake.[28]

Step 4: Validate Your Sample

Next you need to make sure you have a valid sample size. That starts with identifying your unit of analysis. For example, if you are testing an offer sent to individuals in your database, then the unit of analysis is the individual respondent. But if you are testing two versions of a retail store layout, then the unit of analysis is the store. (You are only able to compare the effects of one store to those of another.)

Once you know your unit of analysis, your sample size is simply the number of units that you place in each of your test and control groups. For example, if you have 600 e-mail addresses and you send three versions of an e-mail, each to 200 recipients, then your sample size is n = 200.

What is a statistically valid sample size? The typical rule of thumb is to have n = 100, at a minimum, in each group you are comparing. However, depending on your signal-to-noise ratio, you may need a larger sample size. If the impact of your innovation is large, you may be able to measure it with a sample of n = 100. But if the impact is much more subtle (e.g., a small lift in customer conversion rate), you will need a larger sample so that the effect of your treatment is greater than the margin of error. (A larger sample yields a smaller margin of error.)

Step 5: Test and Analyze

Now you are ready to run your test. The team conducting your experiment will gather data over a predetermined time span. Then they will need to analyze the data to see whether there are differences in the dependent variables you are measuring and, if there are, whether those differences are statistically significant.

When you do measure and analyze the results, it is important to gather data beyond the dependent variables that you chose in step 1 to define success for your experiment. Even if you have a clear answer ("yes" or "no"), you will also want to know why. When the Family Dollar discount store chain tested a plan to add a new section with refrigerated foods, it measured whether customers bought enough of the cold foods to justify the cost. The test said yes. But the chain also found that customers purchased more dried goods after stores introduced the refrigerated section; the result was a much greater boost to profitability.[29]

Step 6: Decide

After analyzing the results of your convergent experiment, it is time to make a decision based on the findings. This is where having agreed on your definition of success in step 1 will pay off.

If you do find a desired improvement from your innovation test, the story may not be over. This should often lead to further iteration and testing of additional ideas to see if they can lead to greater improvement. In the 2008 presidential contest, the Obama campaign ran test after test, examining the effects on fund-raising appeals of changing many different elements—the subject of the request, the kind of photos and videos, the "call to action" words on the button that led you to a donation page. Each subsequent test added a bit more learning, but the cumulative effect was to raise the final rate of conversions—from e-mail to website to volunteer sign-up to donation—by 40 percent, or an estimated $57 million of additional fund-raising.[30]

Step 7: Share Learning

Once you complete your analysis, it is essential to capture and share the learning of your experiment. If you are doing a battery of experiments on the same variables, this process can happen at the end rather than after each step. But it is critical to both document what you learned and communicate your findings to others in your organization who could benefit (and could avoid any of the same mistakes).

You can find a list of sample questions to use in capturing and sharing learning from any convergent experiment with your team in the Tools section of http://www.davidrogers.biz.

Tool: The Divergent Experimental Method

The second tool is a guide for running divergent experiments. This method is particularly useful for innovations that are less defined from the outset, such as new products, services, and business processes for your organization. Innovation projects using divergent experimentation tend to be highly iterative and may span weeks or months.

You can see the ten-step Divergent Experimental Method in figure 5.3. Its steps fall into three stages: preparation, iteration (steps that repeat several times), and action.

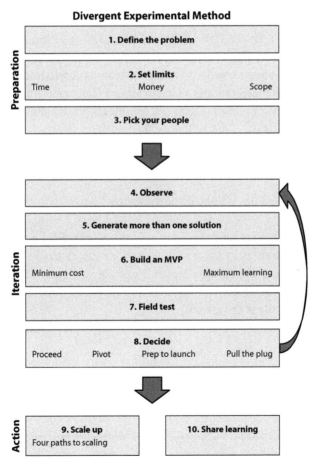

Figure 5.3
The Divergent Experimental Method.

Step 1: Define the Problem

The first step of a divergent experiment is to define the problem you are seeking to solve. The problem should be rooted in an observed customer need or market opportunity and be a challenge that your organization is particularly well suited to solve. The advantage of defining your innovation in terms of a problem is that it forces you to take the customer's point of view. Your innovation should always focus on delivering value to the customer (even if that customer is an internal constituency) rather than on deploying the latest exciting technology or product feature or defeating your competitors.

The problem definition may include a quantified goal, but that goal should be both challenging and broad. Recall the experimentation that led to Intuit's Fasal product: the defined goal was to raise Indian farmers' income by 10 percent. This allowed the team wide latitude in thinking about how to reach it. When Steve Jobs tasked his team at Apple to develop the first iPod, he challenged them to help customers "put 1,000 songs in their pocket." Notice that the challenge is not technical ("fit this much memory on a hard drive this size") but describes the benefit or experience from the customer's point of view.

Step 2: Set Limits

The second step is to set limits for your innovation process. Because divergent experimentation is iterative and because we are naturally inclined to defer or delay before admitting failure, it is easy for your innovation project to keep running even when the prospects for success are dim. It is therefore essential to set limits at the outset.

Any divergent experiment should begin with three kinds of limits defined:

- *Time limit*: Finite time should be allotted for the project and its key approval stages. Many companies, including Mondelez, AT&T, Intuit, and Amazon, use three months as a limit for iterative project development before a crucial decision is made on whether to proceed.[31]
- *Money limit*: Budgeting for innovation projects is often best done in approval stages. IDEO charges clients for each stage of iterative

product development, requiring buy-in before moving on to the next. As assumptions are tested and project risks are reduced, additional budget can be released.

- *Scope limit*: Companies should define up-front what they are *not* seeking to accomplish. This provides helpful boundaries for even the most wide-open experiments. For Intuit's Fasal project, the desired product and business model were unknown, but the target market (rural Indian farmers) established critical boundaries.

Step 3: Pick Your People

The last step of the preparation phase is to pick which people will work on your innovation experiment.

The first question is the size of your team. As a general maxim, an innovation team should be as small as possible—but no smaller. Intuit's popular SnapTax product was developed by a team of three people.[32] Jeff Bezos is famous for his "2 Pizza Rule" at Amazon: no meeting is to take place if the number of participants is too great to be fed with two pizzas. In my own experience running strategy workshops both within and across companies, a five-person team is usually ideal for innovation. J. Richard Hackman has studied team collaboration and found that the number of network links between team members poses an upper threshold for effective group size. As the number of group members increases linearly, the necessary lines of communication increase exponentially, as $n(n-1)/2$. Hackman advises that a group of five is ideal and warns against ever going above ten.[33]

In addition to size, diversity of team composition is crucial. This should include diverse skill sets that relate to the nature of your project. (For example, an innovation team working on new service options for a bank might include team members with backgrounds in IT, consumer behavior, employee training, and service design.) You should also strive to include participants with diverse biases and backgrounds. Look for people who don't always work together or who may come from different parts of your organization. Include recent hires as well as someone who knows your organizational culture well.

It is valuable to change the innovation team over time rather than keeping the same group for every project. You may want to introduce an element of competition as well, with multiple small teams competing (at least in the initial stages) to develop the best solution to a common challenge.

You have now completed the preparation phase of the Divergent Experimental Method. Next come steps 4–8, the heart of your experiment. They will be done not once but in an iterative cycle until a decision is made to either terminate the project or move on to a public launch.

Step 4: Observe

The iterative development of ideas for your innovation begins with observation. Observation informs and provides the insights you need to solve the next stage of the problem you are working on. The goal of observation is to both *deepen* your understanding of the problem itself and *broaden* the range of ideas you bring to bear in finding a solution.

You should focus first on observing the customer's context—to better understand the problem you're trying to solve. Learn everything you can about the customer, the nature of the problem, and the context into which your solution needs to fit.

In addition, look for ideas from further afield. Look at other markets (how other customers deal with the same issue) and other industries (benchmarking from beyond direct competitors in your industry). You can also look to ideas generated in previous innovation efforts. IDEO, for example, maintains a "Tech Box" in each design studio, where prototypes and product ideas that were intriguing but ultimately not completed can be stored away for future inspiration. Rummaging in past ideas that didn't quite make it may lead to unexpected discoveries for your current project.

Step 5: Generate More than One Solution

The next step is to generate ideas to solve the defined problem. This is the stage where your own intuition plays its proper role in innovation: to help create new ideas and possible solutions (not to evaluate them, which should be done by the customer).

There have been numerous books written on creativity and effective idea generation techniques. If you do not already have an ideation process developed within your company, I would highly recommend you read a few, incorporating the tools and processes that you find most helpful into your practice. Some of my favorite books include Bernd Schmitt's *Big Think Strategy*, Luke Williams's *Disrupt*, Drew Boyd and Jacob Goldenberg's *Inside the Box*, William Duggan's *Creative Strategy*, and Rita Gunther McGrath and Ian MacMillan's *Marketbusters*.

The only strict rule here does not cover *how* you generate ideas; rather, it requires that you generate *more than one* idea. Your aim is not to run an intense brainstorming process and conclude with a single favored solution to the problem (perhaps after heated debate among the team members about the relative merits of others). Rather, your goal in ideation should always be to generate multiple *viable ideas*. (Recall the three very different solutions that Intuit initially proposed for the Indian farmers.) You will then, in subsequent steps, experiment on these ideas and use market feedback to determine which one to pursue and how to develop it.

Step 6: Build an MVP

By now, you should have some promising new ideas. But even brilliant ideas are not enough. "If you build it, they will come" may have worked for Kevin Costner in the move *Field of Dreams*, but in business innovation, great ideas are just the start of the process.

In this step, you need to translate your ideas into prototypes. In the start-up world, the focus is on a *minimum viable product*, often an early website or app launched publicly so customers can start using it, responding to it, and identifying bugs or missing features. For an established enterprise, where it may not be appropriate to share early design ideas in public, I prefer the term *minimum viable prototype*. Either one can be abbreviated as MVP.

The most important point is that your MVP should absolutely not be a full-blown or finished product. The most common way to inflate innovation budgets is to overdevelop prototypes (through long and expensive technical development) before validating them with real customers. Scott Cook says an MVP should have "just enough features to allow for useful feedback from early adopters."[34] Recall the makeshift prototype used to test Intuit's Fasal service. The team didn't build a software platform that could scale to millions of Indian farmers. They sent two employees into markets to gather data in person and had a third sit at a desk and manually send text messages to farmers to see if they used the data and if it actually helped them earn more money. This is a perfect example of the goals of an MVP: *minimal cost + maximum learning*.

If an MVP is successful, it will be followed by further iterations. As you progress, your successive prototypes should evolve from lesser to greater fidelity (e.g., from a sketch to a model to a working product) and from partial to total functionality (e.g., from a test of one key feature to a test of the complete offering).

Step 7: Field Test

After building a minimum viable prototype of your idea, the next step is to actually test it. This is where market validation takes place, as you get feedback on your MVP and test your assumptions.

In choosing how and where to test, you should aim for as natural an environment as possible—that is, as close as is feasible to the actual context where the ultimate solution will be used. You should also test your prototype with an audience as similar as possible to the customers you expect will be using the final version.

Confectionary maker Mondelez set up its "Fly Garage" so that real-world customers can respond to its prototypes for new product innovations. "You capture the idea, you visualize it, prototype with limited resources, and two days after, we have the real people coming in and reacting," says Maria Mujica, the company's Latin American marketing director. "That is amazing because . . . we then get to look at the faces of the real people and ask what they like and what they'd change."[35]

Before each field test, you should identify the assumptions you are seeking to validate, which should include the following:

- *Customer value assumptions*: Do customers value your solution? Will they use it? What will they pay for it? Which customers are the best fit? What additional value are they still looking for from your solution? What parts did they not find necessary?
- *Business model assumptions*: How will you manufacture your offering? How much will this cost? How will you market it, distribute it, and acquire new customers? How might competitors respond?

The assumptions you are testing will be guided by where you are in the iterative development of your innovation. In general, customer assumptions will be tested earlier than business model assumptions.

Step 8: Decide

At the end of each field test of an MVP, you will face a decision point. For start-ups, the decision is often "pivot or persevere" (Ries's formulation), with the presumption that your innovation effort will keep going until you run out of money. But in established enterprises, each innovation project is not meant to risk bankrupting the company!

For an established business, the decision after each field test is one of four options:

- *Proceed*: Your field test has validated your ideas so far. You can move on to the next round of prototype development and assumptions testing. Go back to step 4.
- *Pivot*: Your field test has raised issues. You may need to adjust your idea based on what you learned or go back to test another solution you generated before to see if it is more promising. Go back to step 4.
- *Prepare to launch*: Congratulations! You've finished successive prototypes, have fully validated your innovation, and are ready to bring it to market. Go to step 9.
- *Pull the plug*: If you've tested all your solutions or you've hit the limits of your time or budget, now is the time to stop the process and assess what you've learned. Go straight to step 10.

Step 9: Scale Up

If you completed your iterations of steps 4–8 with an innovation deemed ready to launch, then the next stage is to scale it up. This is where you take the solution you have been testing in minimal viable form and translate it into a full release in the marketplace.

For customer innovations, this may include a rollout plan for manufacturing (where and how), distribution (which channels), and marketing (advance buzz, launch, and beyond). If you have developed an internal innovation, your rollout may focus on training, business process integration, and change management. Scaling up any innovation will also require you to secure more resources: staff, budget, and executive sponsorship.

Even with launch, though, the iterative learning from and improvement of your innovation are not over. You should plan to keep learning from customers' use of your product after the launch and apply that learning to improve (although you may shift to a convergent experimental method to further optimize it).

However, not every product can iterate and evolve in the public eye to the same degree. The way a company iterates after launch will differ greatly between a digital-only consumer start-up and a manufacturer serving business clients with mission-critical equipment. To determine which approach is right for your project, see the next section, "Four Paths to Scaling Up an Innovation."

Step 10: Share Learning

Whether your experiment led to a successful solution that you are preparing to launch or failed to solve the defined problem, it is vital to preserve the learning that came through your process. It is therefore important to have a formalized process for capturing, sharing, and accessing the learning from any divergent experiment. This includes archiving or documenting prototypes you developed, solutions you tried (which may not have worked but could inform others), and lessons you learned.

You can find a list of sample questions to use in capturing and sharing learning from any divergent experiment with your team in the Tools section of http://www.davidrogers.biz.

Four Paths to Scaling Up an Innovation

So you've developed a successful innovation. Now what?

One of the ways that the digital revolution has changed innovation is in defining its end point. Innovation used to focus on a finished, polished product for launch into the market. Now, with the addition of data and software to nearly every offering, businesses have the opportunity to continue rapidly experimenting with and evolving their innovations even after launch.

Companies like Google are famous for launching products as an explicitly incomplete beta to get user feedback on how to finalize the design. Pierre Omidyar launched eBay after coding the first version of its website in three days. This is a classic example of the start-up philosophy of launching a minimum viable product directly to consumers—in essence, running the process of experimentation in the public eye.

But launching an MVP is not an option for every company or every innovation. If you are Ford Motor Company, you can't put an MVP for a new car on the road for customers to buy while you are still testing its market fit. Apple has good reason for maintaining the secrecy surrounding its products before unveiling them rather than releasing product betas for early adopters.

There are four general paths for scaling up an innovation to a full release. To understand which path you should take, you need to answer two questions:

- *Can you iterate this offering quickly after launch?* For software products, iteration is generally easy via online updates. For services, iteration is also often possible (e.g., launching a new sales process that you can adapt based on feedback). However, for physical products or physical designs such as retail environments, rapid iteration after launch is rarely an option. If your innovation is heavily dependent on partners or constrained by regulations, you may also not be able to iterate quickly.
- *Can you limit your rollout to stages, or does the innovation have to be released to all customers at once?* You may be able to limit the rollout of an innovation to specific locations (e.g., a retail design or a local service). You may be able to limit it to a subset of customers (e.g., by invitation only). You may be able to limit the duration of a new offering (e.g., a holiday menu item or a limited prerelease of your next video game). For other projects, though, it is will be necessary to offer your innovation immediately to anyone who is interested.

Your answers to these two questions will place you in one of four quadrants (see figure 5.4). Let's look at the requirements for successfully scaling up an innovation in each quadrant.

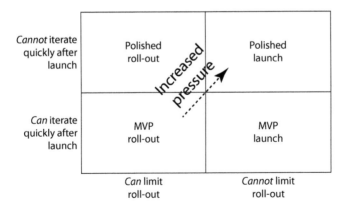

Figure 5.4
Four Paths for Scaling Up.

MVP Rollout

This is the easiest path for introducing an innovation because you can start your rollout with a limited test market and then iterate rapidly as you gain additional feedback from customers. In these cases, you may bleed right from your minimum viable prototype into actual product development. That is, your first public release will be a minimum viable *product* offered to a limited set of customers. The relative ease of this path is one upside to being a little-known start-up: you can iterate and learn with real customers without much public scrutiny.

This was what Rent The Runway did after receiving its first round of capital from Bain. The first website launched with only 5,000 members, by invitation only. This allowed the company to start with a relatively inexpensive inventory of 8,000 dresses from thirty designers. Once they saw the business model was succeeding and press coverage led to a surge in requests to join, the founders secured a second round of financing so they could scale up quickly to meet demand. An example of a locally limited MVP rollout is the launch of Zipcar. This was one of the first services to allow members to rent a car by the hour, picking the cars up at street locations identified online rather than having to visit a car rental office. Founder Robin Chase launched Zipcar as an MVP only six months after beginning work on the business and having raised just $75,000. She was able to do this partly because she began only in Boston, waiting more than a year to extend to a second location. This allowed her to test out the business model and iterate her service with feedback from paying customers.

MVP Launch

The second path for scaling up is harder. In this quadrant, your business is forced to iterate very quickly after launching your innovation because you are not able to able to effectively limit the scope of the launch. (As a result, your first release could make a lasting impression on a larger audience.)

One reason this path may be necessary, even for a digital service, is that the business has to rely on network effects. For example, eBay was predicated on a platform business model that required both buyers and sellers. Growing each side of that equation as quickly as possible was essential (no one wants to sell on an auction site with few customers or to browse on an auction site with few products). Omidyar could not afford to restrict the website to a small pool of customers while he iterated and perfected it.

A business also may not be able to limit the release of an innovation due to the high visibility of its brand or the expectation that the initiative may draw wide attention. American Express launched Small Business Saturday with the idea of putting a spotlight on America's small, local businesses for one day. The campaign launched in just six weeks with its scope still undetermined. An outpouring of energy and involvement came in from social media, consumers, business owners, and even an act of Congress. The company had to move quickly, but it was able to rapidly evolve the program and its goals as Small Business Saturday quickly became an annual phenomenon during the holiday shopping season.

Polished Rollout

The third path for scaling up is also harder than the first—but for different reasons. In this quadrant, you are able to launch your innovation in limited locations or for limited customers, but you cannot quickly iterate it once it is public. It therefore needs to be much more polished at the point of release.

Still, you are able to take advantage of rolling your innovation out in stages by validating your initial findings and testing how it is received by different customers or in different markets. Retail design typically follows this path. Starbucks has tested diverse ideas, such as offering local wines and craft beers, in a set of store locations in Seattle. The company first tested wireless charging mats for phones at stores in Boston before rolling them out nationwide. It even tested a coffee delivery service (via mobile app) by making it available exclusively to customers working in New York's Empire State Building.

When Settlement Music School, an education nonprofit in Philadelphia, developed an innovative plan for a new music program aimed at adults, it chose to roll it out one location at a time. After the first two locations succeeded but the third foundered, the school realized the program would need to be adapted based on the musical interests and cultural networks of each surrounding neighborhood.[36]

Polished Launch

The fourth path for scaling up a new innovation is the hardest of all. In this quadrant, you must offer your new innovation to all customers at once, and you are unable to iterate it quickly. This creates maximum pressure for your company to polish and carefully test an innovation before its public release.

This is the path for innovations like new automobiles, pharmaceuticals, and hardware products. In cases where a physical product can be updated in a year or less (e.g., some consumer electronics), you may want to aim for a streamlined first product, withholding some of your eventual features until the first edition is on the market. This is the pattern of Apple's most successful products, which typically have made large leaps in features between their first and second years (in that sense, some would say the first-generation iPads and iPhones were both "MVPs").

By contrast, we can look at Google Glass. The wearable eye-frame computing device was released publicly while it was still buggy and before Google was even clear on the value proposition for the user. The company failed to iterate Glass meaningfully within a year because it was still just trying to get the device to work consistently. It was probably used to operating in the MVP rollout quadrant (where it had launched Gmail and countless other software products), and it underestimated the discipline necessary when releasing a hardware product, especially one that would be attracting massive media attention. Although Google released Glass to only a few thousand customers, the prominence of its brand and the controversial nature of the product (with its ability to record video incognito) ensured that the release was subject to prolonged and intense scrutiny. A national conversation ensued about what Glass meant for the future of computing and privacy, and the company, which grew up with the most casual of beta-style launches, learned that not every new innovation can be released the same way.

Knowing which of these four quadrants your innovation fits in—polished or MVP, rollout or launch—will clarify your path to bringing it forth and scaling it up successfully. Any new innovation should continue to iterate and improve after launch. Knowing how to best do so is essential.

Organizational Challenges of Innovation

Putting rapid experimentation at the heart of the innovation process is not easy for many large or traditional organizations. As they have grown, most businesses have relied on decision making by committee or by seniority and chain of command. In Silicon Valley, it is commonly said that HiPPOs make the decisions at more-traditional firms. (No, not the river-dwelling mammal you see in the zoo. This is decision based on the Highest Paid Person's Opinion.) Rethinking innovation requires significant organizational changes, beginning with how decisions get made.

Building a Test-and-Learn Culture

Historian Yuval Noah Harari describes the birth of the Scientific Revolution as "the discovery of ignorance." In his view, the birth of modern human societies began with this credo: "We don't know everything ... the things that we think we know could be proven wrong ... no concept, idea or theory is sacred and beyond challenge."[37]

For a business to embrace experimentation requires a similar recognition: we do not know what we think we do. This sobering truth is particularly clear to companies already steeped in the practice of running experiments. One survey of experiment-focused businesses reported that two-thirds of the new ideas tested by Microsoft failed to deliver any of their expected benefits. Only 10 percent of Google's experiments were successful enough to lead to business changes. And Netflix has estimated that 90 percent of what it tries turns out to be wrong.[38]

As technology journalist Alexis Madrigal has observed, "It turns out that our creativity is good but our judgement is lousy."[39]

There is a solution. Companies can compensate for the fallibility of management's own judgment if they instill in their employees a culture of testing and learning about every aspect of their business. One company that has done so is Amazon. We can see this in the experience of Greg Linden, a former Amazon developer. He was working on Amazon's checkout process when he came up with the idea of offering shoppers a final set of product recommendations as they checked out, based on the items that were already in their shopping cart. When he presented the idea, senior management hated it. It was a cardinal rule of e-commerce to not distract or get in the way of the shopper once they have begun the checkout process. But Linden kept thinking about how checkout shelves in real-world supermarkets are ideal for getting customers to pick up just one more item on their way out. Although he had been forbidden to work further on the project, he went ahead and built a quick test version of the feature. The senior vice president who had voted down his idea couldn't have been happy, but the company let Linden run the test anyway. (At Amazon, it was hard for even a top executive to block a test experiment.) The data came back, and Linden's innovation turned out to be extremely profitable. Resources were immediately applied to developing and launching a full version of it.[40]

In how many companies would Linden's story have ended this way?

Leading Without Deciding

The antithesis of Greg Linden within the world of retail might be Ron Johnson. In 2011, Johnson left Apple to take over as CEO of struggling retailer JCPenney. Johnson had a bold vision to reinvent the discount department store with a more modern, Apple Store–like environment. The retail experience was to be transformed—featuring smaller shops within the store, cool coffee bars to hang out in, and new outside brands like Martha Stewart. Eventually, all cash registers and checkout counters would be replaced with high-tech product-tracking and self-checkout systems. Johnson pledged to reinvent pricing as well, shifting from heavy use of coupons and sales promotions to reliance on standardized pricing year-round. It was a truly bold hypothesis, but would JCPenney's customers respond positively to a radically different type of store? Unfortunately, after years of success leading retail teams at Apple, Johnson felt no need to test his hypothesis. Instead, he simply rolled it out, with no pilots and no limited test markets. The result was a catastrophe. The company, which had already been suffering for years, fell into much steeper decline. A little after a year under Johnson's leadership, its quarterly results showed a 32 percent drop in same-store sales—what some observers suspected was the worst decline ever reported by a major retailer in history.[41] Seventeen months into his tenure, Johnson was ousted as CEO.

One can only imagine what might have transpired if Johnson had instructed his team at JCPenney to test the assumptions behind his new strategy in a series of early and focused experiments. Rapid experimentation requires more than curious and empowered employees like Linden in the trenches; it requires a different kind of leadership from the top, too. Nathan Furr and Jeff Dyer talk about this as a shift in role from "Chief Decision Maker" to "Chief Experimenter."[42] In the experiment-driven organization, leadership becomes less about making the big decisions on behalf of the organization. The role of a leader, whether CEO or head of a small team, shifts from providing the right answers to posing the right questions.

Involving Everyone

Intuit's CEO Brad Smith has said that "Intuit has 8,000 employees, and we want them all thinking about how to improve the design of products and services, even if those offerings are intended for internal support only."[43] But how do you make that happen? Can innovation really be something that the entire organization can, or even should, be doing?

Some firms do find it useful to sequester innovation teams, isolating them at least partially from the politics and priorities of those maintaining the current business. This may make sense if you are trying to pursue innovation in an area outside your current business or ventures that may cannibalize or challenge parts of your existing business model. Earlier I mentioned Mondelez's innovation "Garage," where it tests out product ideas that may seem too far-fetched for some managers in the organization. Similarly, AT&T has set up a series of innovation labs it calls "Foundries," each with 40–50 staff.[44]

Other firms seek to engage the entire organization, but they do so during innovation "sprints" or "boot camps." Typically, these are open to all employees, with an innovation challenge, a crowdsourced vetting process for picking the ideas to receive funding, team coaching on innovation methods, and a limited time frame within which final results are announced. Amy Radin has served as a chief innovation or chief marketing officer at top financial services firms such as Citi, AXA, and E*TRADE. While at E*TRADE, she led an initiative called Innovation Unleashed, for which a core objective was to use innovation to build morale and cultural cohesion and tap into employees to create new growth opportunities. "Success really came down to empowering the employees," Radin told me. "Making it easy to participate. Making sure bosses knew that their staff can do it on work time. Making it clear that it's sanctioned by the leadership team." She focused the incentives on recognition rather than compensation. "If your idea wins, we will invest ten or twenty thousand dollars to prototype it, and you will get to participate in the workshops building it." The response far exceeded expectations: 120 teams registered to participate in the innovation competition, out of 3,000 employees in the entire company.[45]

The last, and likely hardest, approach is to try to train everyone in the organization to adopt experimental methods year-round in their daily work. This is the approach that Intuit takes, having now trained hundreds of "catalysts" who, in turn, work with teams throughout the company to help them experiment effectively. The same experimentation method that was used to develop the Fasal product for India is being used internally to improve processes in departments like legal, HR, and order management. By instilling innovation methods broadly, businesses can benefit from a wider range of perspectives, including those of their newer junior staff. Retailer Tesco trains the junior analysts at its UK headquarters to conceive and conduct experiments on small samples of customers. This gives them free rein to try unconventional ideas that executives who have been at Tesco longer would not even think of.[46]

Planning to Fail and Celebrating It

The hardest challenge for many organizations as they learn to embrace innovation by experimentation is accepting, planning for, and even celebrating failure.

Let me be clear. In some quarters, the embrace of failure has gone so far as to mistake it as a noble goal in and of itself. But failure—learning that an idea for an innovation does not work—is not actually the *goal*. Learning through failures is the *process* that takes us to the goal of great innovation.

But singing the praises of failure, done right, is probably needed at most companies. After all, it is human nature to avoid failing and being perceived as having failed. Most large organizations tend to reinforce this strenuously with rewards systems. But an organizational culture that shuns failure poses three severe risks to any innovation efforts:

- *Incremental innovation efforts*: The first big risk is risk aversion. When those involved in failed projects are punished or stigmatized, employees tasked with innovation will shy away from any unknowns, including big growth opportunities for the firm. When Bank of America set up a group of branches in the Atlanta area to serve as test sites for the use of technology to reinvent the banking experience, it established a 30 percent failure rate as a goal in hopes that teams would try genuinely new and risky ideas. But in practice, the innovation teams felt intense pressure to show successes and opted for testing what they acknowledged were the safest of the ideas they generated. The actual failure rate in the first year was only 10 percent.[47]
- *Loss of learning*: When failures are punished, there is no incentive to bring failures to light. Even innovation teams that find successful

solutions are unlikely to reveal the early blunders and blind alleys they stumbled through along the way. If teams aren't comfortable sharing their mistakes, then the learning at the heart of experimentation will never be captured by the organization. Peers will be doomed to repeat the same mistakes.

• *Throwing good money after bad*: When failures are punished, any team with a budget will find a way to justify their underperforming initiative as "just needing a little more time," adjusting their future projections and endlessly postponing any decision to shut it down. Scott Anthony, David Duncan, and Pontus Siren call these "zombie projects" and describe them as initiatives that "fail to fulfill their promise and yet keep shuffling along, sucking up resources without any real hope of having a meaningful impact on the company's strategy or revenue prospects."[48]

To avoid these three hazards, businesses need to plan to fail and celebrate smart failure. Planning to fail simply means developing a process for evaluating every innovation initiative on a predefined schedule, against predetermined criteria, and with incentives to encourage employees to declare their own project fit for termination. Failure planning should be structured so that shutting down one project is directly tied to freeing up resources (indeed, reallocating the same people) to work on new opportunities for innovation. When Finnish game maker Supercell shut down a year-long IT development project that had gone off course, it celebrated the team members' hard work with champagne and shifted them to another project. That project turned out to be the wildly successful mobile game *Clash of Clans*.[49]

Celebrating smart failure means creating occasions for senior leaders to celebrate innovation projects that failed, alongside those that succeeded. (Commemorating them on the same occasion ensures that attendees see the connection between the two.) In celebrating innovation failures, it is important for senior management to communicate both *why* employees should fail (i.e., in pursuit of important strategic opportunities) and *how* they should fail (e.g., cheaply and early). By celebrating the *virtues* of smart failure (i.e., learning from mistakes, applying them to strategy, and sharing the learnings with others), leadership can instill them in the organization. This approach is taken by India's Tata Group. Each year, the global conglomerate celebrates innovations from its 100 operating companies around the world. In addition to categories like Product Innovations and Core Process

Innovations, teams are invited to submit for the Dare To Try category—an award that "recognises and rewards the most novel, daring and seriously attempted ideas that did not achieve the desired results." In its first year, only three companies dared to submit a failed project for the Dare To Try award. Five years later, the category had 240 entries (more than for some of the "success" categories). The winner that fifth year (Tata Consultancy Services) also won in the Service Innovations category. The example showed employees how real innovation and smart failures go hand in hand.[50]

To innovate in the digital age, businesses must learn to experiment continuously and effectively. By continuously iterating and testing new ideas and by getting real data and real customer feedback, even the largest enterprises can become as agile as a lean start-up. Only then will they be able to innovate in a way that is fast enough, cheap enough, and smart enough to create new value for customers in a constantly changing world.

However, launching new products and new ventures and refining existing ones are not the end of the story if businesses are to innovate and evolve. When faced with deep and profound changes in market needs, businesses and entire industries can find that the value they offer to customers is no longer the same, or as relevant, as it used to be. This uncertainty means that every business must be prepared to adapt its value proposition to customers over time. Rather than waiting until a profound change is essential to survival, or even until it is too late to change, businesses in the digital age need to develop a forward-looking attitude. The new imperative is for businesses to adapt their value to customers when they can rather than when they must. The next chapter explores how to do that.

6

Adapt Your Value Proposition

VALUE

One of the long-standing industries most severely affected by the digital revolution is the recorded music business. It is now bouncing back—but after some brutal mistakes and a steep decline in the early years of the Internet. A look back at that history may be instructional as businesses consider the future.

In 1993, an industry body called the Moving Pictures Expert Group publicly released a new technical standard that would allow for effective compression of the audio portion of motion pictures, what came to be known as the MP3 format. This new format allowed musical recordings to be compressed into much smaller digital files, with minimal loss in audio quality for the listener. That same year, the first popular Web browser (Mosaic) launched the World Wide Web as a mass medium for communication. The opportunity created by the two in combination was unmistakable. For the first time, it would be possible to transmit music recordings in digital format, almost instantly, and to store them effectively on the disc drives of that era's computing devices.

For the music industry, this opened the door to an incredible range of new value that could be offered to music customers. With digital files and distribution, record labels could offer customers instant access, a vast selection of music unencumbered by the limits of a physical store, and the ability to pick and choose just the album or even just the songs they wanted. But instead of offering any new value to customers, the music industry, as represented by the Recording Industry Association of America (RIAA), pretended nothing had changed. Actually, the RIAA did take one step: it sued the companies trying to create the first portable devices for storing and playing MP3 files.

There are many possible lessons to draw from the dramatic decline of the recorded music industry from 1999 to 2012, as worldwide sales dropped from roughly $28 billion to $16 billion.[1] One of the starkest, though, is that if your business does not take advantage of a new opportunity to offer value to your customers, someone else will.

In this case, that someone was a start-up called Napster. Launched in 1999, Napster offered a peer-to-peer service for swapping MP3 music files over the Internet, with no payment to the copyright holders whatsoever. Yes, it was illegal. But the value proposition was irresistible for many customers. On the one hand, they had the RIAA, offering them great recordings of their favorite music. On the other hand, they had Napster, offering them all those same great recordings, plus instant access over the Internet, a selection that outstripped that of any physical retail store, and the ability to find and choose just the songs they wanted—and, oh yes, it was all free.

After four years of punishing declines in sales, the major record labels agreed to let Steve Jobs and Apple enter the market with a competing offer: the iTunes Store, a legal MP3 superstore linked to Apple's recently launched portable player, the iPod.

MP3 players were niche products until the iPod, and even afterward, MP3 owners lacked an easy way to legally purchase music. With Apple's design and branding savvy, combined with the RIAA's deep catalog of popular music, the iTunes Store became the first mass-market platform for legal digital music sales.

Suddenly, a new value proposition was available to customers besides the RIAA's compact discs in retail store bins and Napster's illegal digital cornucopia. With iTunes and an iPod, customers could reap all of the benefits of a service like Napster, except the free price, but with an entry price point so low ($0.99 for one song) as to seem negligible. In addition,

		napster. 1999	iTunes 2003
Great music	×	×	×
Instant access		×	×
Vast selection at your fingertips		×	×
Choose the songs you want		×	×
Free		×	
Popular portable device			×

Figure 6.1
Three Value Propositions: Recorded Music.

they were offered the first real lifestyle-branded digital music device and store, with a pleasing and intuitive user interface that made iTunes accessible even to those who had no idea what peer-to-peer file sharing meant. (See figure 6.1.)

From its opening in 2003, the iTunes Store grew quickly, while sales of physical music formats continued to drop. Gradually, the industry's misery lessened until 2012, when global music sales finally bottomed out, and even posted a modest upward tick on the back of iTunes and other online services (such as streaming, the next growing trend). "At the beginning of the digital revolution it was common to say that digital was killing music," Edgar Berger, CEO of Sony Music International, commented to the *New York Times*. Since 2012, he says, "digital is saving music."[2]

The RIAA's desire to resist the evolution of its industry was understandable. It was sitting on a streak of record-breaking profits with its existing business model of selling compact discs. But in 1993, it was already clear that this business model was unsustainable in the Internet era. By waiting as long as possible to adapt what it offered to customers, the music industry trained millions of young listeners to expect digital music to be free and delayed putting in place an effective strategy for dealing with the changes coming to the industry.

Rethinking Value: What Business Are You In?

The fifth and final domain of digital transformation is your business's value to its customers. Traditionally, a company's value proposition has been treated as fairly constant, ideally a source of sustained competitive advantage for the long haul. Successful businesses found a differentiated offer, used it to position themselves in the marketplace, and then did their best to optimize that business model for as long as possible. But in the digital age, unswerving focus on executing and delivering the same value proposition is no longer sufficient. (See table 6.1.)

Think of the real estate business, which went relatively unchanged for decades. Real estate agents were essential brokers between home sellers and purchasers. With the arrival of the Internet, the core value of the broker—providing access to listings of homes on the market—vanished. With transparency of information online, buyers and sellers no longer needed a middleman just to find each other. The real estate broker could have gone the way of the travel agent, made superfluous for most customers and transactions. But, instead, real estate firms adapted by finding new ways to add value for home buyers and sellers. Modern brokers go beyond providing tools for searching for just the right listing (including mobile apps with customizable searches and geolocation alerts to "open house" events near you). They use digital tools to curate all sorts of information for home buyers who are comparing neighborhoods (maps, video tours, information on schools, and online forums to see how residents rate a suburb's

Table 6.1
Value: Changes in Strategic Assumptions from the Analog to the Digital Age

From	To
Value proposition defined by industry	Value proposition defined by changing customer needs
Execute your current value proposition	Uncover the next opportunity for customer value
Optimize your business model as long as possible	Evolve before you must, to stay ahead of the curve
Judge change by how it impacts your current business	Judge change by how it could create your next business
Market success allows for complacency	"Only the paranoid survive"

pros and cons). They have become expert advisors, using blogs and social media to share information on how to decide when to list your home, what closing a credit card does to your credit score, and FAQs on titles and liens. To survive in the digital age, brokers have shifted from being a gatekeeper of home listings to becoming a resource for buyers and sellers in a high-stakes decision process.

Every business today should follow the example of the real estate broker. Instead of defining its job by what its industry has done in the past, your business must define its job to match your customers' ever-changing needs. It should judge each new technology not by how it impacts your current business model, but by how it might create your next one. You need to constantly examine the core value your business offers to customers and ask these questions: Why does my business exist? What needs does it serve? Are they still relevant? What business am I really in?

This chapter explores how businesses manage to adapt their value proposition, why every business should adapt before it needs to, and why many firms fail to do so. It compares different concepts for thinking strategically about your value to the market. And it examines the organizational barriers that may be preventing your business from adapting how it serves customers. This chapter also presents a strategic planning tool: the Value Proposition Roadmap. This tool allows any business to identify its key customer types, define the elements of its value proposition for each customer, identify potential threats, and develop new offerings to deliver value in a rapidly changing environment. By expanding the business's focus beyond current revenues and near-term profits, this tool gives incumbents the opportunity to identify new sources of value in the face of emerging threats.

Let's start, though, by defining the fundamental challenge of maintaining growth when your industry is under attack.

Three Routes Out of a Shrinking Market Position

There may be many reasons that businesses face a declining market. New technologies can bring rapid changes in customer needs, the appearance of substitute offerings, or a decline in the relevance of a once-valued product or service. In some cases, product innovation and marketing can rejuvenate growth in a business or even an entire industry. But in other cases, businesses find themselves in a truly constrained market position, where their

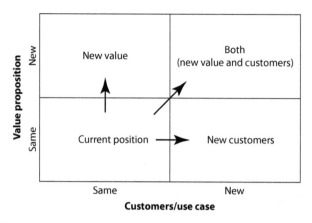

Figure 6.2
Three Routes Out of a Shrinking Market.

current offering and their current customers show almost no chance for continued growth.

What options exist for such a business? Igor Ansoff proposed two general dimensions for growth: new versus existing products and markets.[3] For a business whose current product-market mix is trapped in decline, we can adapt his Ansoff Matrix to help identify three routes out of a shrinking market (see figure 6.2). Let's look at the dynamics and challenges of each route.

New Customers (Same Value)

The first route out of a shrinking market is to find new customers to buy your same offering. This can be extremely difficult in an era where markets are already relatively flat and open (with even small businesses using digital communications to sell around the world). But in some cases, creative thinking can identify a new customer or use case for the same value that your business has been offering.

Like many paper manufacturers, Mohawk Fine Papers found itself in a declining market at the start of the twenty-first century as the rise of digital communications enabled customers to reduce their use of paper. Founded in 1931, the firm had built its business selling high-quality paper to large corporations like GE and Exxon Mobil for use in annual reports and other glossy corporate brochures. Mohawk found its market declining severely as its traditional customers relied more on digital communications. The shift accelerated once the Securities and Exchange Commission started allowing firms to submit financial reports digitally and the New York Stock Exchange stopped requiring that annual reports be printed for shareholders (these had made up a third of Mohawk's revenue). Mohawk's management led a turnaround by finding a new type of customer that could make use of their fine-quality papers: online stationery services. With the growth of websites for printing photos, greeting cards, and business cards, the firm convinced companies like Shutterfly.com and Moo.com to try offering the kind of high-quality papers that were Mohawk's specialty. Stationery consumers took to them immediately, happily paying extra for paper that gave their materials a look and feel of real quality. Within a few years, Mohawk's sales to online businesses had increased dramatically, offsetting the loss of its old customers and putting the company back on steady footing.[4]

Around the same time, Salt Lake City newspaper *The Deseret News* found itself facing a declining market, just like many other smaller urban newspapers across the United States. After thriving for 150 years, the paper was losing two kinds of customers: reader subscriptions were slipping, and advertisers were fleeing for cheaper opportunities to advertise on the Web. The *News'* classified ad revenues fell 70 percent from 2008 to 2010 as advertisers shifted to free sites like Craigslist and national portals like Monster.com. As the owners struggled to reverse the fortunes of their print newspaper, they looked to see if they might be able to sell their same product to new customers besides Utah residents. They realized that the paper's unique focus on a set of core issues—the Mormon faith, family, care for the poor, and the impact of mass media on social values—could resonate with a national audience of readers who shared similar values and concerns. The paper launched a new weekly print edition for subscribers outside of Utah in 2009. By 2012, *Deseret's* total print circulation had doubled, to 150,000 readers nationwide, with growth in advertising revenue that made it one of the fastest-growing print papers in the United States.[5]

There are often limits, though, to how many new customers can be found for a value proposition that is losing relevance in its existing market. If a new customer base is found, it may simply be a smaller niche that has a unique reason to remain loyal while the larger customer base departs.

Westfield, Massachusetts, was home to forty different companies that manufactured whips for the horse-and-buggy industry in the nineteenth century. With the rise of the automobile, the buggy industry that supported whip manufacturers vanished. One whip maker, Westfield Whip, managed to survive by shifting its focus to new customers in the livestock industry as well as those involved in horse riding and dressage competitions. Although the company managed to find enough new customers to continue selling whips into the twenty-first century, the other thirty-nine whip makers in Westfield did not.[6]

New Value (Same Customers)

The second route out of a shrinking market is to continue serving your same customers but to adapt your value proposition to stay relevant to their changing needs. This is what the recorded music industry did once it begrudgingly teamed up with Apple to launch the iTunes Store for music consumers. It's also what real estate agents have done as they continually find new ways to stay relevant to home sellers and buyers.

Adapting its value proposition requires a business to be willing to depart from what has brought it success in the past. When faced with a decline in relevance and demand for its offerings, a business must resist asking "How can I get my customers to still pay me?" and instead ask "How can I become as valuable to my customers as I used to be—or more so?"

Remember the story of *Encyclopædia Britannica* from chapter 1. When, after two centuries, sales of the printed encyclopedia began to drop with the arrival of personal computers, the company knew it wouldn't survive by looking for new customers to buy its existing product. Instead, Encyclopædia Britannica, Inc. tried to reinvent the value it offered while staying rooted in its mission to bring expert, fact-based knowledge to the public. This led to experiments with a CD-ROM encyclopedia, then a free online version with advertisements, and, finally, a successful new offering: a paid online site for home users paired with a wider range of digital teaching tools for educators in the K–12 market. Today, more than half of U.S. students and teachers have access to Britannica content for the classroom, and half a million households subscribe to Britannica Online. When the company finally chose to end its print edition, it was simply because it was relevant to so few customers. "Our people have always kept the mission separate from the medium," said Britannica President Jorge Cauz.[7]

A major ongoing example of value proposition adaptation can be seen in the *New York Times*, a journalistic institution founded in 1851 that many feared would not survive the dramatic shift to the digital age. Ever since the Internet made the distribution of content nearly free, news as a product has looked more and more like a low-value commodity. The prices that publishers like the New York Times Company can charge advertisers have dropped dramatically as readers have moved away from print editions. At the same time, digital start-ups like BuzzFeed and Vox have proven more adept at generating viral sharing in social media. In 2011, the documentary *Page One* depicted the Times as an organization struggling to adapt to a digital future; in 2014, an internal innovation report was leaked, showing the company in the midst of rethinking its value proposition to customers in the digital age. The Times knew it still had unique value in the reporting abilities of its 1,300 newsroom employees and the credibility of its brand. But it knew that value would need to evolve.

Over several years, the Times has shown a steady commitment to rethinking journalism and finding new ways to add value for customers. It has pursued innovations in distributing its content via mobile apps and social media channels. It has experimented with new digital formats to help advertisers engage readers, including Page Posts based on a native advertising model. And its content has embraced new digital forms from blogs by diverse columnists to regular video content to interactive storytelling through data visualizations and interactive graphics. One watershed example is a dialect quiz developed with the help of a statistician intern and based on scientific research in the demographics of regional American vernacular. Combining the best of the Times' rigor with a BuzzFeed-like irresistible format, that quiz quickly became the publication's most read online article of all time. A few months later, the paper established The Upshot, a seventeen-person laboratory that is reimagining what a news story can look like.

The results of this years-long shift can be seen in a news organization that is clearly offering new value to readers whose media habits are rapidly evolving. By 2015, the Times' share price had rebounded 150 percent from its 2013 level; the company had $300 million in net cash, and total revenue was growing again, thanks to digital subscribers and digital advertising.[8] That same year, the company announced it had reached over 1 million digital-only paid subscribers.

New Value + New Customers

In some cases, a third route out of a shrinking market may be possible with both new value and new customers. Usually, this may come when a dramatic shift in the value proposition succeeds in capturing a new market of customers.

One business that made such a leap is Williams, a leader for decades in the manufacture of pinball machines, those popular twentieth-century arcade games. With the emergence of electronic video games in 1972, the company realized that the entire pinball category could be headed toward irrelevance. It decided to reinvent itself by moving into a new kind of gaming that was just emerging: electronic gambling. By the time Sony's PlayStation had arrived and the pinball and arcade industries had collapsed, Williams had established itself with a string of hit casino games. Its new products attracted a different customer base—and a much more profitable one at that. After more than a decade of growth, the company was the third-largest manufacturer of casino slot machines when an even bigger competitor, Scientific Games, bought it for $1.5 billion.

An even more remarkable example of revival through new value and new customers is Marvel Comics. Despite being the progenitor of such classic superheroes as Spider-Man, the Avengers, and the Fantastic Four, by 2004 the comic book company was facing an unpromising future. Youngsters were turning away from printed paper comics in favor of digital media. Licensing deals negotiated in the 1990s with vastly more powerful movie studios had provided only a modest lifeline of income (e.g., $62 million for two Spider-Man films that grossed nearly $800 million).[9] The company decided to take a leap and redefine its value proposition entirely by creating a movie studio to produce high-budget films featuring its own comic book characters. To raise capital, it had to put up its own rights to those characters as collateral. But the bet paid off with huge new audiences and financial success for such movies as *Iron Man, Thor*, and *The Avengers*. Once a struggling company making printed comics for a narrow base of enthusiasts, it had transformed into a major movie studio with an enormous fan base, an arsenal of sequels in production, and a small print publishing unit that could serve as a lab for testing new characters and storylines. Within five years, this burgeoning Marvel empire was purchased by the even larger Walt Disney Company for $4 billion.

It is worth noting that in the cases of Williams and Marvel, a new customer base was discovered only after a reinvention of the value proposition (from pinball machines to gambling games, from pulp-paper superheroes to silver-screen blockbusters).

In the digital age, a mature business that is facing decline is less likely to uncover some previously unreached markets for its same products and services. Digitization has simply removed too many barriers to entry for markets. The customers were already reachable. It is much more likely that adapting and extending the value of your offering is what will lead you into new markets. (Indeed, the New York Times Company has reached many more international readers as it pushes into digital delivery.)

In sum, for any business in a shrinking market, focusing on adapting its value proposition to provide new relevance to customers is absolutely essential.

Adapt Before You Must

There is no need to wait for a crisis, though. Value proposition adaptation is a strategy that every business can apply even when it appears to be doing well. In a rapidly changing digital environment, it is worth remembering Andy Grove's maxim: "only the paranoid survive."

This attitude toward customer value can be clearly seen in today's digital titans, whether Google, Amazon, Facebook, or Apple. Even as they are achieving great success, they are looking ahead to shifts in customer needs and preparing to enter new markets with new value propositions. (This year's impregnable monopoly might be next year's declining incumbent—think Microsoft Windows.)

But we can find examples among pre-digital enterprises, too, that are focused on staying ahead of the curve of change.

Founded in 1870, the Metropolitan Museum of Art has long been one of New York's top tourist attractions. With over 6 million annual visits, it is far from in decline. But the museum is keenly aware that its audience's lives are changing dramatically due to the digital revolution in media and communications. It also knows that if it hopes to continue to be an integral and enriching part of people's lives, it needs to think differently about the value it provides. In 2013, my friend Sree Sreenivasan was hired as the museum's first chief digital officer, in charge of a team of seventy staff. Their task has been to extend and enrich the experience of the art in the museum for both the 6 million who walk through its doors and the 30 million who visit its website and digital properties each year.

For those inside the Met, this includes new mobile apps for discovering curator recommendations; mobile games for kids, like "Murder at the Met" (which challenges teens to study various artworks for clues to a mystery about a John Singer Sargent painting); and hashtags for visitors to use when sharing their own photos of each exhibit on social media (#Benton-Mural or #AsianArt100). "Our audience was demanding it!" Sreenivasan told me. The museum is also using social media to engage those outside its halls—not just on Facebook and Instagram but also on Pinterest, where curators collaborate on joint pinboards, and on the Chinese network Sina Weibo, where the Met received 3 million views of its first sixty posts. Online interactive tools to explore the collection include the kaleidoscopic One Met. Many Worlds, which allows for keyword-based exploration in eleven languages, and the Timeline of Art History, a teachers' favorite that receives one-third of all the museum's Web traffic. Sreenivasan told me that they are still learning how best to engage their diverse audiences. "One thing we've learned is that everyone wants a peek behind the scenes." After acquiring a seventeenth-century family portrait by Charles Le Brun, instead of working in secret to prepare it for exhibition, the museum began blogging and posting photos and videos that show the restoration work. One post showed Michael Gallagher, the head of painting conservation, using a cotton swab to clean the oxidized varnish off a baby's toes. "Now you're interested, because you want to see what happens to the rest of the painting," Sreenivasan said. "And when you come to the Met, you'll get to see that!"[10]

The Met is a perfect example of an organization changing before it has to and staying ahead of trends in customer needs. This kind of forward thinking and willingness to invest in new capabilities before an old business model falls into decline is essential to strategy today. My Columbia Business School colleague Rita McGrath describes this as strategy focused on "transient advantage" (in her excellent book *The End of Competitive Advantage*). In today's world, no advantage enjoyed by any company can be treated as defensible for the long term. Instead, businesses need to think in terms of developing transient advantages, which drive profitability for a time but must be constantly buttressed by new value drivers as old positions of strength may quickly come under threat.

The speed with which a position of strength can flip to one of decline can be seen in the experience of Facebook. In 2012, the social networking colossus seemed to dominate the digital world, disrupting traditional media and advertising companies as it attracted a billion users and ever more hours of their precious attention each day. But just as it was preparing for its IPO, the firm disclosed in its securities filings that it faced a huge unknown threat: the shift of users to mobile devices. All of its revenue had been based on advertising on its desktop display. Companies like Google were struggling to retain the profitability of their advertising as consumers switched to the small screen. Facebook had no mobile revenue at all. At the peak of its triumph on the desktop, the burning question was, How will Facebook deliver value to advertisers in a mobile world without turning off its users?

Facebook succeeded by adapting its value proposition for both audiences. For users, it added value through simplicity. Its mobile app kept the focus on the News Feed (the stream of posts by your friends) and split off other features into separate apps, like Messenger. When it bought photo-sharing app Instagram, it kept that separate as well. Within its main app, it dropped the website's sidebar full of countless cheap and irrelevant ads; it raised the price for the ads that remained and formatted them so they wouldn't overwhelm the user's field of vision. For advertisers, it similarly rethought the value it offered in mobile. It dropped the old ad formats that wouldn't work on a small screen and developed new ones like video ads, which performed much better. By harnessing its data with its new Custom Audiences, it allowed advertisers to, in effect, pay to reach just the right and most relevant audience, both inside Facebook and in ads placed anywhere else on the Web. The result: mobile advertising became the company's biggest growth engine, quickly taking over as its top source of revenue. Total profits soared, and the company's stock bounced back from a dip after the IPO, doubling in price over two years.

Five Concepts of Market Value

Value proposition is just one of several strategic concepts available for thinking about your offerings and value to the market. But it is a particularly useful, and underutilized, concept. To better understand the concept of value proposition, let's compare it with four of the most common ways of thinking about market value (see table 6.2).

- *Product*: Thinking about products is something every manager is comfortable doing. If you're an automaker, you spend a lot of time thinking about your different models of SUVs, sedans, and minivans. Product thinking is useful (indeed essential) when making decisions about engineering, design, launch dates, pricing, and other factors as you prepare to go to market. But product is probably the most overused strategic lens in companies. Thinking about products can limit your vision. It allows you to ignore the customers who are actually using

Table 6.2
Five Concepts of Market Value

Concept	Concept pros and *cons (in italics)*	Examples as applied to automotive
Product	Important in portfolio decisions *Ignores customers and value to them* *Leads to strategic myopia*	SUV Sedan Minivan
Customer	Customer-centric Helps identify whom to focus on *Not focused on value*	College student drivers Parents with small kids
Use case	Value-centric and customer-centric Helps with better segmentation *Obscures that a customer may have multiple use cases*	Night out with friends Driving and carpooling with kids
Job to be done	Value-centric and customer-centric Helps identify nontraditional competitors *Lacks concrete specifics*	Safely and comfortably transport several kids from points A to B
Value proposition	Value-centric and customer-centric Helps assess threats and ideate new innovations outside of existing products More concrete and specific (includes multiple elements)	Reliable transportation Accommodates several passengers Safety in an accident Personalization of car zones (e.g., for climate or audio) Communication for driver (e.g., hands-free calling) Entertainment for passengers (e.g., Wi-Fi or video)

the product as well as the value that it may provide them. An excessive product focus has long been recognized as a source of what Ted Levitt called "marketing myopia," where a company assumes it is in the business of making a particular line of products (e.g., daily newspapers) rather than being in the business of meeting a particular need (e.g., to stay informed).[11]

- *Customer*: Another very common approach is to think about your business in terms of your customers—who they are and how they differ from one another. This is certainly the first step toward becoming a customer-centric company. By focusing deeply on customers, you can begin to learn which customers matter more, have different needs, and should therefore be treated differently. However, looking at traditional profiles and "personas" of customers (fictional stand-ins based on demographics, attitudinal data, and product consumption) can sometimes take the place of actually talking to flesh-and-blood customers to find out why they are using your products and what needs you may not yet be meeting. Again, you are still short of focusing on the value delivered.

- *Use case*: This concept arose in software engineering and is credited to Ivar Jacobsen,[12] but it has been applied more broadly in design and marketing. In the broader sense, a use case is the context within which a customer utilizes your product or service. For example, if your product is a minivan and your customers are parents with small children, one important use case is driving and carpooling with children. The use case concept combines a focus on the customer with a focus on the context, which helps you think about the value being delivered. However, it is important to recognize that the same customer may have different use cases for the same product (e.g., parents of small children may use the same minivan for a night out socializing with friends). But, used properly, use cases can lead to better customer segmentation and a focus on the value of your products in customers' lives.

- *Job to be done*: This concept has been popularized by Clayton Christensen and Michael Raynor.[13] In the job-to-be-done framework, the concern is not just the context in which a customer is using a product but also the customer's purpose for using it. By focusing on the underlying problem that the customer is trying to solve, your business becomes more customer-centric and more value-centric. You can also begin to identify nontraditional competitors: if the job your customer is "hiring" your minivan to do is to safely and comfortably transport their children from point A to point B, there could be another competitive solution besides a different brand of minivan. Perhaps Uber will develop a verified "child-safe" service that will become popular with overbooked parents. The fact that using the job-to-be-done concept results in a high-level summation is valuable (it can focus your thinking), but it can also sometimes be a limitation (it can lack specificity).

- *Value proposition*: This term was coined by Michael Lanning and Edward Michaels.[14] It has come to be used broadly in marketing and strategy as a concept that defines the benefits received by a customer from a company's offering. Like job to be done, it is a concept that is both value-centric and customer-centric. However, it is often used to identify multiple elements of value to the customer (that is how I will use it in this chapter's tool). For example, if the job to be done for parents by a minivan is to transport their children safely and comfortably, the value proposition you offer them could include several elements: reliable transportation, spacious accommodation for passengers, safety features for accidents, personalization of different zones in the car (for climate or audio), hands-free communication for the driver, and entertainment options for the passengers. By breaking the customer value down into more-concrete and more-specific elements, you can assess threats to each one (e.g., your minivan's entertainment options may become irrelevant to customers as their children acquire more portable devices) and innovate new elements that can be added.

All five of these strategic concepts are useful at different times in decision making and planning. (I certainly wouldn't recommend that you never discuss your product portfolio or customer segments.) But the value proposition is especially useful when you face the challenges of adapting and evolving your value to customers in response to changing needs and new opportunities posed by technologies. This is why it is used in this chapter's tool.

Now that you've seen the importance of value proposition adaptation for any business in today's fast-changing environment, let's take a look at a strategic planning tool for making this happen.

Tool: The Value Proposition Roadmap

The Value Proposition Roadmap is a tool that any organization can use to assess and adapt its value proposition for its customers. You can use it to identify new and emerging threats as well as new opportunities to create value for your customers. It will help you synthesize those findings into a plan to create new, differentiated value in a changing landscape. Above all, if your company is under pressure, the tool will force you to challenge your assumptions, step back from focusing on defending your past business, and use your customers' perspective to imagine new ways forward.

The Value Proposition Roadmap uses a six-step process to map out new options for your business (see figure 6.3). Let's look at each of the steps in detail.

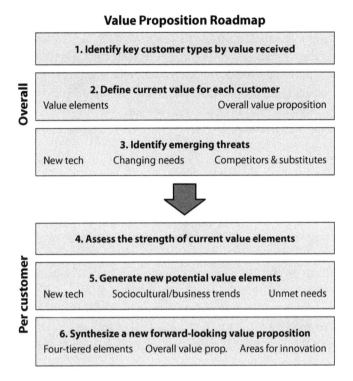

Figure 6.3
The Value Proposition Roadmap.

Step 1: Identify Key Customer Types by Value Received

The first step is to identify your key customer types, distinguished by the different kinds of value they receive from your business.

For a hypothetical University XYZ, for example, the key customer types might include undergraduate students, their parents, alumni, and employers (looking to recruit students and alumni). Note that each of these customer types gains somewhat different value from the university. For undergraduate students, the value may be a mix of education, social environment, and certification to help in job seeking. For alumni, the value of their ongoing relationship with the university may be based more on career networking or a sense of pride in the school's athletics, research efforts, or reputation. For employers, the value of the school may be in preparing graduates with certain skills (topical knowledge, critical thinking, or technical skills) as well as credentialing and assisting in finding the right recruits.

If you are having trouble identifying different customer types, look to differences in customers' motivations or jobs to be done (For what different reasons do they do business with me?) or in their use cases (In what different circumstances do they do business with me?). Looking at these is more useful than looking at differences in demographics (students come from all over the world; alumni are of all different ages; neither of these factors is as critical to their relationship with the university as the different kinds of value they receive).

Step 2: Define Current Value for Each Customer

The next step is to define your current value proposition for each customer type.

This starts with a list of value elements—the various benefits that each customer type gains from the relationship with your business. After listing the value elements, write a summary statement of the value that this type of customer receives from your business—the overall value proposition.

In table 6.3, you can see value proposition definitions for University XYZ's key customer types.

Notice that nowhere in the university's value propositions is there a list of products or services or a list of fees paid or ways that it will monetize each customer type. Your value proposition should always be defined in terms of benefits that matter to your customers.

Notice also that each of the university's customer types has a distinct overall value proposition. Customer types may have some value elements in common (undergraduate students and alumni both care about a career network; parents and employers both care about credentialing). But no two customer types should have identical lists of value elements. If you arrive at identical value propositions for two customer types, dig deeper. If you still don't find a significant difference in the value they receive from your business, combine them into a single customer type.

Step 3: Identify Emerging Threats

Now that you understand your current value to customers, it is important to understand emerging threats that could undermine it. They could do so by competing with the value you offer, substituting for it, or simply making it less important to your customers.

Table 6.3
Value Proposition Definitions for University XYZ's Customers

Customer type	Value elements (What benefits do they gain?)	Overall value proposition
Undergraduate students	Foundational knowledge (e.g., chemistry) Exploration of interests/ self-discovery Socializing and formation of friendships School pride (athletics, etc.) Career network (peers who will be part of their career network after graduation) Credentialing (i.e., a degree, which provides opportunities)	"Launchpad for your personal and professional life as an adult"
Parents	Foundational knowledge (e.g., chemistry) Critical thinking (e.g., writing, analysis) Credentialing Career network Career counseling and assistance (to help their children in finding a first job) ROI (average boost in graduate's expected income vs. total cost of education)	"Foundation for your child's independence and career success"
Employers	Foundational knowledge (e.g., chemistry) Critical thinking (e.g., writing, analysis) Applied/job skills (e.g., programming languages) Credentialing Recruiting (helping them recruit students on campus)	"A source of talent for your firm's long-term growth"
Alumni	Career network (those met during school as well as fellow alumni met later) Career counseling and assistance School pride (athletics, professional reputation, etc.)	"A lifelong network and source of pride"

At this point, you are not looking for factors that you *know* will undermine your business but simply ones that *might* have the potential.

Following are three sources to consider for potential threats to your current value proposition:

- *New technologies*: Look for emerging technologies that seem relevant to your industry and your customers' experience. For the recorded music industry, the MP3 compression format was one such technology. For pinball machine maker Williams, early video games like Pong were identified as a potential threat to established games.
- *Changing customer needs*: These can include changes in consumers' habits, lifestyles, and social behaviors. Facebook recognized the shift in its users' computing time from desktop to mobile devices as a potential threat. For B2B companies, changing customer needs may include changes in laws, regulations, or the business environment. Think of Mohawk Fine Papers and the shift in financial reporting rules, which meant that its client businesses had less need of printed documents.
- *New competitors and substitutes*: A threat to your current value proposition can often come from an asymmetric competitor entering from another industry. For Encyclopædia Britannica, Inc., that included Microsoft, when the software maker bundled a free encyclopedia with its operating system. Other times, the new entrant may substitute for your value proposition by meeting your customers' need in a new way. The publishers of *The Deseret News* saw this as websites like Craigslist filled the need that used to be met by newspaper classified ads.

In table 6.4, you can see emerging threats to University XYZ from each of these three sources.

The rest of the tool will focus in detail on each of your customer types. You may want to start by completing steps 4 through 6 for a single customer type and then repeat the process for the next customer type. Alternatively, you can analyze all your different customer types as you go through each step.

Step 4: Assess the Strength of Current Value Elements

At this point, you should return to the lists of value elements you developed for your customer types in step 2. You can now assess the strength of the specific elements of value that you provide.

Table 6.4
Emerging Threats to University XYZ's Value Proposition

Source	Examples
New technologies	Video
	Podcasts
	Telepresence
	MOOCs
Changing customer needs	Millennial students seeking more digital, anytime experiences
	Alumni needing more lifelong learning
	Employers seeking different skills for new job hiring
	Government funders looking for more measurable economic impact
New competitors and substitutes	Universities offering purely online degrees: ASU Online, etc.
	Nonuniversities offering online courses: Coursera, etc.

For each value element that you listed, ask three questions:

- *Are there any ways that this is a source of decreasing value to the customer?* This decrease could come from one of the emerging threats identified in step 3 (a new technology, customer need, or competitor). Other factors could include declining relevancy to the customer, cheaper options, and underinvestment by your business (e.g., if cost cutting has led you to deliver less value here than in the past).
- *Are there any ways that this is a source of increasing value to the customer?* New innovations by your business may mean you are increasing the value you deliver through this particular element. Or the value may be increasing due to this element's growing importance to the customer, scarcity in the market, or differentiation compared to your competitors.
- *What is the overall verdict?* Based on these combined factors, you should now make an overall assessment for each value element. Is it strong (still a powerful source of value for your customer); challenged (under threat and perhaps not as strong a source of value as in the past); or disrupted (no longer relevant or meaningful to this customer type and uncertain to recover in value).

This process should provide a clear assessment of the strength of your current value elements. Table 6.5 shows University XYZ's assessment of value elements for its undergraduate students.

Table 6.5

Assessing the Strength of University XYZ's Current Value Elements

Company: University of XYZ
Customer type: Undergraduate students
Overall Value Proposition: "Launchpad for your personal and professional life as an adult"

Value element	Decreasing value to customer?	Increasing value to customer?	Overall verdict
Foundational knowledge (e.g., chemistry)	Large introductory lecture classes have worst ratings MOOCs provide cheaper access to this content Best students are testing out via AP exams		Challenged
Exploration of interests/ self-discovery		New internship and study-abroad programs have had very strong interest	Strong
Socializing and formation of friendships	More socializing happens through online networks (but not all)		Challenged
School pride (athletics, etc.)	Less relevant to many students (rank low on surveys) International students not participating		Challenged
Career network (peers who will be part of their career network after graduation)	Underinvested for several years (no strong programs to support students)		Challenged
Credentialing (i.e., a degree, which provides opportunities)		Reputation continues to be strong Is attracting increasing numbers of international students	Strong

Step 5: Generate New Potential Value Elements

Your next step is to try to identify new value elements that you could offer to this customer type. This is a chance to examine some of the external forces that may be weakening your value proposition and use them as a source of opportunity for new value that you can create for your customers.

Table 6.6
Generating New Value Elements for University XYZ's Undergraduate Students

Source	Examples	Possible new value elements
New technologies	Video, podcasts, MOOCs Telepresence	On-demand learning experiences (e.g., versions of large lecture classes) Telepresence to provide more internship and professional work exposure
Trends in customer environment	Millennial students seeking more digital, anytime experience	Micro-classes to explore student interests between semesters before enrolling in classes
Unmet customer needs	Career counseling Interpersonal skills coaching on "emotional intelligence"	New "life coaching" program that combines career and social skills

To generate new value elements that you could offer to your customers, look in three areas:

- *New technologies*: How could new technologies allow you to create additional elements of value for your customers?
- *Trends in your customers' sociocultural or business environment*: Consumer lifestyle and business trends may provide new opportunities for you to create value, even with the same products.
- *Unmet customer needs*: Get close to your customers. Observe them directly. Talk to lead users. You're sure to find some unmet needs that no one is fulfilling; one of them may be an opportunity for your business to add new value.

Table 6.6 shows some new value elements that University XYZ might consider adding for its undergraduate students.

Step 6: Synthesize a New Forward-Looking Value Proposition

The final step of the Value Proposition Roadmap is to synthesize everything you have learned about your value proposition for each customer type.

Review your value elements, and place each into one of four columns:

- *Core elements—to build on*: These elements are a source of strength that you plan to use as a focus of continuing innovation.
- *Weakened elements—to bolster*: These are current value elements that are losing their impact for your customers and that you have chosen to try to reinforce and improve.
- *Disrupted elements—to deprioritize*: These are former sources of value that have lost their ability to deliver for your customers and that you have chosen to move away from and drop from your strategic focus.
- *New elements—to create*: These are new value elements that you have identified as opportunities to add more value for your customers and that you have chosen to invest in for future growth.

Now you can craft a revised overall value proposition for each customer type. This should be a forward-looking statement of how you intend to create value as you continue to evolve your offerings for this particular customer type. Finally, list any ideas you have for specific initiatives (new product features, service offerings, etc.) you can use to deliver on your revised value proposition.

Table 6.7 shows a new forward-looking value proposition for University XYZ's undergraduate students.

If you are looking at your customer types separately, you can now go back and complete steps 4–6 of the tool for the remaining customer types that you identified in step 1.

When you have finished, you will have in your hands a complete roadmap for adapting your value proposition. This roadmap includes a strategic analysis of emerging threats, an innovation brief that can be used by those working on your next-generation products and services, and a customer-centric analysis of where your business is today and where it is going in the future.

If applied as a regular part of strategic planning, the Value Proposition Roadmap can be a helpful tool for anticipating customer needs, assessing new technologies proactively, and applying resources to new strategic opportunities.

Organizational Challenges of Adapting Your Value Proposition

The benefits of continuously adapting a business's value proposition may be clear. But that does not make it easy. It requires the business to step outside

Table 6.7
Synthesizing University XYZ's New Value Proposition

Company: University of XYZ
Customer type: Undergraduate students
Existing Overall Value Proposition: "Launchpad for your personal and professional life as an adult"

Core elements— to build on	Weakened elements— to bolster	Disrupted elements— to deprioritize	New elements— to create
Exploration of interests/ self-discovery	Foundational knowledge (especially large lectures)	Expensive school pride events and social activities	On-demand learning and preprofessional experiences
Credentialing and international brand reputation	Peer network for careers		Career and personal "coaching"

Revised Value Proposition	"Your launchpad for personal discovery and professional success"

*Specific areas for
innovation*
	On-demand learning experiences (e.g., versions of large lecture classes)
	Expanded international internships and telepresence-based work
	  projects
	Online micro-classes for students to explore interests between semesters
	"Life-coach" program for final two years that combines career and
	  social skills
	Alumni-to-student mentoring programs

the inward-looking habit of focusing on its own products and processes and, instead, to take the point of view of the customer. It also requires the business to imagine a version of itself that is different than what perhaps worked very well in the past. In particular, a larger or longer-established organization may find it much harder to gain a clear view of its value to the customer and of the opportunity, and necessity, to adapt while it still has the chance.

Dedicating Leadership

The first challenge for value proposition adaptation is leadership. Who will be in charge of making the change happen? Even when a strategy team is effectively set up to identify opportunities for evolving the business's value proposition, someone needs to be in charge of acting on the new opportunities. For years, the U.S. Postal Service has struggled to balance its finances as technology has changed the needs of customers for its services (When did you last send anyone a post card?). In 2014, its inspector general released a report arguing that the USPS should move into providing nonbank financial services (bill payments, money orders, prepaid cards, international money transfers, etc.) to its customers, many of whom are underserved by traditional banks.[15] The report was praised in the press, on Capitol Hill, and even in the pages of *American Banker*.[16] But more than a year later, no action had been taken, despite support for the idea from the American Postal Workers Union. A newly sworn-in postmaster general had focused on the current value proposition (e.g., whether to trim Saturday mail delivery), but no one appeared to be in charge of turning innovative ideas for new customer services into a reality.[17]

Leadership tenures may be another important factor in value proposition adaptation. As Henry Chesbrough has observed, many large firms move their general managers in two- or three-year rotations among different business units in order to develop their leadership and knowledge of the whole firm. However, undertaking significant change to a unit's value proposition or business model often takes more than two years. These kind of short-term leadership roles encourage managers to simply continue to optimize the existing model rather than pushing the company to adapt for the future.[18]

Allocating Talent and Treasure

Another key challenge for an organization seeking to adapt is the need to allocate the necessary human and financial resources away from existing areas of business and into new, unproven ventures.

New managers with appropriate skills and authority are often the driving force behind new strategic direction. At the New York Times Company, adapting the value proposition of its business for both readers and advertisers required organizational changes as well. The company hired Alexandra MacCallum, founding editor of the digital Huffington Post, to lead a unit focused on audience development in an age of social media. Chris Wiggins was named chief data scientist and assigned to help guide a burgeoning engineering division. Its job was to harness data and analytics to help inform decisions by both editors and publishers on the Times' content, distribution, audience, and new advertising products.

Often, adapting a business's value proposition requires changing the lines of reporting of existing employees. When Facebook began its strategic shift to focus on the best mobile experience for users and advertisers, it had to redesign the organization chart for the company's engineering teams. In the old organization, the desktop team led the development of each new feature, and separate teams handling mobile apps for iOS and Android were left to play catch-up. To support the new strategy, all engineers were reassigned to teams focused on a single Facebook feature (photo albums, group messages, upcoming events, etc.) so they could build it for both mobile and desktop from the very beginning.[19]

Financial resources must also be allocated carefully to support the evolution to new value propositions. This often requires leveraging revenue or assets from existing units to finance the launch of new ones. During Williams's strategic transition, the firm was simultaneously taking money out of its existing pinball machine business and launching its first casino games. Marvel Comics had to leverage its prized rights to its comic book characters as collateral to secure funding for its move into film producing. This kind of transition is critical. McGrath describes this as a process of "continuous reconfiguration" of assets, people, and capabilities as businesses adapt from one transient advantage to another.[20]

Avoiding Myopia

Perhaps the biggest challenge to adapting the value proposition of an organization is that it requires looking beyond the conventional wisdom of its current business. Bold new opportunities (like selling music as digital files over the Internet rather than as physical products) can often provoke a response of "That's not how we do things around here!" To paraphrase entrepreneur Aaron Levie, "Businesses evolve based on assumptions that eventually become outdated. This is every incumbent's weakness and every startup's opportunity."[21]

Numerous psychological experiments have illustrated the power of confirmation bias. When faced with new information, we have a strong tendency to selectively notice facts that fit our preexisting theories of the world and to discount or filter out the ones that conflict. Think of the pinball machine industry. When computer games first arrived in arcades, pinball machine sales actually improved temporarily because the new games were bringing in more customers. It would have been easy for Williams to have concluded that video games posed no threat to its legacy business. Actually, that is what their competitors concluded; almost all of them vanished while Williams was making its pivot to casino gaming.

Avoiding myopia requires a business to take the customer's point of view rather than its own. This kind of customer-centric thinking is difficult, as an organization naturally focuses its energy and attention on its own processes, strategies, and immediate self-interest. If a company has been making encyclopedias for 200 years, it would be easy for it to focus on all the hard work that goes into making them and to wish customers would just pay for its new CD-ROM version rather than cultivating the perspective to see that its CD-ROM isn't really the best solution for those customers.

To cultivate the customer's point of view, a business needs to institutionalize listening to its own customers, particularly lead users (as discussed in chapter 4). These avidly involved customers actually drive most commercially successful new innovations because they tend to face new needs earlier than the general population.[22]

The challenge, though, is often not in finding the right customers to listen to but in keeping our ears open. My friend Mark Hurst has spent his career trying to help companies develop customer empathy through direct customer observation. "The difficult truth is that customers often bring the bad news when something is wrong," Hurst says. "Some executives simply don't want to hear it."[23]

In a world of rapidly changing technology and customer needs, it is no longer sufficient for a business to deliver the same value that has brought it success in the past. A rapid pace of change demands that every business continuously adapt how it serves its customers, what problems it solves, and what value it delivers. By taking a truly customer-centric attitude, a business can stay ahead of the curve of change. If it can learn to continuously reevaluate the value it delivers, identify changing customer needs, and spot emerging opportunities, it can continue to be the most valuable option for its customers.

We have now examined all five domains of digital transformation. We have seen, in detail, how businesses today need to think quite differently about customers, competition, data, innovation, and value to customers. By applying new tools and concepts to each of these five domains, any organization can move beyond the assumptions of the analog age. By transforming its strategic thinking across the five domains, any business can adapt and create new value in the digital age.

But success in the digital age also requires us to prepare for the unexpected: the most challenging ruptures and dislocations that can strike any industry. This requires a clear understanding of what we mean when we talk about business *disruption*. That concept is surrounded by many misconceptions. True business disruption does not happen every day. But there might be times when a business must face a truly disruptive challenge—an asymmetric threat that radically undermines its current position, calling into question its core value proposition and threatening to make it unattractive to customers or, worse, irrelevant. In such times, that business needs additional tools: a theory to understand the difference between competition and true disruption, a rubric to assess any potentially disruptive threat, and a guide to judge what the appropriate response is.

The prevailing theory of disruption, developed just as the Internet age was dawning, was based in the prior revolutions of the late industrial and early information ages. Successful leadership today requires an updated theory of disruption for the digital age. That is the subject of the next and final chapter.

7

Mastering Disruptive Business Models

There is a specter that lurks in the background of almost every discussion of digital transformation. For many, the need to rethink and adapt their organizations arises in response to a fear of a different, dire outcome: disruption.

This concern is prudent. Even if your business absorbs the best strategic thinking of the digital age and works diligently to apply it toward your own strategies, no method is foolproof. It is still possible—in some cases, even inevitable—that you will wind up faced with a truly disruptive threat from an asymmetric competitor. It is critical, then, to be prepared to cope with disruption.

In this last chapter, we will examine the nature of business disruption and its relationship to everything we have learned about the five domains of digital transformation. I will present two final strategic tools. The first tool, the Disruptive Business Model Map, allows you to assess any emerging threat to determine whether it truly poses a disruptive challenge to your business. (*Spoiler*: in most cases, it does not.) If you are dealing with a true case of disruption, the second tool, the Disruptive Response Planner, reveals the full scope of the threat and helps you choose among the six responses possible for an incumbent business under attack. In order to do all this, we will first need to revisit the existing theory of disruption and update it to account for the changed dynamics of the digital age.

Throughout this chapter, our understanding of disruption will be informed by all that we've learned about the five domains of digital transformation—customers, competition, data, innovation, and value. We will see why disruption differs from most cases of innovation. We will see how it is best understood as an asymmetric competition between business models. We will discover why value proposition is an essential lens to understanding and mastering disruption. And we will discover how platforms, data assets, and customer networks are among the key drivers of disruptive value in the digital age.

But to start, let's be clear about what we are trying to understand when we talk about business disruption.

Disruption Defined

The idea of disruption has grown in relevance as every industry faces increasingly unpredictable threats. But at the same time, *disruption* has become a buzzword, bandied about indiscriminately. Any new business or product is heralded as disruptive to lend it credibility. ("You have to fund our new start-up; it is going to disrupt the XYZ industry!") Countless speeches have been made exhorting entrepreneurs to be disrupters. At times, the rhetoric seems to mistake the point of innovation, which is not simply to disrupt existing enterprises but rather to create new value for customers.

If we are to inform our own business strategy by thinking constructively about disruption, it is essential that we develop a clear understanding of the phenomenon.

To start, let me offer a definition:

Business disruption happens when an existing industry faces a challenger that offers far greater value to the customer in a way that existing firms cannot compete with directly.

Let's unpack that definition.

- *Business disruption*: We are talking specifically about disruption in the sphere of business. I state this because the idea of disruption is frequently applied to changes in culture, society, politics, and other domains. For example, one can argue that the birth control pill was a disruptive innovation in terms of its impact on social mores, marriage law, and political ideologies. But it may not have transformed business or industry. In a case like this, an innovation may be disruptive to society but not be an example of business disruption.

- *Existing industry*: *Disrupt* is a transitive verb! In order for something to be disruptive, something else must be disrupted. When we see a radically innovative new business or product, we sometimes leap to the conclusion of disruption before considering its impact on existing industries. Think of the self-driving car first pioneered by Sebastian Thrun and others in Google's Google[x] division. A mainstream, affordable self-driving car may soon be commonplace—and even become the dominant mode of transportation within a decade or two. If so, this will clearly be a transformative technology for drivers. But it is less clear that self-driving cars will disrupt existing automakers. So far, Google has shown little interest in entering car manufacturing and is looking to partner with major automakers. Some of them, like Toyota, are even launching their own parallel efforts in this area. It is quite possible that self-driving cars will radically transform the experience of driving and the world of transportation but do so without undermining the existing automobile industry.

- *Offers far greater value to the customer*: Whenever disruption occurs, it is because a new offering is suddenly much more attractive to customers than the offering that the existing industry provides. Photographic film maker Kodak did not collapse into bankruptcy because digital cameras offered somewhat better value for consumers. It did so because digital cameras—with nearly unlimited shots, instant display of the picture taken, and free replication and transmission of images— were *vastly* better than film cameras for the average snapshot taker. The first thing that separates disruption from traditional competition is this wide gap in value, which can lead to a tipping point when customers shift en masse to the new offer.

- *Cannot compete with directly*: This is the other key distinction between disruption and traditional competition. In traditional competition, roughly similar businesses duke it out to offer the customer better product features, lower prices, or greater personalization and service.[1] When Ford Motor Company comes out with a faster, more fashionable, or more fuel-efficient car, Chrysler redoubles its efforts to compete on the same dimensions. When Macy's draws traffic with holiday sales, JCPenney does the same. When British Airways uses data to offer more personalized service to its travelers, Virgin Airways may aim to do the same for its customers. But disruption is different. Disruption is caused by asymmetric competitive threats. A disruptive challenger is not selling a different version of the same product or service. It meets the customer's needs with a product, service, or business model that the existing industry does not, and cannot, offer.

The most important lesson to take from a clear definition of disruption is this: not all innovation is disruptive. I stress this because many times *disruptive* is used simply to mean "extremely innovative." In fact, many new business ideas create new customer value, and they do so by defying common assumptions, or sacred cows, in their industry. But most of these innovations don't actually disrupt the preexisting shape of the market. The result is a better product or a new brand but not disruption.

Take, for example, socks. In 2004, Jonah Staw and three cofounders launched LittleMissMatched, a company selling socks by the threes, each set intentionally not matching but with playful colors and patterns that looked stylish when paired with each other. It was a new lifestyle brand aimed at girls aged eight to twelve, and it went on to great success. The socks were a brilliant idea, one that defied conventional wisdom and added new value for the right customer. But they were not disruptive. The socks were still manufactured, sold, distributed, priced, and used roughly the same as other socks. So there was no hurdle to existing sock manufacturers competing directly. Indeed, as LittleMissMatched proved to be a winner, other brands copied the product idea.

Even an innovative business model is not necessarily disruptive—as long as the jobs and revenues it creates are entirely additive to the market. In their book *Blue Ocean Strategy*, W. Chan Kim and Renée Mauborgne describe how "value innovation" can be used to create new value and growth by opening up new uncontested space; they use examples like Cirque du Soleil's invention of a new hybrid form of entertainment combining circus and theater.[2] In this and many such cases, the innovator is not undermining an existing industry but simply carving out a new market space (the "blue ocean").

None of this is to dismiss the value of blue oceans, unconventional thinking, or innovative products, services, or brands. It is simply to make clear that innovation is not always disruption.

Disruption in the Digital Age

Now that we have an understanding of what we mean by disruption, why does it seem to be on the rise in the digital age?

The answer is simple. As we have seen throughout the last five chapters, digital technologies are rewriting the rules of business. These new rules have created opportunities for countless new challengers to take on long-profitable businesses that have failed to adapt. No industry is immune. If the Industrial Revolution was about machines transforming nearly every physical act of labor and value creation, we are still at the beginning of a revolution in which computing will transform nearly every logical act of value creation.

Marc Andreessen has famously said that "software is eating the world." He invented the first Web browser, the software that unleashed the Internet as a network for mass participation. In chapter 6, we saw the existential threat that it posed to the recorded music industry. Today, Andreessen sees the digitization of every industry leading to ever more battles between incumbents and software-powered disrupters.[3]

It's certainly easy to find examples.

Think of Craigslist, the online classified service, and its impact on newspapers' business model. Traditional newspapers were very expensive to produce. Certain sections, such as international news coverage, would never pay for themselves if sold alone, but newspapers were always sold in bundles so the more profitable sections could support the cost. One of the most profitable parts of every newspaper was the classified ads, where individual readers would pay to place a small advertisement announcing items for sale (a used car, furniture, a television) or services (college movers, lawn mowing). Then along came Craig Newmark, a software programmer in San Francisco with the simple idea of using the Internet to allow anyone to publish their classified ads for free. His small hobby project was called Craigslist, and it quickly grew from an e-mail list into a self-service website and a global enterprise that operates in seventy countries and thirteen languages, with 50 billion page views per month.[4] Craigslist's success was inevitable. For customers, it offered a vastly better deal than using newspapers: the ads were free to post (in almost all categories), appeared instantly, and could be searched through a simple interface. Newspapers, watching one of their highest margin sources of revenue disappear, found themselves unable to do much but wish the Internet had never been invented. Certainly, they could have created their own free classifieds listings, but that would have done little to stanch the loss of income. With their completely different cost structure, newspapers were unable to compete with this disruptive challenger.

We've already seen the example of Airbnb, the software-powered challenger to the traditional hotel industry. Rather than building expensive properties and renting rooms to travelers, Airbnb provides an online platform that allows homeowners to rent out their homes when they aren't using them and travelers to find them. With over 10 million guests per year staying in more than 192 countries, the start-up surpassed InterContinental Hotels Group and Hilton Worldwide to be "the world's largest hotel chain" without owning a single hotel.[5] For many customers, Airbnb offers a much better deal than a traditional hotel in New York or Paris—a better price, more choice among neighborhoods, and a more "local" and personalized experience. It is also a deal that hotel chains cannot hope to replicate, given their investment in completely different business assets. Their best hope to restrain the disrupter may be local governments, many of which are losing tax revenue on these nontraditional hotel stays.

Another example can be seen in the category of restaurant food delivery with the digital challenger GrubHub. For hungry residents in cities like Chicago, New York, and London, GrubHub (and its local brands, like Seamless) offers a great experience. Using a single, well-designed GrubHub app or website, customers can browse numerous nearby restaurants, pick items off their menus, and order for delivery with a preregistered credit card. It's a far superior experience to clicking through an assortment of badly maintained websites, calling a restaurant, and dealing with sometimes poor phone service. For individual urban restaurants, GrubHub's platform offers access to new customers and an online ordering system they couldn't afford to build themselves. But as its app becomes more popular and its power grows, individual restaurants feel they have no option but to join up and give a share of their already thin profit margins to the new digital platform. Trying to compete directly with GrubHub is out of the question. Even if it had the technical savvy, a single restaurant could never offer the variety of GrubHub's aggregated menus.

In each of these industries, a new digitally powered business has created great value for the customer while weakening or undermining the position of the traditional incumbent businesses. Although the digital challenger is eating into their profits, traditional incumbents find themselves unable to respond by competing directly with the same offer.

The exact strategy of the digital disrupter may vary. It may be offering a new service for free, like Craigslist. It may use intermediation, like GrubHub, to place itself between traditional businesses and the final consumer. It may offer a substitute solution to a long-standing customer need, like Airbnb does in place of a traditional hotel.

In every case of disruption, though, the challenge arises from a new business offering new value to the customer. Incumbent businesses may wring their hands and declare an unfair advantage for their challenger. But whether the disrupter is a well-monetized new business (Airbnb is valued at over $10 billion) or not (Craigslist is run almost like a nonprofit), every disrupter is creating new value *for the customer*. No one ever created a disruptive business without creating an incredibly appealing new value proposition.

But is that it? Are we simply talking about new value propositions—or something more? What really defines disruption? And can we model it, understand it, and even predict it?

Theories of Disruption

The first major theorist of business disruption was the Austrian economist Joseph Schumpeter. He didn't use the word itself, but he wrote influentially on a phenomenon he called "creative destruction," whereby capitalism inherently destroys old industries and economic systems in the process of innovating new ones. In describing the arrival of railroads like the Illinois Central to the midwestern United States, he wrote, "The Illinois Central not only meant very good business whilst it was built and whilst new cities were built around it and land was cultivated, but it spelled the death sentence for the [old] agriculture of the West."[6]

Schumpeter identified industry disruption as an inherent pattern in capitalism. Successive cycles of capitalist invention birth new industries while destroying their predecessors. But it was Clayton Christensen who offered our first theory of how disruption happens and began to delve seriously into its mechanisms. His brilliant and elegant theory of disruptive technology (later redubbed disruptive innovation) was laid out in a 1995 article and subsequent book, *The Innovator's Dilemma*.[7]

Christensen's theory shows how disruptive challengers can unseat long-standing incumbents. The disrupter always starts out selling to buyers in a new market—that is, buyers who are outside the market of customers currently served by the incumbent. This "new market" disrupter offers an innovative product that is inferior in terms of performance and features but is cheaper or otherwise more accessible to those who cannot make use of the incumbent's offering. The pattern that follows is predictable: the incumbent ignores the challenger's inferior product because its own customers aren't interested and instead continues to improve the performance of its higher-priced products. Over time, though, the performance of the challenger's innovation gets gradually better while it remains much cheaper or more accessible. At a critical juncture, the new technology becomes good enough to be a viable alternative for the incumbent's own customers, and they begin to defect rapidly in favor of the much cheaper or more accessible alternative. The incumbent, who has remained wedded to its long-standing product and business model, finds it almost impossible to compete. Rapid decline follows.

It is a powerful theory and one that fits uncannily well in cases from many, many industries—computer hard drives, mechanical excavators, steel mills, stock brokerages, printing presses, and more.

But as tech analyst Ben Thompson has noted, "Christensen's theory is based on examples drawn from buying decisions made by businesses, not consumers."[8] In the mid-1990s (when Christensen's book was written), technology was mostly sold to businesses, not consumers. Not surprisingly, this allowed for a very straightforward theory of disruption. Customer motivations were driven by a few clear, functional attributes: price, accessibility, and performance. Incumbent businesses were particularly blind to new customer markets. Due to their B2B sales process (with a dedicated salesforce visiting corporate customers), incumbents found it extremely difficult to switch from serving their current customers to focusing on the emerging customer populations that their disrupters served.

Its origins in B2B industries may be the reason Christensen's theory explains a great many cases of disruption but has missed others. Famously, when Christensen was interviewed about Apple's iPhone, he predicted that it would fail to disrupt the incumbent mobile phone manufacturers like Nokia. "The iPhone is a sustaining technology relative to Nokia. In other words, Apple is leaping ahead on the sustaining curve [by building a better phone]. But the prediction of the theory would be that Apple won't succeed with the iPhone. They've launched an innovation that the existing players in the industry are heavily motivated to beat: It's not [truly] disruptive. History speaks pretty loudly on that, that the probability of success is going to be limited."[9]

After the colossal success of the iPhone, Christensen said that it had, in fact, been a disrupter but that the incumbent was actually the personal computer industry.[10] This is an interesting point and is still playing out as global PC sales have flattened and been overtaken by smartphones. But it would be nonsensical to argue that Nokia was not disrupted by the iPhone as well. The incumbent king of the mobile phone industry before the iPhone was completely unable to match the new challenger; Nokia fell rapidly into irrelevance, and its phone division was sold to Microsoft six years later.

But I don't believe that Christensen spoke hastily or misapplied his theory. Clearly, the case of iPhone versus Nokia didn't fit his original model. From the start, the iPhone sold to the kind of affluent, technology-adopting consumers who were a mainstay of Nokia's customer base. The iPhone was neither cheaper nor more accessible than Nokia's phones. It did not start out performing at a lower level and gradually build up to overtake the incumbent. So how did Nokia come to be so thoroughly disrupted?

I will attempt to answer that question by offering a new theory. My aim here is not to replace Christensen's theory but to extend it to account for newer dynamics of disruption that are now visible in the marketplace— disruption that is driven by consumer purchase behaviors, disruption that starts with the incumbent's core customers (rather than starting with new markets), and disruption that is driven by values other than price or access. As we will see, Christensen's theory of new market disruption is actually a specific case of the broader theory that I will present.

A Business Model Theory of Disruption

My theory begins with the assumption that the best lens through which to view disruption is business models. Many of today's biggest disrupters are not introducing a new fundamental technology to the market (e.g., a new type of hard drive or mechanical excavator). Instead, they are applying established technology to the design of a new business model. (Craigslist invented neither e-mail lists nor websites; GrubHub invented neither e-commerce nor mobile apps.) Business disruption is, at its core, the result of the clash of asymmetric business models.

As with disruption, *business model* is a term that has taken on varying definitions with its growing popularity as a tool for strategy formation. I'll use the common definition: a business model describes a holistic view of how a business creates value, delivers it to the market, and captures value in return.[11]

A detailed business model may comprise several components. Alexander Osterwalder and Yves Pigneur describe it as including nine "building blocks": customer segments, value propositions, channels, customer relationships, revenue streams, key resources, key activities, key partnerships, and cost structure.[12] Mark Johnson, Clayton Christensen, and Henning Kagermann define it in terms of four parts: customer value proposition;

profit formula (including revenue model, cost structure, margin model, and resource velocity); key resources; and key processes.[13]

My intent is to use the business model specifically as a predictor of business disruption, and for this purpose, the schema can be simpler.

Two Sides of a Business Model

For the purpose of understanding disruption, let's split the business model into two sides.

The first side is the value proposition—the value that a business offers to the customer. Due to the extreme importance of value creation and its role in business disruption, for this framework I'll consider it on par with all the other elements of a business model combined. I am not alone in this priority: Johnson, Christensen, and Kagermann picked value proposition as "the most important to get right, by far."[14] And although it is just one of nine building blocks in Osterwalder and Pigneur's first book, their next book was focused entirely on value propositions.[15]

The second side of the business model is the value network—the people, partners, assets, and processes that enable the business to create, deliver, and earn value from the value proposition. This includes things like channels, pricing, cost structure, assets, resources, and the customer segments on which a business is focused. The term *value network* emerged in the 1990s to provide a model of value creation that is less atomistic, less manufacturing-oriented, and less confined inside the firm than the model of value chains.[16]

A quick example: I often present this framework when teaching short programs for international executives through Columbia Business School Executive Education (often in partnership with leading universities in Asia, Europe, or Latin America). I introduce it by asking the executives to describe the value proposition of an executive program like the one they are participating in: "What is the benefit you gain as a customer?" They typically identify several things: cases studies and best practices, exposure to new industry trends, and practical frameworks and tools—but also peer relationships, access to faculty, the recognized credential of a certificate, and a chance to step outside their daily rush for some big-picture perspective taking. In any complex business, the value proposition will include numerous elements such as these.

I then ask the participants about the value network: "What enables the business school to create and deliver this value and to earn revenue from it?" They typically point to the faculty, the campus (being in New York is sometimes important), and the program development staff—but also the brand name and reputation of the school, relationships with industry, a network of partner business schools, and being part of a broader research university. Each of these, in different ways, helps to make the value proposition possible.

Once we can see any business model in terms of these two sides— value proposition and value network—we are ready to apply them in a new theory of how disruption happens.

The Two Differentials of Business Model Disruption

The theory of business model disruption is simply this: in order to disrupt an existing business, a challenger must possess a significant differential on each side of the business model:

- A difference in value proposition that dramatically displaces the value provided by the incumbent (at least for some customers)
- A difference in value network that creates a barrier to imitation by the incumbent

Business disruption happens when both of these conditions are met— and only then.

Without the first differential, there is no disruption, just traditional competition. If the challenger's offer is merely incrementally better (slightly better price, availability, simplicity, features, etc.), then there may be some loss of business, but the incumbent can simply respond with normal competitive tactics to catch up, close the gap, or minimize losses. For disruption, the challenger's offer must be dramatically better. For at least some types of customers, it should be no contest at all to decide whether to switch to the challenger. When local newspaper readers discovered Craigslist, the option of instant, free online listings of their advertisements (as compared to slow, expensive newspaper listings) was incontestably better. Not every traveler wants to stay in an apartment like the ones they can find via Airbnb, but for those who do, the various benefits (price, availability, choice of location, personal interaction, and local flair) mean that a traditional hotel room simply can't compete.

Without the second differential, however, an incumbent would simply be able to watch the success of an innovative new challenger and profitably imitate it with a copycat offering of its own. An incumbent that gets disrupted is unable to replicate its challenger for varied reasons, but they all stem from the value network that the incumbent established in building its business. For newspapers facing Craigslist, their high cost of operations meant they saw no benefit in imitating a free service run by a small group of iconoclasts who persisted for years with no revenue and never attempted to build a large for-profit enterprise. For global hotel chains like Hyatt, offering a bed-sharing service like Airbnb's would make no use of their real estate, confuse their brand image, irritate their partners (many of the hotels are owned by franchisees), and draw even more tax scrutiny from local governments than Airbnb has. In both cases, the existing value network of the incumbent prevents it from imitating the appealing new offering of its challenger.

Let's look at both differentials in a bit more detail.

Value Proposition Differential

Every disrupter requires a difference in value proposition that dramatically displaces value provided by the incumbent. That difference can come from many possible sources, which I call *value proposition generatives* (a term I am adapting from Kevin Kelly).[17]

Key value proposition generatives that are common to digital disrupters include the following:

- *Price*: Digital business models often allow for the same product or service to be offered at a substantially lower price.
- *Free or "freemium" offer*: Research has shown that free offers stimulate many more customer trials than a low price, even a penny.[18] Many new business models add customer value with a freemium offer, where some level of service is available for free but a premium paid version offers additional benefits.
- *Access*: One of the most common generatives of a digital business model is the ability to access content or services remotely, anywhere, any time.

- *Simplicity*: Many digital business models disrupt by removing friction from the sales process, making decision, purchase, and enjoyment of a product much simpler and easier.
- *Personalization*: Customers prefer to have more choices to pick from (provided there are tools to assist) and the choice of a product or service that fits their particular needs. Sometimes this personalization occurs through recommendation engines like Netflix's; in other cases, a new business offers customers the chance to customize a product.
- *Aggregation*: Many platform business models add value by aggregating many sellers for the customer to choose from.
- *Unbundling*: A lot of digital innovation involves splitting apart traditional bundles—groups of products, services, or features that customers needed to purchase together. The added value can come from letting the customer buy only the part they need or from focusing on and improving the one part of the bundle that matters most.
- *Integration (or rebundling)*: In the opposite direction, businesses can generate new customer value by bundling together services that are currently separate. (Think of the first iPhone customers, carrying one device rather than a phone, an MP3 player, and a personal digital assistant.) The real value of integration comes when the various parts work together in a seamless way that was not possible when they were separate. (Think of how your address book, maps, calendar, e-mail, phone calls, and texts all work together and interact in a smartphone.)
- *Social*: The ability to share the experience of a product or service with others is increasingly valuable to many customers.

This list is not meant to be exhaustive. Other value proposition generatives that may be less tied to digital technologies include purpose (e.g., how each purchase from Warby Parker or Patagonia supports a social cause), authenticity (e.g., how Etsy allows shoppers to interact with and buy directly from craft artisans), or freedom from ownership (e.g., how Rent The Runway allows customers to rent a different designer dress each time they go out rather than owning any of them).

You will notice that the generatives above arise from many of the strategic concepts we have seen throughout the book—such as customers' networked behavior, the path to purchase, the use of data for personalization, and the aggregating value of platforms. All of them are applied in the service of adapting or inventing new value propositions, the subject of chapter 6.

Value Network Differential

Every disrupter also requires a difference in value network that creates a barrier to imitation by the incumbent. Recall that the network includes anything—people, partners, assets, processes—that enables a business to create, deliver, and earn value from its value proposition. The differences can be found by looking at many different elements—what I call *value network components*.

Key components to consider in analyzing a challenger's value network include the following:

- *Customers*: The challenger may be pursuing different customer segments or types than the incumbent currently serves.
- *Channels*: These may include retail or online distribution, direct delivery to the customer, or distribution through intermediaries. (Is the challenger using different channels to come to market?)
- *Partners*: These may include sales, manufacturing, supply chain, or other key partners that are critical to the challenger's offer.
- *Networks*: If the challenger has a platform business model, then an established network of customers or partners may be essential to how it delivers its offer. (This may include networks of consumers, advertisers, app developers, etc.)
- *Complementary products or services*: The challenger may already provide the customer other products or services that are essential to the value created by its new offer. (Think of Apple's iTunes music service, which predated the iPhone and added to its value.)
- *Brand*: Reputation, brand image, and the prior relationship with the customer may be essential to the challenger's ability to provide the value of its offer (and to charge the right price for it).
- *Revenue model*: This includes the pricing and profit margin as well as the payment model. (Is the customer paying for the offer on a product basis, per use, monthly subscription, revenue share, etc.?)
- *Cost structure*: This includes both the fixed and the variable costs incurred by the challenger in order to provide its offer to the customer.
- *Skills and processes*: The challenger may have unique or differentiated processes and organizational skills that are essential to the value it delivers (from Apple's design capability behind the iPhone to Zappo's highly developed customer service).

- *Physical assets*: These may include factories, equipment, stores, and so on owned by the challenger.
- *IP assets*: Critical intellectual property may include patents, rights, licenses, and unique technologies.
- *Data assets*: The challenger's value proposition may rely on unique data assets and capabilities, such as Amazon's and Google's use of their customer data to deliver all kinds of personalized offerings.

The Two Differentials in Christensen's New Market Disruption

As mentioned earlier, Christensen's original model of business disruption, often called new market disruption, is actually a specific case of this more general theory of business model disruption.

Within this new theory, Christensen's new market disruption is simply a description of all those cases of disruption where the value proposition differential is a difference in *price* or *access* and the value network differential includes a difference in *customer segment* (the challenger is pursuing a different customer segment).

By expanding our model to include other differentials of both value proposition and value network, we can account for and explain many additional examples of business disruption, particularly those involving some of the biggest disrupters of the digital age.

Digital Disrupters: iPhone, Netflix, Warby Parker

Let's see how this model applies to three recent cases of business disruption. All three are in consumer businesses, and the disruption did not follow the traditional new market theory of disruption.

Two of the incumbents were completely disrupted and left the business where they had recently been the market leader; one disruption is newer and still ongoing. (As we shall see, a disruptive challenger does not always spell doom for the incumbent.)

iPhone Versus Nokia

Why did Apple's iPhone so thoroughly supplant Nokia's mobile phones?

By looking at the differences in their value propositions, we can see why customers quickly came to see the iPhone as not slightly better but vastly better—no comparison at all, really. (See table 7.1.)

Certainly, one difference was in the physical design—the iPhone's shape, weight, and large glowing screen and the tactile experience of its touchscreen provided a totally different customer experience. Simplicity was another critical difference. Mobile phones in 2007 were notoriously difficult to navigate, even for common features like managing voice mail messages. The iPhone's operating system offered a much easier user interface. Another important difference was integration—rather than carrying around a phone (for calls), a PDA (for address book and calendar), an MP3 player (for music), and a GPS device (for maps), the user had all these integrated seamlessly into one device. Lastly, there were the apps—starting with a Web browser and a few others and then exploding into thousands of programs in the iPhone's second year when Apple opened it up to outside developers to create programs. The apps turned the iPhone into a true computing device.

Why couldn't Nokia compete? It was very clear within a couple of years that the iPhone was a huge hit with enviable profit margins. But Nokia, despite being the global leader in mobile phones (and valued at over $100 billion), was unable to imitate Apple's success with a copycat smartphone of its own. The reasons can be seen in the difference between the value networks of the two companies.

Much attention is often paid to Apple's highly developed design capabilities, which were doubtless critical to the creation of the iPhone's compelling physical design and touchscreen interaction. But there were several other differences in Apple's value network that allowed it to create, deliver, and monetize the iPhone. One was the partnership Apple had struck with its retail partner, AT&T. This included a large price subsidy, with AT&T

Table 7.1
Business Model Disruption: iPhone (Disrupter) Versus Nokia (Incumbent)

Value proposition differential	Value network differential
Physical design	Design capability
Simplicity of use	Retailer subsidy
Integration (music, phone, PDA, browser, e-mail, maps)	Unlimited data
	OS design experience
Apps	iTunes integration
	App developers

covering most of the consumer purchase price of the iPhone and rolling it into consumers' (higher) monthly payments for data over two years. Without this, the iPhone would have been so expensive as to remain a niche luxury product. AT&T also offered unlimited data usage for a fixed price in the early years of the iPhone; this led consumers to fully explore the apps and features of the new device, thereby cementing radically new habits and expectations for mobile devices. Other key elements of the iPhone's value network lay in Apple itself: its skill in designing simple computing operating systems (from years of designing desktop computing products) and its ownership of the iTunes music platform. Thanks to the iPod, Apple already had the dominant digital music platform for U.S. consumers, and who really wanted to buy their music all over again in a new market from Nokia or anyone else? Lastly, once the App Store was opened up, explosive growth in users and sales attracted an ecosystem of tens of thousands of developers who learned to program apps for the iPhone. Nokia could never program the same number of apps for any phone of its own and was badly behind in the race to attract outside developers. Taken together, these differences in the companies' value networks made it impossible for Nokia to imitate the iPhone's strategy.

Netflix Versus Blockbuster

Let's take a look at another recent case of massive disruption: how Netflix's original DVD service defeated the leading retail chain for movie rentals, Blockbuster.

Blockbuster was an extremely entrenched and dominant player in the retail space, so Netflix chose to compete by offering a dramatically different value proposition to the customer. (See table 7.2.)

Table 7.2
Business Model Disruption: Netflix DVD Service (Disrupter) Versus Blockbuster (Incumbent)

Value proposition differential	Value network differential
No late fees	Subscription pricing model
Easy access (product comes to you)	E-commerce website
Wider choice	Data assets and recommendation engine
Personalized recommendations	Warehouse and mail distribution system
	No retail costs

The first difference was the elimination of late fees. In the retail model, the customer picked up a movie and paid for a fixed number of days. If they returned it past that time period, they were charged a late fee—aggravating and unavoidable. But Netflix did away with the hated late fees entirely, with a flat monthly fee that allowed the customer to keep three movies at home at a time, exchanging them as quickly or as slowly as they wanted. The product was also more accessible. Rather than going to a retail store, the customer simply picked the movies out on Netflix's website. A few days later, they arrived in the mail, with a handy return envelope to send them back. Because Netflix was shipping from centralized warehouses, it was able to offer every customer 100,000 movies, a much wider product choice than at any of Blockbuster's retail stores. To help the customer choose among all those (potentially overwhelming) options, Netflix's website also offered a sophisticated recommendation tool. The cumulative effect of these differences in value proposition was that consumers who tried Netflix loved it, never went back, and recommended it to their friends. Blockbuster quickly realized it was a facing a real threat.

Why didn't Blockbuster launch a copycat of Netflix—a mail-order service of its own? Actually, it did. Once the threat of Netflix's service was clear, the retailer tried to launch its own mail-order service. The hurdles it faced could have been predicted, though, by looking at the differences between the two companies' value networks. One difference was the pricing model (subscription pricing vs. per product fees)—but that was easy enough for Blockbuster to simply adopt as part of its copycat effort. The next difference was Netflix's website and recommendation engine. Although Blockbuster could build an e-commerce website, it lacked the massive data sets as well as the sophisticated technology assets to provide movie recommendations as good as Netflix's. Another difference was Netflix's sophisticated warehouse and mail distribution system. With great expense, Blockbuster was able to build one of its own. But, critically, Netflix had spent years carefully iterating and optimizing every aspect of its mailing system (including the precise shape and size of the mailing envelopes and DVD sheaths) to allow for maximum automation, minimum errors, the fastest possible turnaround, and minimal cost. It was possible for Blockbuster to replicate the delivery service—but not at the same price and with the same profit margins. Lastly, a huge difference was that Netflix lacked the overhead costs of running 9,000 retail stores. In the end, Blockbuster was able to offer a roughly comparable value proposition to customers for a while, but it could not do so profitably at the same customer price. After years of rapid decline, Blockbuster closed its final 300 stores in 2014.

Warby Parker Versus Luxottica

Warby Parker is an American eyeglasses brand that is seeking to disrupt the way prescription glasses and sunglasses are sold to consumers. The traditional behemoth in this industry is Luxottica Group, which controls more than 80 percent of major eyewear brands (including Ray-Ban, Oakley, Persol, and licensed designer brands such as Armani and Prada).

Perhaps because of the highly consolidated market, the traditional customer experience when purchasing glasses is far from inviting. Glasses cost upward of $300, and buying them involves going to a retail store, placing an order, and returning later for the product. Warby Parker offers its own brand of fashionably designed glasses primarily through e-commerce sales at a price of $95. To surmount the challenge of picking out glasses from afar, the company allows consumers to select five frames to be mailed to them free to try on. Once they choose the frame they like, the prescription lenses are added, and the final product is delivered.

Does Warby Parker pose a disruptive threat to the incumbent? Let's take a look at the two differentials to judge (see table 7.3).

The biggest difference in Warby Parker's value proposition is its price—less than one-third the traditional price for the product. There is also a potential difference in access: for consumers who want to avoid multiple trips to a store or who don't have many retailers in their area, the online service may be another big advantage. (To appeal to customers in major cities, the start-up has launched a limited number of retail stores and showrooms.) In addition, it donates one pair of glasses, via nonprofit VisionSpring, for each pair that it sells to consumers. This and other social causes (Warby Parker is a certified B corporation and 100 percent carbon neutral) matter a lot to some consumers. So it would appear that, at least for

Table 7.3
Business Model Disruption: Warby Parker (Disrupter) Versus Luxottica (Incumbent)

Value proposition differential	Value network differential
Much lower price ($95)	Online channel
Accessibility	Low retail costs
Social cause	Vertical integration
	B corporation status

some consumer segments (price sensitive, preferring to avoid retail hassles, or favoring social cause brands), the company offers a dramatically more attractive value proposition.

What about the value networks? Is there any difference that allows Warby Parker to deliver this value? The first differences are its online sales channel and its much lower retail costs. It also can keep prices low due to its vertical integration (it owns the brand, manufactures the product, and owns the entire sales channel). By contrast, Luxottica licenses many of its brands, and although it owns large retail chains, it also sells products through other retailers. It could certainly launch an e-commerce portal for its own brands, but its cost structure would likely prevent it from coming close to Warby Parker's price. As a standard, publicly listed corporation, Luxottica would also have difficulty matching Warby Parker's level of support for social causes.

Clearly, Warby Parker poses a disruptive threat for Luxottica—having a much better value proposition that the incumbent cannot emulate. But it is not yet clear how broad the disruption will be. Perhaps many customers are willing to pay the higher prices for global brands like Prada, or prefer to shop in a nearby store, or won't care as much about carbon footprints and donated eyeglasses.

These kinds of issues will determine the scope and impact of a disruptive challenger like Warby Parker. Such variables can significantly affect success. Let's take a look at some of the key variables that impact the outcome of business model disruption.

Three Variables in Business Model Disruption Theory

The theory of business model disruption can identify and explain the cause of disruption by a wide variety of challengers and in different industries. But just because a challenger poses a genuine disruptive threat does not mean that others in the industry are doomed. Incumbents may have some choices in how they respond. And the nature of the disrupter itself—its value proposition and its value network—can predict much of how the disruption will play out.

Three important variables that complete the theory of business model disruption are customer trajectory, disruptive scope, and multiple incumbents.

Customer Trajectory

The first variable to consider in any case of business model disruption is the customer trajectory. Which customers will provide the initial basis for the challenger's market entry, and are they already customers of the incumbent?

Business model disrupters can enter the market through one of two trajectories:

- *Outside-in*: The disrupter starts by selling to buyers that are not currently served by the incumbent (that are "outside" the incumbent's market), and over time, the disrupter works its way in until it starts to steal customers directly from the incumbent's own market.
- *Inside-out*: From the beginning, the disrupter starts by selling to some subsegment of the incumbent's current customers. This initial subsegment may be small (sometimes the most affluent or the most eager to try new things), but over time, it grows as the successful disrupter expands outward to claim more and more of the incumbent's customers.

Christensen's new market theory of disruption is based solely on cases that follow the outside-in customer trajectory. Indeed, one of the fundamental keys to his theory is that by starting outside the incumbent's customer base, the disrupter makes it very hard for the incumbent to respond.

However, many cases of business disruption today take the opposite customer trajectory: inside-out. All three of the cases we just saw were inside-out cases. The iPhone did not start by selling to buyers who were not previously in the market for a mobile phone. Rather, it began with a small subsegment of the type of customers who would certainly have owned a Nokia previously. At first, Nokia could reason that Apple was stealing a profitable but small part of the market and that Nokia could aim to hold on to the much larger majority of customers who were so far unwilling to pay the higher monthly fees for a smartphone. But over time, the iPhone's customer base expanded outward to attract more and more of these customers. Similarly, Netflix did not start by appealing to customers who had never used video rental services like Blockbuster. Instead, its appeal was specifically to those who had—pointing to their frustration with late fees and promising a better customer experience. And Warby Parker obviously had no option but to go after customers served by the incumbents like

Luxottica. If you didn't already own or need prescription glasses, you were unlikely to sign up for Warby Parker. The company's rise may have started with some of the more price-sensitive customers from the current customer base (those who would give online ordering a try primarily for the $95 price tag), but it then expanded outward as it proved itself capable of delivering a true high-fashion brand as well as a superior customer experience.

Disruptive Scope

The second important variable in cases of business model disruption is the likely scope of the disruption. There is sometimes an assumption that whenever disruption occurs, the incumbent's business, product, or service will be replaced 100 percent by the disruptive challenger. Out with the old, in with the new. In some cases, this does happen. When Henry Ford's mass-produced automobile arrived, it was only a matter of years before the horse and buggy had basically vanished as a means of transportation. (Kevin Kelly has argued persuasively that no technology ever disappears from use entirely[19]—and, indeed, you can still enjoy a carriage ride around New York's Central Park as an expensive tourist treat.)

But in many cases of business disruption, the scope is not 100 percent. Even after being disrupted, the incumbent's product or business model hangs on, confined to a diminished portion of the market but still a notable player in the industry.

A recent example of this can be seen in bookselling, with the arrival of e-books. Thanks to Amazon's development of the Kindle e-book format and electronic readers, consumers discovered they had a new choice for reading. The e-book and its online bookstore offered many compelling advantages: a lower price per book, a vast selection of choices, nearly instant purchase and download, and the ability to carry hundreds of books in your purse or bag at the weight of a paperback. The threat to booksellers was clear: there is no need for a customer to walk into their local bookstore to download an e-book.

In the first few years after the launch of the Kindle, e-books enjoyed steady growth in market share. Many in the publishing industry looked at that growth curve, projected it outward, and nervously predicted that in a few short years, e-books would comprise the majority of book sales and publishers would no longer be able to afford to produce print editions.[20] But then something unexpected happened. After a spurt of rapid growth, e-book sales leveled off. Various reports, confirmed to me by insiders in the industry, say that the plateau was about 30 percent of book sales by revenue.[21] This was still enough to spark major disruption and shifts in the balance of power in the industry. (Borders, one of the largest retail book-sellers in the United States, filed for bankruptcy in 2011.) Yet printed books, while diminished, certainly did not disappear into obsolescence.

Although this surprised many observers, it was no fluke. In fact, I believe that by looking at the behavior of book buyers, it would have been quite easy to predict the scope of this particular disruption.

One important lens for predicting disruptive scope is the product's different use cases (as discussed in chapter 6). Customers buy books on a variety of occasions, and they read books in a variety of settings. In some use cases for reading, it is quite clear that the e-book provides a far superior value proposition—for example, when you are going on a trip and would like to have a variety of reading options but don't want to be weighed down by a bag of books. In other reading use cases, however, a printed book may be better—for example, if you want to take notes in the margin or read on the beach in direct sunlight (cases where e-book software and screens have continued to lag the paper medium). We can also look at use cases for book purchase. When the customer is seeking to try a new book while lying in bed, there is no match for the benefit of being able to download a sample chapter in seconds to their e-reader (and purchase the rest if they quickly decide they like it). But what about gift giving? No one I have ever asked has thought that an e-book was an acceptable substitute for a printed book when giving a gift. This is not a small point: a large portion of book sales takes place around holidays and other gift-giving occasions. If only a few use cases favor the old value proposition, we might expect consumers to sacrifice those benefits to shift entirely to a new value proposition. But in cases like books, where the customer can easily alternate purchases of the old product and the new one, it is predictable that we will wind up with a split market—with some sales shifting to the disrupter's offer and others remaining with the incumbent.

In addition to use cases, the scope of disruption of a new business model can be influenced by customer segments. Sometimes the disrupter's value proposition is highly preferable for some types of customers but not for others with different needs. In the Warby Parker case, we may see that certain eyeglasses wearers are likely to shift to its sales model, whereas others (those that buy luxury brands and specialty lenses or those that have better access to retail options) will stay with an incumbent like Luxottica.

Lastly, network effects can play an important role in determining the scope of disruption. (This is particularly true for platform businesses, as we saw in chapter 3.) If a disrupter's product or service increases in value as more customers use it (think of a platform like Airbnb, which relies on ample hosts and renters), this will initially be a hurdle to the new business. But it also means that if the disrupter manages to achieve a certain critical mass of adopters, its continued growth is nearly assured, and it will more likely end up with a very large share of the market.

Multiple Incumbents

The third variable to consider is multiple incumbents. A single disruptive business model can actually disrupt more than one incumbent. By multiple incumbents, I don't mean similar companies in the same industry (e.g., the iPhone disrupting Motorola along with Nokia) but entirely different industries or classes of companies that are each challenged by the same new disruptive business model. The iPhone posed a disruptive threat not just to mobile phone companies (like Nokia) but also to desktop software companies (as Microsoft discovered that Windows was no longer the world's dominant operating system) and online advertising companies (as Google had to move rapidly to stay relevant as computing moved to the small screen).

Another interesting case of disrupting multiple incumbents can be seen in the meteoric rise of online messaging apps, such as WhatsApp, WeChat, LINE, and Viber (each of which has grown initially in somewhat different global markets). Their full range of features may vary, but at their core, each service has attracted hundreds of millions of customers with the ability to send mobile messages for free over Internet connections rather than being charged per message by the mobile phone's service provider.

Obviously, one incumbent industry that is being disrupted by this business model is telecommunications—companies like Vodafone and América Móvil. For years, text messages had been a large source of revenue for these companies. By one estimate, services like WhatsApp cost the phone companies over $30 billion in texting fees in a single year.[22]

But telecommunications is not the only incumbent industry threatened by the free messaging apps. When Facebook chose to buy the largest one, WhatsApp, for 10 percent of its own stock (a $22 billion price), it was not because WhatsApp promised to generate huge new revenues for the social network. It was purely a defensive strategy against a new app that was on track to attract 1 billion customers of its own. If consumers spent more and more of their mobile screen time in apps like this one, they would spend less time in the world of Facebook-driven socializing.

There may be another, even less likely industry that is being disrupted in part by WhatsApp. A long article by Courtney Rubin in the *New York Times* detailed the rise of mobile social networking (via text messaging, Instagram, Facebook, and Grindr) in the social life of multiple American college towns. Rubin's ethnographic reporting uncovered a broad shift, described by both students and owners of college bars. Each described how students are spending less time and less money in the bars and coordinating more of their socializing through mobile networking, with alcohol purchased in stores and consumed in residences. College bars have always made their money charging for drinks. But the value they provided to customers was mostly the opportunity for serendipitous encounters and socializing. Now students find they can get that through their phones and are showing up to the bars sometimes only for a last drink before closing time (hardly enough to keep a bar in business). Many college bars are struggling, and some that have operated for decades are closing down. Yet another incumbent industry has been disrupted by the rise of mobile messaging.[23]

Now that we've examined the theory of business model disruption, how it expands on previous theories, and some of the key variables in its application, let's put it to work with two strategic planning tools. These tools will allow businesses to gauge whether a threat they're facing is disruptive to their business and, if so, to assess its likely course and then select among six possible incumbent responses.

Tool: The Disruptive Business Model Map

The first tool is the Disruptive Business Model Map. This strategy mapping tool is designed to help you assess whether or not a new challenger poses a disruptive threat to an incumbent industry or business.

If your business is the incumbent, you can use the map as a threat assessor—to judge whether a challenger poses a traditional competitive threat that you can respond to with traditional countermeasures or whether it is a genuine disrupter. You can also use the map if your business is a start-up or an innovator within an enterprise. As you develop new ventures, the map will help you to identify the industries where you may pose a disruptive threat and those that may be less affected or more able to respond to your challenge.

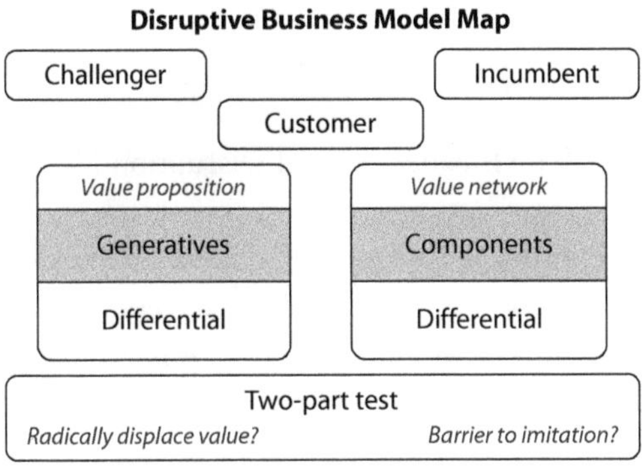

Disruptive Business Model Map

Figure 7.1
The Disruptive Business Model Map.

Figure 7.1 shows the Disruptive Business Model Map. It includes eight blocks, each of which you will fill out in making an assessment of a potentially disruptive threat. Let's look at each block and the question you must answer to fill it in.

Step 1: Challenger

The first step of the Business Model Disruption Map is to answer this question: What is the potentially disruptive business?

The challenger you identify here may be a new competitor to your own established business. It may be your own start-up, attempting to disrupt an existing industry. Or it may be a potential new venture or initiative within your organization whose disruptive potential you are seeking to judge.

Note that we are not yet labeling this challenger as "the disrupter." The point of the map is to apply business model disruption theory to analyze the challenger, incumbent, and customer to determine if there really is a threat of disruption. In my experience running this scenario with numerous executives—both to analyze existing threats and to test the market for a proposed new venture—many challengers who have been dubbed disruptive do not in the end pass the test.

In describing the challenger, you need to include its key offering: What are its unique products and services? What is it bringing to the market that does not exist yet? If your challenger were Netflix, you would include not just the name of the company but also a description of the monthly subscription service model that it is offering for movie rentals.

Step 2: Incumbent

The second question of the Business Model Disruption Map is, Who is the incumbent?

You may choose either a category of related businesses (e.g., video rental retail chains) or a leading example of the category (e.g., Blockbuster) in order to make the analysis more concrete as you compare the business models of the challenger and the incumbent.

The other key point here is that, as we have seen, a challenger may pose a disruptive threat to more than one incumbent. Especially if you are the challenger, you should try to identify multiple incumbents who may be threatened by your new business model. Whenever you do identify more than one possible incumbent, you should complete the map multiple times—once per incumbent. You may well find that your new business model poses a disruptive threat to one incumbent industry but that another incumbent can accommodate the success of your model or can co-opt and imitate it.

Step 3: Customer

The third question of the Business Model Disruption Map is, Who is the target customer?

This is the customer being served by the challenger. In some cases, it may be a direct customer of the incumbent, but it also could be another key business constituency (e.g., a challenger could disrupt an incumbent by stealing away all its employees). It is critical to state who the challenger's target is before you move on to the next stage to consider the value proposition being offered to that target customer.

Once again, it is possible that a challenger could aim to usurp the incumbent's relationship with more than one type of customer. In this case, you should also complete the map multiple times—once per customer type.

Step 4: Value Proposition

The next question of the Business Model Disruption Map is, What is the value offered by the challenger to the target customer?

It is very important to answer this question from the point of view of the customer: What benefits do they stand to gain?

Remember, the aim here is not to describe the product or service offered by the challenger (that should have been done in step 1). Nor it is to describe how the challenger will get customers to pay it (the revenue model will come in step 6, as part of the value network). The focus here is exclusively on the benefit to the *customer*: What value could they gain from the challenger's offer?

You can refer back to the list of value proposition generatives earlier in this chapter to consider some of the many ways that digital business models provide value for customers.

Step 5: Value Proposition Differential

After you have described the challenger's value proposition, the next question is, How does the challenger's value proposition differ from that of the incumbent?

The point here is to identify those elements of the challenger's value proposition that are unique and different—this is the value proposition differential.

There is certain to be some overlap between the values offered by incumbent and challenger (e.g., Craigslist and newspapers both offer users the same core benefit of being able to advertise personal items for sale to a large local audience looking for them). You do not need to include those commonalities here.

For some challengers, such as Craigslist, the differences in value proposition may all be positive—that is, they are ways that the challenger offers additional customer value. In other cases, the value proposition differential may include benefits but also deficits, which you should indicate as such—for example, for e-books as a challenger to print, you might indicate "less easy to read in direct sunlight."

Step 6: Value Network

The next question of the Business Model Disruption Map concerns the value network: What enables the challenger to create, deliver, and earn value from its offering to the customer?

You can refer back to the list of value network components earlier in this chapter as you map out the value network that makes the challenger's offering possible. Your goal is to identify everything—people, partners, assets, and processes—that enables the challenger to offer its value proposition.

If the challenger is new and unproven, this step should help to identify unanswered questions about its business model and whether it will actually be able to deliver the value proposition it is promising to the market.

Step 7: Value Network Differential

After you have described the challenger's value network, the next question is, How does the challenger's value network differ from that of the incumbent?

Again, there may be some points of overlap between the challenger and the incumbent. If so, you can leave these out. The point here is to identify those elements of the challenger's value network that are unique and different.

Does the challenger's offering rely on a unique data asset or on specific skills that the incumbent currently lacks? Does it come to market via different channels than the incumbent uses? Does the challenger have a different pricing model or a different cost structure (e.g., less overhead costs for retail space or staff) than the incumbent? Is the challenger launching with a focus on a different market segment?

The set of all these differences between the challenger and the incumbent is the value network differential.

Step 8: Two-Part Test

You are now ready to answer the ultimate question of the Business Model Disruption Map: Does the challenger pose a disruptive threat to the incumbent?

As described by the business model disruption theory, this question is answered by a two-part test.

First, you need to assess how significant the differential in value is to the customer. Is the challenger's value proposition only slightly better than the incumbent's? Or does it radically displace the value of the incumbent? In some cases, this could be because the challenger offers a comparable product or service but with much better terms (think of Craigslist's free version of classified ads). In other cases, the challenger may solve the same customer problems as the incumbent but also meet other customer needs at the same time (think of the iPhone, which was both a great cell phone and much more). In still other cases, the challenger may provide an offering that simply makes the incumbent's offer much less relevant to the customer (as mobile social networking apps have made college bar rituals less relevant to American students).

The first question of the disruption test, then, is this: Does the challenger's value proposition dramatically displace the value proposition provided by the incumbent? If the answer is no, then the challenger does not pose a disruptive threat to the incumbent. The challenger may be a great innovator with a terrific new value proposition for customers. But if that offer grows to threaten too much of the incumbent's business, the incumbent should be able to respond by matching, or remaining closely competitive with, the challenger's value to the customer. If the answer to the first test is yes, then you can move to the second test of disruption.

Here you need to assess the barriers that are posed by the differences in value networks between incumbent and challenger. Could the incumbent bridge these gaps, if it wished, so that it could deliver the same value to customers that the challenger does? For example, could the incumbent strike deals with channel partners similar to those employed by the challenger? Could the incumbent eliminate any difference in its fixed costs or compensate for them otherwise? Is it possible for the incumbent to overcome the network effects that the challenger may have already built up to its own benefit? Any major difference in value network could be the hurdle that prevents the incumbent from responding effectively.

The second question of the disruption test is this: Do any of the differences in value networks create a barrier that will prevent the incumbent from imitating the challenger? If the answer is no, then the challenger does not pose a disruptive threat to the incumbent. It may be a dire asymmetric competitor, but there is no fundamental obstacle to the incumbent responding by matching its strategy. The incumbent may have to sacrifice some of its current profit margins in the process, just as it would in a price war with a traditional competitor. But the challenger is not truly disruptive. On the other hand, if the answer is yes, then the challenger has passed both tests of business model disruption. The value it offers to the customer will dramatically outstrip or undermine the value delivered by the incumbent, and the incumbent will face intrinsic structural barriers that prevent it from responding directly. This matches perfectly the definition with which we started the chapter: business disruption happens when an existing industry faces a challenger that offers far greater value to the customer in a way that existing firms cannot compete with directly. The challenger is a disruptive threat.

But is all hope lost? In the face of a real disruptive threat, can the incumbent expect complete and rapid extinction (like the horse carriage industry facing automobiles), or is there an opportunity for the incumbent to respond—or at least hold on to some of its glory?

That is where the next tool comes in.

Tool: The Disruptive Response Planner

If you have determined that you are, in fact, looking at a true disruptive challenger to an incumbent business, you are now ready to apply the second tool.

The Disruptive Response Planner is designed to help you map out how a disruptive challenge will likely play out and identify your best options for response.

The first three steps help you to assess the threat from the disrupter in terms of three dimensions: customer trajectory, disruptive scope, and other incumbents that may be affected. You can then use these insights in the last step to choose among six possible incumbent responses to a disruptive challenger. (See figure 7.2)

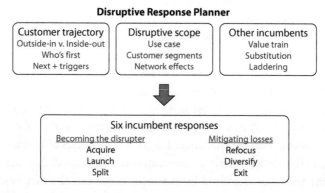

Figure 7.2
The Disruptive Response Planner.

Step 1: Customer Trajectory

The first step in predicting the possible impact of a new disruptive business model is to understand its customer trajectory: What customers are likely to adopt the disrupter's offer first, and how will its market spread from there if it is successful?

OUTSIDE-IN OR INSIDE-OUT?

As we have seen, there are two types of customer trajectories for disruptive business models: *outside-in* and *inside-out*. It is critical to start by judging which of these paths your disrupter is likely to take in entering the market.

Outside-in disrupters begin by selling to noncustomers of the incumbent and then work their way inward to encroach on the incumbent's own customers. As described by Christensen, outside-in disrupters don't appeal at first to the incumbent's customers because of their lesser features, but they do appeal to customers who could not afford or access the traditional incumbent's services. As the disrupter improves, it begins to attract the incumbent's customers as well. Christensen's theory has shown how industries with barriers that exclude many potential customers—higher education, health care, financial services—are ripe for disruption. As he and Derek van Bever write: "If only the skilled and the rich have access to a product or a service, you can reasonably assume the existence of a market-creating opportunity."[24]

Inside-out disrupters follow a different path. They begin by selling to a segment of the incumbent's current customers and then work their way outward to take more of its market. We have seen many examples of these: iPhone versus Nokia (started by selling to existing mobile phone users) and Netflix versus Blockbuster (explicitly marketed to existing movie renters as a better alternative). Rather than starting out as inferior to the incumbent's offer but "good enough" for buyers who could not afford the incumbent, these disrupters offer much better value from the beginning. These are business model innovations that would quickly draw a competitive response from the incumbent except that they rely on a value network that the incumbent finds impossible to imitate.

Who Is First?

Once you know if the disruption will be outside-in or inside-out, you will want to identify which specific types of customers will likely be first to adopt the disrupter's product or service.

For inside-out disruptions, you should ask these questions: Who among your current customers would be most attracted to the disruptive offer? Are there any hurdles to their early adoption (e.g., reliability is not yet proven)? Are there some current customers for whom those hurdles matter less (e.g., they are eager to try out new products or are less concerned about established brands)?

For outside-in disruptions, you should ask these questions: Who is currently most motivated but unable to afford or access your products or services? Which of these hurdles (price or access) is the bigger barrier for them? Which hurdle does the disrupter's offer help them more to surmount?

Who Is Next, and What Will Trigger Them?

Once you identify the likely first customers for a disrupter's offer, you need to identify who will be attracted to the offer next. For inside-out disrupters, that is likely another subgroup of your customers. For instance, if Warby Parker starts by appealing to the supporters of social causes, will its next customers be tech-savvy eyeglasses wearers? For outside-in disrupters, the key question here is this: When will the disrupter "tip" from selling to noncustomers and start to reach your own customers?

You also need to think about what will trigger these second-wave customers to come on board. These triggers can often be other customers' behaviors; wait-and-see customers, for example, may become interested as they see others using a product, or they may be persuaded by word of mouth. The trigger may be some further innovation by the disrupter, such as dropping prices further or improving features or both. Or the trigger may simply be visibility—as press coverage, marketing, or geographical distribution brings the disrupter's offer to the attention of the next wave of new customers.

Knowing the likely customer trajectory has important implications. As the incumbent, you need to know which of your current customers to keep an eye on first to see if they defect. You must also know if the challenger doesn't need any of your customers to get started (an outside-in disrupter). In that case, you should develop a strategy to compete for these same "outside" customers, where the disrupter may grow first before moving into your own market.

Step 2: Disruptive Scope

The next step in assessing the threat from a disruptive business model is to consider its likely scope. This describes how much of the market (how many customers) are likely to wind up switching to the disrupter once it is well established. Disruptive scope can be predicted by looking at three factors: use case, customer segments, and network effects.

USE CASE

You should first identify various use cases where customers purchase and use your product or service. Make two lists: In what situations do customers purchase your offering? In what situations do they utilize it? (There should be overlap in the lists but also some differences.) Then, for each use case on both lists, consider the disrupter's value proposition. In which cases is the disrupter clearly preferable for the customer? In which cases is there an advantage for your offer?

As we saw in the case of e-books versus print books, a disrupter may have a clear advantage for some use cases (e.g., boarding a plane with a variety of reading material) but be at a disadvantage in other use cases (e.g., giving a gift to a friend). You should also consider whether there are costs to multihoming (as discussed in chapter 3). How difficult is it for a customer to buy from your business for some use cases and from the disrupter for others? For readers, it is not that difficult to buy printed books as gifts while keeping an e-reader stocked for their own travel.

Customer Segments

Next you should subdivide the customers for which you and the disrupter are competing. Rather than seeing them as one monolithic group, try to divide these customers into segments based on their shared needs. What drives them to use this product category? What are their relevant needs? (This may sometimes correspond to some of your use cases.) Then, for each segment, consider whether the disrupter is extremely attractive in comparison to your business.

Recall Zipcar (discussed in chapter 5). This on-demand car rental service seemed to pose a disruptive challenge to traditional car rental companies when it launched. Zipcar members pay a small monthly fee to have access to any of the Zipcars parked in their metropolitan area. They simply look on their phone app, walk up to a nearby car, and type an entry code into the keypad lock on the car door. This self-service model appears much more convenient than the customer service experience of picking up a car at a traditional rental agency. But Zipcar never supplanted the traditional rental model for most customers. It turns out that certain types of consumers (e.g., those in dense cities with regular needs for short-term car rentals) were ideally suited to the membership model. But other consumers (e.g., those in rural areas or those with more infrequent rental needs) did not benefit as much from that model. While expanding to four countries and nearly a million members, Zipcar has stayed focused on college campuses and major cities.

Network Effects

The third factor to consider in predicting a disrupter's scope is network effects. Many services, especially platform businesses, become more valuable with each new customer that participates. As more customers bought iPhones, it became easier for Apple to attract more developers to create apps for the platform. As more developers built apps, the advantages of the iPhone versus an incumbent like Nokia grew as well. If you look at a cryptocurrency like Bitcoin, there is certainly the possibility that it could disrupt various incumbents that provide traditional financial services (credit card payments, savings accounts, foreign exchange). But the biggest hurdle to a currency like Bitcoin is that currencies are extremely dependent on network effects. As long as few merchants accept Bitcoin and few other customers are using it, the benefits to a new user are mostly hypothetical. On the other hand, incumbents watching Bitcoin need to realize that enough momentum in user adoption could quickly lead to a snowballing effect (much like users flocking to a fast-growing social network such as Instagram or Snapchat) that transforms it quickly from a curiosity to a major disruptive force.

IMPLICATIONS

Now that you have examined use cases, customer segments, and network effects, you should be able to make an informed prediction of the likely scope of impact of a new disrupter. Broadly, we can think of three likely outcomes of a disruptive business model. One is a *niche* case, where the disrupter is attractive to only a very specific portion of the market. Other disrupters may wind up *splitting the market*, with the disrupter's and the incumbent's business models each taking large shares. And in cases of a *landslide*, the disrupter quickly takes over the entire market, pushing the incumbent into obscurity.

Step 3: Other Incumbents

We saw earlier how a single new business model can disrupt multiple incumbent industries. When assessing a disrupter to your business, it is easy to focus on its impact on only one industry (your own). But to understand the competitive dynamics at work, it is critical to expand your reference frame to consider other incumbent businesses and how they will be impacted and respond to the disrupter.

VALUE TRAIN

The first place to look for additional businesses that may be disrupted is in your own value train (as discussed in chapter 3).

Start by asking which product or service the disrupter most resembles. For example, the product most like e-books would be printed books. You can then look at a value train of everyone involved in delivering that product or service—from the originator (authors), to producers (book publishers), to distributors (book printers, distribution companies, and retail and e-tail booksellers)—until the value reaches the final consumer. Then ask which of these different types of companies may be disrupted if the new business model is successful? For e-books, the answer would likely be retail booksellers, printers, and distributors; authors and publishing houses are most likely able to adapt to the new business model.

SUBSTITUTION

Another way of identifying additional incumbents is to think of products or services for which the customer may substitute the disrupter's offering. Ask yourself two questions: If a customer starts spending more money on the disrupter's product or service, where else might they spend less money? If the customer starts spending more time on the disrupter, where might they spend less time?

Considering the early iPhone, you can easily see that if customers spend money on an iPhone, they are less likely to spend money on a phone by another handset maker like Nokia. (Digging deeper, you might determine that if they spend more money on iPhone apps, they are likely to spend less on other entertainment.) If you ask where avid iPhone users spend their time, you might realize that they spend less time conducting Web searches on their desktops (a hugely profitable business for Google) and more time on mobile Web searches (much less profitable).

One other question about substitutes is worth asking: If the disrupter's current product continues to become much better in terms of performance and quality, for what other products or services might it start to become a substitute? Looking at the initial iPhone, it is possible to imagine that if it continues to get faster, more powerful, and a bit bigger, it does indeed pose a threat as a substitute for laptop computers, televisions, and other categories.

LADDERING

The last way to identify more incumbents who may be impacted by a disrupter is to look at both immediate and higher-order customer needs.

You start by asking these questions: What problem or need does the disrupter solve or meet for its customers? Who else tries to solve that problem? For example, looking at messaging apps like WhatsApp, you can see that customers use them to meet their need for expedient text messaging with friends (especially friends in different countries). That need was previously met by telecommunications providers, which, as we saw, lost billions of dollars in texting fees due to this disruption.

Next you can attempt to unearth higher-order customer needs through a process known as laddering. In this market research technique, you ask a customer a series of "Why?" questions to get at the reasons behind their immediate motivations. For example, if you ask college students why they use WhatsApp, they might say "to message easily with my friends." If you ask why they use it for that, they might say "to be able to make plans and swap photos." If you ask why that matters, they might say "so we can meet up and find out wherever the cool get-togethers are happening." This might lead you to realize that mobile messaging apps are meeting the need for convening social interactions, which was formerly met by visiting the college bar. This kind of laddering can reveal products or services that are made less necessary for customers by the disrupter, even though the disrupter doesn't appear to be competing directly.

IMPLICATIONS

By looking at value trains, different means of substitution, and different levels of customer needs, you may have identified multiple incumbents—types of companies that will be disruptively challenged by the same new disrupter. As an incumbent, it is always valuable to know who else may be threatened by the same disrupter that is threatening you. In planning your own response, it is important to see how these other incumbents are responding or consider how their responses might parallel yours. You may also find that these "enemies of my enemy" could serve as allies in response to the disruptive threat. As described above, Google saw that it was threatened just as much by the rapid rise of the iPhone as were cell-phone handset makers. As we will see, this led to Google's choice of response to the disruptive threat.

Step 4: Six Incumbent Responses to Disruption

The final step of the Disruptive Response Planner is to plan your response as an incumbent. To do so, you will use what you have learned regarding the trajectory, scope, and other incumbents of the disrupter you are facing to help you choose which strategic responses are most promising for your circumstances.

As an incumbent, you have six possible responses when faced with a disruptive challenger:

THREE STRATEGIES TO BECOME THE DISRUPTER

- Acquire the disrupter
- Launch an independent disrupter
- Split the disrupter's business model

THREE STRATEGIES TO MITIGATE LOSSES FROM THE DISRUPTER

- Refocus on your defensible customers
- Diversify your portfolio
- Plan for a fast exit

These six strategies are not exclusive; you can combine them (and, in fact, some of them work best together). The first three responses seek to occupy the same ground as the disrupter. The last three responses seek to reduce its impact on your core business. Depending on your own circumstances, only one or a few of these incumbent responses may be workable, so it is best to be familiar with each of them.

Let's look at each response and see where and how you might best apply it.

ACQUIRE THE DISRUPTER

The most direct response for an incumbent faced with a disruptive challenger is to simply acquire the challenger. This is how Facebook dealt with the challenge of WhatsApp. When Google's Maps product faced a potential disrupter in Waze, it bought the company. When the car rental giant Avis saw that Zipcar had invented a disruptive business model, Avis also bought its challenger. If you are considering buying your disrupter, knowing who the other incumbents are will help you predict who else might compete with you to drive up the price.

If you do acquire your disrupter, you should continue to run it as an independent division. That's what Facebook, Google, and Avis did in all the above cases. That means the disrupter you own will continue to steal customers from your core business (and possibly at a lower profit margin).

But if you don't take measures to keep the acquired disrupter independent, you will inevitably put the interests of your core business above the goal of serving your customers. And that will create an opportunity for someone else to launch a similar business and steal away your disappointed customers.

Acquiring the disrupter is not always possible. A start-up with sufficient venture capital may refuse to sell, as was the case with Facebook's failed $3 billion bid for messaging app Snapchat. Or the disrupter may be part of a bigger company than the incumbent. Amazon's e-books posed a clear disruptive threat to retail booksellers like Barnes & Noble, but the retailers were much smaller than Amazon (for whom e-books was just a part of its business).

Often, acquiring the disrupter is overlooked or rejected in the early stages, when acquisition is still an option. In 2000, shortly after Netflix launched its subscription DVD model, the start-up's CEO, Reed Hastings, flew to Dallas to meet with Blockbuster's CEO, John Antioco. Hastings proposed the video giant and the newcomer form a partnership, with Netflix handling online distribution and Blockbuster the retail channel. Hastings was laughed out of the office.[25] Blockbuster didn't get a second chance. Acquisition does not always need to be 100 percent (a partnership with Netflix would have proved a godsend for Blockbuster), but it does require swallowing your pride and recognizing the disrupter's advantages before it scales so big as to no longer need your help.

LAUNCH AN INDEPENDENT DISRUPTER

The second incumbent response is to launch a new business of its own that imitates the business model of the disrupter. Instead of purchasing the disrupter outright, the incumbent leverages its scale and resources to try to beat the disrupter at its own game. This is the response Christensen proposes: "Develop a disruption of your own before it's too late to reap the rewards of participation in new, high-growth markets."[26]

In order to launch your own disrupter, however, you, the incumbent must be willing to cannibalize your own core business. After all, you are trying to re-create the very business model that is disruptively attacking your traditional business. Charles Schwab implemented this strategy when it saw the growth of online brokerages like Joe Ricketts's TD Ameritrade, launching its own online service that competed with its full-service offerings.

This strategy again requires you to keep the new disruptive initiative walled off in an independent part of your company. You should run it on its own P&L, with no responsibility to save or support your core business. Although the independent unit should have access to some of the main company's resources, it should maintain a small and lean organization so that it can evolve quickly rather than becoming a sclerotic version of the nimble disrupter it is trying to beat.

You may even launch an independent disrupter preemptively—as you see a possible new business model based on emerging trends and technology. Saint-Gobain, a leading global retailer of construction materials, looked at the trends in e-commerce and recognized the opportunity for an online store in its industry. Rather than waiting for a start-up to capture this opportunity, Saint-Gobain launched Outiz, an online-only retailer in the French market. Outiz has been tasked with competing directly with the parent company's own brick-and-mortar retail brands.

Launching an independent disrupter is not easy, but it is plausible if the differences in value networks are your company's organizational culture, cost structure, revenue model, and customer segments. You can potentially overcome these kinds of barriers by insulating the self-launched disrupter from the rest of your business.

SPLIT THE DISRUPTER'S BUSINESS MODEL

What if the incumbent lacks some core capabilities—like intellectual property, brand reputation, essential skills, or the right partners—that are needed to re-create the disrupter? In that case, simply insulating a new initiative from the rest of the organization is not sufficient. But the incumbent may still be able to re-create the disrupter's business model by splitting the job with other businesses.

This may be a good strategy if your prior analysis uncovered multiple incumbents and their value networks are complementary to your own. This was the strategy used by Google when it launched the Android operating system in response to Apple's iPhone, which was threatening its advertising business. Google already had a core mobile operating system from its 2005 acquisition of Android Inc. It also had the key software assets required for an iPhone-like device: Google Search, Google Maps, YouTube video, and the Chrome Web browser. But Google knew it lacked the skills and assets required to design and manufacture hardware to compete with Apple, so it licensed its operating system and mobile software to diverse companies—Samsung, Sony, HTC, and others—with the capabilities to build great smartphone hardware. By splitting the iPhone's business model with these firms, Google was able to bring Android phones to market with a value proposition that rivaled that of the iPhone.

The key to splitting a disrupter's business model is to find other businesses that complement your own value network and partner with them to bridge the gaps that are preventing you from launching your own disrupter. Ideally, those partners are also threatened by the same disrupter, so they will be motivated to collaborate.

Refocus on Your Defensible Customers

Incumbents don't have to react just by becoming the disrupter; they can also act defensively in shoring up their own core business. That is the focus of the next two incumbent responses. These strategies can often be deployed in combination with the previous ones.[27]

The first of these defensive strategies is to refocus the incumbent's core business on those customers it has the best chance of retaining. You should use this strategy whenever you have identified a likely split market or niche market for your disrupter.

It is essential that you not engage in wishful thinking and simply continue to invest in your traditional business as if its future will look the same as its recent past. Refocusing should appeal to the customers that you think are most likely to stay with you despite the disrupter. Remember, they won't stay with you out of loyalty; they will stay because your business model still offers more value to them. Look back at your scope analysis and the customer segments and use cases that favored your product. Look also at the customer trajectory you predicted: Who will likely depart for the disrupter first, and who may follow? Then plan to shift your core business to focus on them, even while that business is likely shrinking.

When book retailer Barnes & Noble found its business disrupted by online book delivery, it refocused its business model on high-margin products like children's books and coffee-table books because the customers buying these still valued the ability to browse the products in a store environment.[28]

In refocusing your core business, you should aim your marketing, messaging, and continued product innovations at these most defensible customers. If your strategy involves cutbacks, focus on reducing the operations serving those customers that you are likely to lose and on continuing to deliver value to those you are likely to retain.

DIVERSIFY YOUR PORTFOLIO

The next way that incumbents can mitigate the disruption of their core business is by diversifying their portfolio of products, services, and business units. They can accomplish this by repurposing the firm's unique skills and assets in new areas and by acquiring smaller firms in the areas into which they want to extend.

When digital photography was going mainstream and disrupting the business of photographic film, the top two incumbent businesses were Kodak and Fujifilm. While Kodak slid into a long decline that ended in bankruptcy, Fujifilm managed to adapt and survive. "Both Fujifilm and Kodak knew the digital age was surging towards us. The question was, what to do about it," said Fujifilm's CEO, Shigetaka Komori. "Fujifilm was able to overcome by diversifying." Under Komori's leadership, the firm spent years applying its technical expertise in chemicals, developed in producing film, in diverse areas such as flat-panel electronic screens, drug delivery, and skin care. By the time Kodak filed for bankruptcy, Fujifilm's film business was only 1 percent of its revenue, but health care and flat-panel displays were 12 percent and 10 percent, respectively.[29]

Diversification allows you to leverage the strengths in your value network in new business areas, and although these areas may not initially be as profitable as your core business, they can create new opportunities for growth and make your firm less susceptible to total disruption.

PLAN FOR A FAST EXIT

The last strategy for an incumbent response to disruption is the least desirable one. When a disruptive challenger poses an irresistible threat to an incumbent's entire market and there is no feasible way to launch a disruption of its own, the incumbent needs to plan for a fast exit. This is the case when the disruptive scope is a landslide because all customers and use cases are vulnerable or because strong network effects lead to a winner-take-all scenario.

In planning to exit a market, you should assess all your firm's assets, especially intangible assets (patents, brand names, etc.) that can be sold.

You may also choose to spin off the indefensible part of your business from other divisions that can survive on their own rather than letting the vulnerable part bring down your entire enterprise. In most cases, you can pursue one or a combination of the first five incumbent responses, but sometimes an orderly liquidation of assets is the necessary call.

Beyond Disruption

The fact of disruption is inescapable. The very strategies that comprise the digital transformation playbook for traditional enterprises are also the source of their biggest disruptive threats. And yet disruption is both more and less than it seems.

Disruption is more diverse than our prevailing theory has held. Disruption is driven by more than just lower prices and accessibility for new customers; it can be triggered by any dramatically greater value proposition for the customer. Disruption can happen not just on the familiar trajectory of outside-in but from inside an existing market outward as well.

But disruption is also less than we sometimes imagine it to be. First and foremost, not every innovation (no matter how breathtaking) is necessarily a disrupter of an existing industry. Disruption is rarely total; most disrupters attract a significant part of an incumbent's market without taking 100 percent. Disruption is also less than irresistible. Even though it may pose an existential threat to an incumbent's business model, there are strategies the incumbent can use to adapt, diversify, and continue its enterprise by adding new value for customers.

More than anything else, responding to disruption requires that a business be willing to question its own assumptions and focus on the unique mission of how it serves customers.

Conclusion

Digital transformation is fundamentally not about technology but about strategy. Although it may require upgrading your IT architecture, the more important upgrade is to your strategic thinking.

Traditionally, digital leaders, such as CIOs, were tasked with focusing on automating and improving the processes of an existing business. Today, digital leadership requires the ability to reimagine and reinvent that business itself. What business are you in? How do you create value for customers? What do you keep inside the borders of your organization, and what processes, assets, and value should reside in your relationships outside? How do you balance your relationships with customers and other organizations to ensure profitability, sustainability, and growth?

Reimagining your business requires challenging some of its underlying core assumptions. It requires recognizing blind spots you may not realize you have. It requires thinking differently about every aspect of your strategy—customers, competition, data, innovation, and value. This kind of rethinking is difficult—but certainly possible. Just as factories built before the era of electrification were able to revamp their entire way of working and manufacturing, businesses today that were born before the Internet are quite capable of transforming for the digital age.

So why don't more businesses do this successfully? The sober truth is that for every Encyclopædia Britannica that succeeds in transforming for the digital age, there is a Kodak or a Blockbuster that fails. Why are so many of our institutions struggling to adapt and keep up?

One of the key reasons is organizational agility. It is not enough just to recognize and overcome your strategic blind spots—or even to see how the principles of digital transformation apply to your own industry and business. Legacy organizations must be ready to make change happen—and at a very rapid pace. The curse of successful enterprises is often their very size and scale: their enviable resources can become a trap as future decisions are held hostage by past success.

To develop true organizational agility, your business needs to focus on three areas:

- *Allocating resources*: How will you decide what to invest in? Are you able to disengage from initiatives and lines of business that lack future potential? Can you apply resources from older business lines to support new ventures?
- *Changing what you measure*: What outcomes are being measured by senior decision makers? Do they simply relate to existing business practices, or can they support new directions? What should you be measuring at different stages of a transition to a new business model?
- *Aligning incentives*: What kind of behavior is enabled, supported, and rewarded in your organization? What are managers held accountable for? How are they assigned to new positions? Do compensation and recognition support or hinder the necessary changes in your strategy?

It may be helpful to conduct an audit of your business's readiness for digital transformation. At the end of this book, you can find such a diagnostic tool, titled Self-Assessment: Are You Ready for Digital Transformation? It includes questions to assess your own organization's current readiness for digital transformation—in terms of both strategic thinking and agility to carry out new strategies.

You can think about the challenge of digital transformation in terms of mastering two different kinds of management. To succeed in any transformation, your organization must be able to develop truly new ideas, processes, ventures, and ways of thinking. But it must also be able to spread these ideas or processes throughout the organization. This is quite a different task—and one that is particularly hard for large organizations.

The head of British Airways' Know Me program explained to me how the company is tackling this transition. Having built a powerful data asset, developed tools to capture customer insight and apply it in customer interactions, and launched pilot programs to prove the impact for the business, she now faces a different challenge. The next stage is to scale up the program, to embed the use of data for customer service into the company's DNA, and to transition Know Me from an innovative initiative to a part of British Airways' day-to-day operations.[1]

My colleague Miklos Sarvary, who teaches in my digital strategy executive programs at Columbia Business School, talks about this transition as a shift from "incubation" (seeding and nurturing new strategies) to "integration" (building the best ones into the fabric of the organization).

But incubation and integration require very different skills in an organization. The ability to incubate is seen best in start-ups and venture capital firms. It relies on specific skills: tolerating risk, seeding diverse ideas with resources, welcoming outsiders who don't fit your organizational culture, empowering entrepreneurs, developing a robust innovation process based on discovery and assumptions testing, maintaining a customer-centric view, and being willing to let new ventures cannibalize existing ones.

By contrast, the ability to integrate and replicate successful ideas at scale is most often seen in larger enterprises. It involves a different set of skills: building a compelling business case, developing a clear proof of concept, selling new ideas to diverse internal constituencies, finding the right executive sponsorship, working with budgets based on business outcomes, managing accountability to multiple stakeholders, and being able to scale up operations.

The organizations that flourish in the digital age will combine the right strategic mindset with the right leadership skill set. They will understand the new strategic fundamentals of the digital age and use them to craft new products, services, brands, and business models. Whatever their size, they will maintain the organizational agility to seize new opportunities, and they will balance the art of incubating and learning like a start-up with the art of scaling and integrating like an enterprise.

These organizations will be guided, as their strategies and business models change, by a focus on continuous value creation. Going back to Peter Drucker, management thinkers have argued that the true and ultimate purpose of business should always be creating value for the customer: "to create a customer," as Drucker wrote,[2] or "to get and keep a customer," as Ted Levitt put it.[3] Today, though, this doctrine may require a slight update.

Amidst constant digital change, no business can thrive for long just delivering the same value proposition to customers. The need for value creation is now intertwined with the need to constantly relearn and reinvent what that value will be. The purpose of business, then, may be thought of as the continuous creation of *new* value for the customer.

The digital revolution is still just getting started. With an ever-unfolding cascade of new technologies and all the potential they provide, it is impossible to predict how the digital future will impact your business or any industry. But if you are savvy, your business can choose to use each new wave of change as an opportunity to create new value for your customers.

Onward!

SELF-ASSESSMENT:
ARE YOU READY FOR DIGITAL
TRANSFORMATION?

Even extremely successful companies built in the pre-digital age struggle to adapt their strategic thinking in order to thrive and grow in the digital age. This self-assessment tool is designed to assess the readiness of your own business or organization for digital transformation.

For each pair of statements, reflect on the current state of your own business. Choose the number, on the scale from 1 to 7, that reflects where your organization stands in relation to the two statements: 1 indicates fully aligned with the left, 7 with the right.

The first group of questions relates to the strategic concepts presented in this book. These questions are designed to measure the degree to which your organization has adapted its strategic thinking to the digital reality. The second group of questions relates to organizational agility. These questions are designed to measure your organization's ability to put into practice these new strategic principles and successfully drive change in your business.

After completing the self-assessment, look back at your results. Those areas with a score on the left (e.g., 1–3) are where change is most needed. You can use this diagnostic tool to focus your leadership attention and efforts as you guide your own organization into the future.

Strategic Thinking

We are focused on selling to and interacting with customers through the usual channels.	1 2 3 4 5 6 7	We are focused on our customers' changing digital habits and path to purchase.
We use marketing to target, reach, and persuade customers.	1 2 3 4 5 6 7	We use marketing to attract, engage, inspire, and collaborate with customers.
Our brand and reputation are what we communicate to our customers.	1 2 3 4 5 6 7	Our customers' advocacy is the biggest influence on our brand and reputation.
Our sole competitive focus is beating our rivals.	1 2 3 4 5 6 7	We are open to cooperating with our rivals and to competing with our partners.
We look to create value exclusively through our own products.	1 2 3 4 5 6 7	We look to create value through platforms and external networks.
We are focused primarily on own industry and on direct competitors.	1 2 3 4 5 6 7	We view our competition as broader than our current industry.
Our data strategy is focused on how to create, store, and manage our data.	1 2 3 4 5 6 7	Our data strategy is focused on how to turn data into new value.
We use our data to manage day-to-day operations.	1 2 3 4 5 6 7	We manage our data as a strategic asset we are building over time.
Our data stays in the division or business unit where it is generated.	1 2 3 4 5 6 7	Our data is organized to be accessible by all divisions of the company.
We make decisions by analysis, debate, and seniority.	1 2 3 4 5 6 7	We make decisions through experiments and testing wherever possible.
Our innovation projects always go over time or over budget.	1 2 3 4 5 6 7	We innovate in rapid cycles, using prototypes to learn quickly.
We try to avoid failure in new ventures at all costs.	1 2 3 4 5 6 7	We accept failure in new ventures but look to reduce cost and increase learning.
Our value proposition is defined by our products and our industry.	1 2 3 4 5 6 7	Our value proposition is defined by changing customer needs.
We assess new technologies by how they will impact our current business.	1 2 3 4 5 6 7	We assess new technologies by how they could create new value for our customers.
We are focused on executing and optimizing our current business model.	1 2 3 4 5 6 7	We aim to adapt early to stay ahead of the curve of change.

Organizational Agility

Our IT investments are seen as operational.	1 2 3 4 5 6 7	Our IT investments are seen as strategic.
It is hard to allocate resources away from existing lines of business.	1 2 3 4 5 6 7	We are able to invest in new ventures even if they compete with our current business.
Our key performance metrics relate only to sustaining our existing businesses.	1 2 3 4 5 6 7	Our business metrics adapt to suit changes in strategy and the maturity of a line of business.
Managers are accountable and rewarded for immediate results on past objectives.	1 2 3 4 5 6 7	Managers are accountable and rewarded for long-term goals and new strategies.
We have difficulty developing new ventures far from our existing business.	1 2 3 4 5 6 7	We are able to seed and develop new ideas that are unusual for our business.
The sharing of best practices across our organization is slow and inconsistent.	1 2 3 4 5 6 7	We are skilled at taking successful new ideas and integrating them across the organization.
Our first priority is maximizing shareholder return.	1 2 3 4 5 6 7	Our first priority is creating value for customers.

MORE TOOLS FOR STRATEGIC PLANNING

You can find additional resources to assist you in applying the digital transformation playbook by visiting the Tools and Blog sections of http://www.davidrogers.biz. These include the following:

PRINTABLE VERSIONS OF:

- Self-Assessment: Are You Ready for Digital Transformation?
- One-page overview of *The Digital Transformation Playbook*
- Diagrams for each of the nine strategic planning tools

DETAILED INSTRUCTIONS FOR THE STRATEGY MAPPING TOOLS:

- Drawing and using the Platform Business Model Map
- Drawing and using the Competitive Value Train

You can also find there additional case studies and tips for leading digital transformation in your own organization.

NOTES

1. The Five Domains of Digital Transformation

1. Jorge Cauz, "How I Did It . . . Encyclopædia Britannica's President on Killing Off a 244-Year-Old Product," *Harvard Business Review* 91 (March 2013): 39–42.

2. I'm grateful to Rita McGrath for the analogy to factory electrification, whose strategic impact she describes in "How 3-D Printing Will Change Everything About Manufacturing," *Wall Street Journal*, June 4, 2015, http://blogs.wsj.com/experts/2015/06/04/how-3-d-printing-will-change-everything-about-manufacturing/. A fuller history, and the story of the Detroit Edison Company's evangelizing for electrical motors, can be found in Warren D. Devine Jr., "From Shafts to Wires: Historical Perspective on Electrification," *Journal of Economic History* 43, no. 2 (June 1983): 347–72.

2. Harness Customer Networks

1. Bobby Gruenewald, Twitter post, January 24, 2015, https://twitter.com/bobbygwald/status/559133099540234241.

2. Amy O'Leary, "In the Beginning Was the Word; Now the Word Is on an App," *New York Times*, July 26, 2013, http://www.nytimes.com/2013/07/27/technology/the-faithful-embrace-youversion-a-bible-app.html.

3. Ibid.

4. David L. Rogers, *The Network Is Your Customer: Five Strategies to Thrive in a Digital Age* (New Haven, Conn.: Yale University Press, 2012), 3–50.

5. Edelman, "Brandshare: How Brands and People Create a Value Exchange," *Edelman Insights*, 2014, http://www.edelman.com/insights/intellectual-property /brandshare-2014/about-brandshare-2014/global-results/.

6. For a summary of research into the hierarchy of effects, see Thomas Barry, "The Development of the Hierarchy of Effects: An Historical Perspective," *Current Issues and Research in Advertising* 10 (1987): 251–95.

7. Matthew Quint, David Rogers, and Rick Ferguson, *Showrooming and the Rise of the Mobile-Assisted Shopper*, Columbia Business School and Aimia, September 2013, http://www8.gsb.columbia.edu/rtfiles/global%20brands/Showrooming_Rise_Mobile _Assisted_Shopper_Columbia-Aimia_Sept2013.pdf.

8. Sunil Gupta and Donald R. Lehmann, *Managing Customers as Investments: The Strategic Value of Customers in the Long Run* (Upper Saddle River, N.J.: Pearson Education, 2005).

9. Quint, Rogers, and Ferguson, *Showrooming*.

10. Alexis C. Madrigal, "How Netflix Reverse Engineered Hollywood," *The Atlantic*, January 2, 2014, http://www.theatlantic.com/technology/archive/2014/01/how -netflix-reverse-engineered-hollywood/282679/.

11. Brian Stelter, "Strong Quarter for Netflix, but Investors Hit Pause," *New York Times*, July 22, 2013, http://www.nytimes.com/2013/07/23/business/media/netflix -revenue-tops-1-billion-for-the-quarter.html.

12. Tim Grimes, "What the Share a Coke Campaign Can Teach Other Brands," *Media Network Blog* (blog), *The Guardian*, July 24, 2013, http://www.theguardian.com /media-network/media-network-blog/2013/jul/24/share-coke-teach-brands.

13. Thomas H. Davenport, Leandro Dalle Mule, and John Lucker, "Know What Your Customer Wants Before They Do," *Harvard Business Review*, December 2011, https://hbr.org/2011/12/know-what-your-customers-want-before-they-do.

14. Suzanne Kepner, "Citi Won't Sleep on Customer Tweets," *Wall Street Journal*, October 4, 2012, http://www.wsj.com/articles/SB10000872396390443493304578035132643293660.

15. Zsolt Katona and Miklos Sarvary, "Maersk Line: B2B Social Media—'It's Communication, Not Marketing,'" *California Management Review* 56, no. 3 (2014): 142–56.

16. Joerg Niessing, "Social Media and the Marketing Mix Model," *INSEAD Blog* (blog), August 29, 2014, http://knowledge.insead.edu/blog/insead-blog/social-media -and-the-marketing-mix-model-3540.

17. Quotations in this section are from Joseph Tripodi, telephone interview with author, November 6, 2014.

18. Mukund Kaushik, "Client Perspective" (panel discussion at the IBM ThinkMarketing CMO Executive Leadership Forum, New York City, April 10, 2014).

19. Frank Eliason, e-mail interview with author, August 4, 2015.

3. Build Platforms, Not Just Products

1. Jessica Salter, "AirBnB: The Story Behind the $1.3bn Room-Letting Website," *The Telegraph*, September 7, 2012, http://www.telegraph.co.uk/technology/news/9525267/Airbnb-The-story-behind-the-1.3bn-room-letting-website.html.

2. Zainab Mudallal, "Airbnb Will Soon Be Booking More Rooms than the World's Largest Hotel Chains," Quartz, January 20, 2015, http://qz.com/329735/airbnb-will-soon-be-booking-more-rooms-than-the-worlds-largest-hotel-chains/.

3. Rafat Ali, "Airbnb's Revenues Will Cross Half Billion Mark in 2015, Analysts Estimate," Skift, March 25, 2015, http://skift.com/2015/03/25/airbnbs-revenues-will-cross-half-billion-mark-in-2015-analysts-estimate/.

4. Jason Clampet, "Airbnb's CEO Explains the Sharing Economy to Stephen Colbert," Skift, August 8, 2014, http://skift.com/2014/08/08/airbnbs-ceo-explains-the-sharing-economy-to-stephen-colbert/. (The interview aired August 7, 2014.)

5. Brad Stone, "AirBnB Is Now Available in Cuba," Bloomberg, April 2, 2015, http://www.bloomberg.com/news/articles/2015–04–02/airbnb-is-now-available-in-cuba.

6. Jean-Charles Rochet and Jean Tirole, "Platform Competition in Two-Sided Markets," *Journal of the European Economic Association* 1 (June 2003): 990–1029.

7. Thomas Eisenmann, Geoffrey Parker, and Marshall W. Van Alystyne, "Strategies for Two-Sided Markets," *Harvard Business Review*, October 2006, https://hbr.org/2006/10/strategies-for-two-sided-markets.

8. Andrei Hagiu and Julian Wright, "Multi-Sided Platforms" (working paper, Harvard Business School, Cambridge, Mass., March 16, 2015); also, Andrei Hagiu and Julian Wright, "Marketplace or Re-seller?" (working paper, Harvard Business School, Cambridge, Mass., January 31, 2014).

9. David Evans and Richard Schmalensee, "The Industrial Organization of Markets with Two-Sided Platforms," *CPI Journal* (2007, vol. 3).

10. Andrei Hagiu and Julian Wright, "Do You Really Want to Be an eBay?" *Harvard Business Review*, March 2013, https://hbr.org/2013/03/do-you-really-want-to-be-an-ebay.

11. Frederic Lardinois, "Evernote's Market for Physical Goods Now Accounts for 30% of Its Monthly Sales," TechCrunch, December 10, 2013, http://techcrunch.com/2013/12/10/evernotes-market-for-physical-goods-now-accounts-for-30-of-its-monthly-sales/.

12. Derek Thompson, "AirBnB CEO Brian Chesky on Building a Company and Starting a 'Sharing' Revolution," *The Atlantic*, August 13, 2013, http://www.theatlantic.com/business/archive/2013/08/airbnb-ceo-brian-chesky-on-building-a-company-and-starting-a-sharing-revolution/278635/.

13. Tom Goodwin, "The Battle Is for the Customer Interface," TechCrunch, March 3, 2015, http://techcrunch.com/2015/03/03/in-the-age-of-disintermediation-the-battle-is-all-for-the-customer-interface.

14. Gregory Ferenstein, "Uber and AirBnB's Incredible Growth in 4 Charts," Venturebeat, June 19, 2014, http://venturebeat.com/2014/06/19/uber-and-airbnbs-incredible-growth-in-4-charts/.

15. Ali, "Airbnb's Revenues Will Cross Half Billion Mark in 2015."

16. Companies were selected from the Forbes Global 2000 list but ranked on market value, not Forbes's weighted ranking formula. Market values were updated to market capitalization as of September 5, 2015. Companies from the Forbes list were excluded if they were founded before 1994 or if they were founded from a spin-off or merger of companies that were founded before 1994. The Forbes list was published in "The World's Largest Public Companies," *Forbes*, May 6, 2015, http://www.forbes.com/global2000.

17. Joan Magretta, *Understanding Michael Porter: The Essential Guide to Competition and Strategy* (Boston: Harvard Business Review Press, 2011), 21–33.

18. Adam M. Brandenburger and Barry J. Nalebuff, *Co-opetition* (New York: Currency Doubleday, 1997), 11–27.

19. Josh Dzieza, "Why Tesla's Battery for Homes Should Terrify Utilities," *The Verge*, February 13, 2015, http://www.theverge.com/2015/2/13/8033691/why-teslas -battery-for-your-home-should-terrify-utilities.

20. Nick Bilton, "For Some Teenagers, 16 Candles Mean It's Time to Join Uber," *New York Times*, April 8, 2015, http://www.nytimes.com/2015/04/09/style/for-some -teenagers-16-candles-mean-its-time-to-join-uber.html.

21. Rita Gunther McGrath, *The End of Competitive Advantage: How to Keep Your Strategy Moving as Fast as Your Business* (Boston: Harvard Business Review Press, 2013), 9–12.

22. Russell Dubner, telephone interview with author, July 29, 2015.

23. Danny Wong, "In Q4, Social Media Drove 31.24% of Overall Traffic to Sites," *Shareaholic* (blog), January 26, 2015, https://blog.shareaholic.com/social-media- traffic-trends-01–2015/.

24. You can find a great discussion of this competitive shift between Facebook and publishers in Ben Thompson, "Publishers and the Smiling Curve," *Stratechery* (blog), October 28, 2014, https://stratechery.com/2014/publishers-smiling-curve/.

25. Gregory Sterling, "German Publishers to Google: We Want Our Snippets Back," Search Engine Land, October 23, 2014, http://searchengineland.com/german -publishers-google-want-snippets-back-206520.

26. Jason Dedrick and Kenneth L. Kraemer, *Asia's Computer Challenge: Threat or Opportunity to the World?* (New York: Oxford University Press, 1998), 152–57.

27. Julia King, "Disintermediation/Reintermediation," *Computerworld*, December 13, 1999, 54.

28. Peter Thiel, *Zero to One: Notes on Start-ups, or How to Build the Future* (New York: Crown Business, 2014), 42.

4. Turn Data Into Assets

1. John A. Dutton, "Opportunities and Priorities in a New Era for Weather and Climate Services," *Bulletin of the American Meteorological Society* 83, no. 9 (2002): 1303–11.

2. Vikram Somaya, "The Invisible Impact of Weather on Brands" (speech given at the Advertising and Data Science Congress, New York, January 26, 2013).

3. Alexis Madrigal, "Keynote Speech" (speech given at the Advertising and Data Science Congress, New York, January 26, 2013).

4. Rita McGrath, "To Make Better Decisions, Combine Datasets," *Harvard Business Review*, September 4, 2014, https://hbr.org/2014/09/to-make-better-decisions-combine-datasets/.

5. Steve Lohr, "The Origins of 'Big Data': An Etymological Detective Story," *Bits* (blog), *New York Times*, February 1, 2013, http://bits.blogs.nytimes.com/2013/02/01/the-origins-of-big-data-an-etymological-detective-story/.

6. Miklos Sarvary, "In Mobile Marketing, the Value Is in the Journey, Not the Destination," *Columbia Business School Ideas at Work*, September 24, 2014, http://www8.gsb.columbia.edu/ideas-at-work/publication/1690/in-mobile-marketing-the-value-is-in-the-journey-not-the-destination.

7. McKinsey on Marketing & Sales, "CMO View: Making Data Easy to Use," YouTube video, 2:44, August 26, 2014, https://www.youtube.com/watch?v=GwB6LWwifLg.

8. Christopher Mims, "Most Data Isn't 'Big,' and Businesses Are Wasting Money Pretending It Is," *Quartz*, May 6, 2013, http://qz.com/81661/most-data-isnt-big-and-businesses-are-wasting-money-pretending-it-is/.

9. Matthew Quint and David Rogers, *What Is the Future of Data Sharing? Consumer Mindsets and the Power of Brands*, Columbia Business School and Aimia, October 2015, http://www8.gsb.columbia.edu/globalbrands/research/future-of-data-sharing.

10. Eric Von Hippel, "Lead Users: A Source of Novel Product Concepts," *Management Science* 32 (1986): 791–806. doi:10.1287/mnsc.32.7.791.

11. Alexandre Choueiri, telephone interview with author, June 10, 2014.

12. Anca Cristina Micu, Kim Dedeker, Ian Lewis, Robert Moran, Oded Netzer, Joseph Plummer, and Joel Rubinson, "Guest Editorial: The Shape of Marketing Research in 2021," *Journal of Advertising Research* 51, no. 1 (March 2011): 213–21.

13. Oded Netzer, Ronen Feldman, Moshe Fresko, and Jacob Goldenberg, "Mine Your Own Business: Market-Structure Surveillance Through Text Mining," *Marketing Science* 31, no. 3 (2012): 521–43.

14. Rachael King, "Sentiment Analysis Gives Companies Insight Into Consumer Opinion," *BusinessWeek*, March 1, 2011, http://www.bloomberg.com/bw/stories/2011-03-01/sentiment-analysis-gives-companies-insight-into-consumer-opinionbusiness week-business-news-stock-market-and-financial-advice.

15. Ki Mae Heussner, "Meet the Startup Helping Sites Like Fab and Etsy Court Their Customers," Gigaom, June 4, 2012, https://gigaom.com/2012/06/04/meet-the-startup-helping-sites-like-fab-and-etsy-court-their-customers/.

16. Steven Rosenbush and Michael Totty, "How Big Data Is Changing the Whole Equation for Business," *Wall Street Journal*, March 11, 2013, http://www.wsj.com/news/articles/SB20001424127887324178904578340071261396666.

17. Alice Lee, "How Health Care 'Hotspotting' Can Lower Costs, Improve Quality," *The Aspen Idea Blog* (blog), The Aspen Institute, October 2, 2014, http://www.aspeninstitute.org/about/blog/how-health-care-hotspotting-can-lower-costs-improve-quality.

18. Atul Gwande, "The Hot Spotters," *New Yorker,* January 24, 2011, http://www.newyorker.com/magazine/2011/01/24/the-hot-spotters.

19. Mukund Kaushik, "Client Perspective" (panel discussion at the IBM Think Marketing CMO Executive Leadership Forum, New York, April 10, 2014).

20. Jo Boswell, telephone interview with author, August 9, 2015.

21. David Williams, "Connected CRM: Delivering on a Data-Driven Business Strategy" (speech given at Columbia Business School's Annual "BRITE" Conference, New York, March 3, 2014).

22. Boswell, telephone interview.

23. Mike Weaver, "How Data and Insights Are Evolving Digital Consumer Engagement" (speech given at the IBM ThinkMarketing CMO Executive Leadership Forum, New York, April 10, 2014).

24. David Rogers and Don Sexton, "Marketing ROI in the Era of Big Data: The 2012 BRITE/NYAMA Marketing in Transition Study," Columbia Business School Center on Global Brand Leadership, March 2012, http://www8.gsb.columbia.edu/globalbrands/research/brite-nyama-study.

25. Jose van Dijk, "Client Perspective" (panel discussion at the IBM ThinkMarketing CMO Executive Leadership Forum, New York, April 10, 2014).

26. Anindita Mukherjee, "Social Spending: Measuring the ROI of Tweets, Posts, Pics, and 6-Second Vids" (speech given at *The Economist's* "The Big Rethink: The 360-Degree CMO" Conference, New York, March 13, 2014).

27. From a fascinating insiders' account of the Sony Pictures data hack, in an interview with CEO Michael Lynton, "They Burned the House Down," *Harvard Business Review*, July–August 2015, 113.

5. Innovate by Rapid Experimentation

1. Scott Anthony, "Innovation Is a Discipline, Not a Cliché," *Harvard Business Review*, May 30, 2012, https://hbr.org/2012/05/four-innovation-misconceptions.

2. Kaaren Hanson, "Creating a Culture of Rapid Experimentation" (speech given at Columbia Business School's Annual "BRITE" Conference, New York, March 4, 2013).

3. Ibid.

4. Ibid.

5. Ibid.

6. Nathan R. Furr and Jeffrey H. Dyer, *The Innovator's Method: Bringing the Lean Start-Up Into Your Organization* (Boston: Harvard Business Publishing, 2014), 13–14. Intuit was one of several companies singled out in research by Furr and Dyer as applying a lean and iterative approach to innovation; the authors measure the impact of this approach in terms of an "innovation premium"—the premium that investors will pay for a company's stock compared to the net present value of its existing business revenues.

7. Stefan Thomke and Jim Manzi, "The Discipline of Business Experimentation," *Harvard Business Review*, December 2014, https://hbr.org/2014/12/the-discipline-of-business-experimentation.

8. Eric T. Anderson and Duncan Simester, "A Step-by-Step Guide to Smart Business Experiments," *Harvard Business Review*, March 2011, https://hbr.org/2011/03/a-step-by-step-guide-to-smart-business-experiments. (*Note*: I have updated the market capitalization of Capital One from its figure to the amount on September 9, 2015.)

9. I recommend reading Thomke's book *Experimentation Matters*, Thomke and Manzi's article "The Discipline of Business Experimentation," and Anderson and Simester's article "A Step-by-Step Guide to Smart Business Experiments." (Bibliographic information for each can be found in the other endnotes for this chapter.)

10. I highly recommend Furr and Dyer's book *The Innovator's Method: Bringing the Lean Start-Up Into Your Organization* and their article "Leading Your Team Into the Unknown." (Bibliographic information for both can be found in the other endnotes for this chapter.) Readers at start-ups should enjoy Steve Blank and Bob Dorf's *The Startup Owner's Manual* (Pescadero, Calif.: K & S Ranch, 2012) and Eric Ries's *The Lean Startup* (New York: Crown, 2011).

11. Hanson, "Creating a Culture of Rapid Experimentation."

12. John Hayes, interview with author at American Express headquarters, New York, May 29, 2012.

13. Andre Millard, *Edison and the Business of Innovation* (Baltimore: John Hopkins University Press, 1990), 40.

14. John Mayo-Smith, e-mail interview with author, August 4, 2015.

15. Roc Cutri and Tim Conrow, "WISE Mission Operations System CDR," July 18–19, 2007, http://wise2.ipac.caltech.edu/staff/roc/docs/WISE_MOS_CDR_WSDC.pdf.

16. Millard, *Edison and the Business of Innovation*, 15–16.

17. Rae Ann Fera, "How Mondelez International Innovates on the Fly in 8 (Sort of) Easy Steps," *Fast Company*, February 7, 2013, http://www.fastcocreate.com/1682100/how-mondelez-international-innovates-on-the-fly-in-8-sort-of-easy-steps.

18. Hanson, "Creating a Culture of Rapid Experimentation."

19. Joe Ricketts, telephone interview with author, September 25, 2014.

20. Alistair Croll and Benjamin Yoskovitz, *Lean Analytics: Use Data to Build a Better Startup Faster* (Sebastopol, Calif.: O'Reilly Media, 2013), 55–63.

21. Thomke and Manzi, "The Discipline of Business Experimentation."

22. Thomas R. Eisenmann and Laura Winig, *Rent The Runway* (Cambridge: Harvard Business School, 2011).

23. Ibid.

24. Ibid.

25. Rita Gunther McGrath and Ian MacMillan, *Discovery-Driven Growth: A Breakthrough Process to Reduce Risk and Seize Opportunity* (Boston: Harvard Business Review Press, 2009).

26. Carmen Nobel, "Lean Startup Strategy Not Just for Startups," *Forbes*, February 25, 2013, http://www.forbes.com/sites/hbsworkingknowledge/2013/02/25/lean-startup-strategy-not-just-for-startups/.

27. Stefan H. Thomke, *Experimentation Matters: Unlocking the Potential of New Technologies for Innovation* (Boston: Harvard Business Review Press, 2003), 13.

28. Thomke and Manzi, "The Discipline of Business Experimentation."

29. Ibid.

30. Pete Koomen, "Beat the Back Button: How Obama, Disney, and Crate & Barrel Use A/B Testing to Win" (speech given at Columbia Business School's Annual "BRITE" Conference, New York, March 4, 2013).

31. Furr and Dyer, *The Innovator's Method*, 175.

32. Sarah E. Needleman, "For Intuit Co-Founder, the Numbers Add Up," *Wall Street Journal*, August 18, 2011, http://www.wsj.com/articles/SB100014240531119035969 04576514364142860224.

33. Janet Choi, "The Science Behind Why Jeff Bezos's Two-Pizza Team Rule Works," *iDoneThis* (blog), September 24, 2014, http://blog.idonethis.com/two-pizza-team/.

34. Nobel, "Lean Startup Strategy Not Just for Startups."

35. Fera, "How Mondelez International Innovates on the Fly in 8 (Sort of) Easy Steps."

36. Scott Anthony, David Duncan, and Pontus M. A. Siren, "Build an Innovation Engine in 90 Days," *Harvard Business Review*, December 2014, https://hbr.org/2014/12/build-an-innovation-engine-in-90-days.

37. Yuval Noah Harari, *Sapiens: A Brief History of Humankind* (New York: Harper, 2015), 247–54.

38. Ron Kohavi, Alex Deng, Brian Frasca, Toby Walker, Ya Xu, and Nils Pohlmann, "Online Controlled Experiments at Large Scale," in *Proceedings of the Nineteenth ACM SIGKDD International Conference on Knowledge Discovery and Data Mining* (New York: ACM, 2013), 1168–76. doi:10.1145/2487575.2488217.

39. Madrigal, "Keynote Speech."

40. Greg Linden, "Early Amazon: Shopping Cart Recommendations," *Geeking with Greg* (blog), April 25, 2006, http://glinden.blogspot.com/2006/04/early-amazon-shopping-cart.html.

41. Henry Blodget, "TO BE CLEAR: JC Penney May Have Just Had the Worst Quarter in Retail History," *Business Insider*, February 28, 2013, http://www.business insider.com/jc-penney-worst-quarter-in-retail-history-2013-2.

42. Nathan Furr and Jeffrey H. Dyer, "Leading Your Team Into the Unknown," *Harvard Business Review*, December 2014, https://hbr.org/2014/12/leading-your-team-into-the-unknown.

43. Brad Smith, "Intuit's CEO on Building a Design-Driven Company," *Harvard Business Review*, January 2015, https://hbr.org/2015/01/intuits-ceo-on-building-a-design-driven-company.

44. Furr and Dyer, "Leading Your Team Into the Unknown."

45. Amy Radin, telephone interview with author, September 12, 2014.

46. Anderson and Simester, "A Step-by-Step Guide to Smart Business Experiments."

47. Thomke, *Experimentation Matters*, 121–22.

48. Scott Anthony, David Duncan, and Pontus M. A. Siren, "Zombie Projects: How to Find Them and Kill Them," *Harvard Business Review*, March 4, 2014, http://hbr.org/2015/03/zombie-projects-how-to-find-them-and-kill-them.

49. Joshua Brustein, "Finland's New Tech Power: Game Maker Supercell," Bloomberg, June 5, 2014, http://www.bloomberg.com/bw/articles/2014-06-05/clash-of-clans-maker-supercell-succeeds-nokia-as-finlands-tech-power.

50. "Tata Innovista 2013 Receives Record Participation," Tata Group press release, April 26, 2013, http://www.tata.com/article/inside/VWQXoUJo!$$$$!xI=/TLYVr3 YPkMU=.

6. Adapt Your Value Proposition

1. "Something to Sing About," *Economist*, March 2, 2013, http://www.economist .com/news/business/21572811-first-time-13-years-music-business-growing-again -something-sing-about. Figures for worldwide recorded music sales are from the International Federation of the Phonographic Industry and include "physical, digital, and performance rights and licensing."

2. Eric Pfanner, "Music Industry Sales Rise, and Digital Revenue Gets the Credit," *New York Times*, February 26, 2013, http://www.nytimes.com/2013/02/27/technology /music-industry-records-first-revenue-increase-since-1999.html.

3. Igor Ansoff, "Strategies for Diversification," *Harvard Business Review* 35, no. 5 (September–October 1957): 113–24.

4. Katherine Rosman, "U.S. Paper Industry Gets an Unexpected Boost," *Wall Street Journal*, March 7, 2014, http://www.wsj.com/articles/SB10001424052702304703804579385470794476470.

5. Clark Gilbert, Matthew Eyring, and Richard N. Foster, "Two Routes to Resilience," *Harvard Business Review*, December 2012, https://hbr.org/2012/12/two -routes-to-resilience.

6. David Schmaltz, "Whip City," *Pure Schmaltz* (blog), January 13, 2006, http:// www.projectcommunity.com/PureSchmaltz/files/Vaporized1.html.

7. Jorge Cauz, "How I Did It . . . Encyclopædia Britannica's President on Killing Off a 244-Year-Old Product," *Harvard Business Review* 91 (March 2013): 39–42.

8. John McDuling, "The New York Times Is Finally Getting Its Swagger Back," Quartz, April 29, 2014, http://qz.com/203869/the-new-york-times-is-finally -getting-its-swagger-back/.

9. Sharon Waxman, "Marvel Wants to Flex Its Own Heroic Muscles as a Moviemaker," *New York Times*, June 18, 2007, http://www.nytimes.com/2007/06/18/business /media/18marvel.html.

10. Sree Sreenivasan, "Digital, Mobile, Social Lessons from a Year @MetMuseum: What Every Business Should Know" (speech given at Columbia Business School's Annual "BRITE" Conference, New York, March 2, 2015).

11. Theodore Levitt, "Marketing Myopia," *Harvard Business Review*, July–August 2004, https://hbr.org/2004/07/marketing-myopia.

12. Ivar Jacobson, *Object Oriented Software Engineering: A Use Case Driven Approach* (Reading, Pa.: Addison-Wesley Professional, 1992).

13. Clayton M. Christensen and Michael E. Raynor, *The Innovator's Solution: Creating and Sustaining Successful Growth* (Boston: Harvard Business School Press, 2003), 74–80, 96. Christensen and Raynor credit Richard Pedi with coining the phrase "jobs to be done," Anthony Ulwick with developing closely related concepts, and David Sundahl

with assisting in their own formulation. The job-to-be-done concept has been further explored in various articles by Christensen with other coauthors.

14. Michael J. Lanning and Edward G. Michaels, "A Business Is a Value Delivery System," McKinsey Staff Paper no. 41, June 1998, http://www.dpvgroup.com/wp-content/uploads/2009/11/1988-A-Business-is-a-VDS-McK-Staff-Ppr.pdf.

15. Office of Inspector General, United States Post Office, *Providing Non-Bank Financial Services for the Underserved*, January 7, 2014, https://www.uspsoig.gov/sites/default/files/document-library-files/2014/rarc-wp-14–007.pdf.

16. Felix Salmon, "Why the Post Office Needs to Compete with Banks," *Reuters* (blog), February 3, 2014, http://blogs.reuters.com/felix-salmon/2014/02/03/why-the-post-office-needs-to-compete-with-banks/.

17. Donna Leinwand Lager, "Postmaster General to Seek New Tech, New Fleet for USPS," *USA Today*, March 6, 2015, http://www.usatoday.com/story/news/2015/03/06/postmaster-general-brennan-seeks-innovation-technology-for-us-postal-service/24520575/.

18. Henry Chesbrough, "Why Bad Things Happen to Good Technology," *Wall Street Journal*, April 28, 2007, http://www.wsj.com/news/articles/SB117735510033679362.

19. Josh Constine, "How Facebook Went Mobile, in Before and After Org Charts," Techcrunch, December 4, 2013, http://techcrunch.com/2013/12/04/facebook-org-charts/.

20. Rita Gunther McGrath, *The End of Competitive Advantage: How to Keep Your Strategy Moving as Fast as Your Business* (Boston: Harvard Business Review Press, 2013), 27–51.

21. Aaron Levie, Twitter post, November 18, 2013, 12:16 A.M., http://twitter.com/levie/status/402304366234718208. In his original tweet, Levie spoke about "products," not "businesses." But I hope he would agree the point remains just as true.

22. Eric Von Hippel, "Lead Users: A Source of Novel Product Concepts," *Management Science* 32 (1986): 7. doi:10.1287/mnsc.32.7.791.

23. Mark Hurst, e-mail interview with author, August 28, 2015. In his book *Customers Included*, Hurst presents trenchant examples of the benefits of direct customer observation and the failures that result when businesses don't integrate it into their planning. *Customers Included: How to Transform Products, Companies, and the World—with a Single Step*, 2nd ed. (New York: Creative Good, 2015).

7. Mastering Disruptive Business Models

1. Michael Treacy and Fred Wiersema wrote that businesses compete by providing superior customer value in one of three value disciplines: operational excellence, customer intimacy, or product leadership. "Customer Intimacy and Other Value Disciplines," *Harvard Business Review*, January–February 1993, https://hbr.org/1993/01/customer-intimacy-and-other-value-disciplines.

2. W. Chan Kim and Renée Mauborgne, *Blue Ocean Strategy: How to Create Uncontested Market Space and Make Competition Irrelevant* (Boston: Harvard Business Review Press, 2005), 12–18.

3. Marc Andreessen, "Why Software Is Eating the World," *Wall Street Journal*, August 20, 2011, http://www.wsj.com/articles/SB10001424053111903480904576512250915629460.

4. "Craigslist Fact Sheet," accessed November 16, 2014, http://www.craigslist.org/about/factsheet.

5. Robert Safian, "The World's Most Innovative Companies 2014," *Fast Company*, 2014, http://www.fastcompany.com/most-innovative-companies/2014/.

6. Joseph A. Schumpeter, *The Economics and Sociology of Capitalism* (Princeton, N.J.: Princeton University Press, 1991), 349.

7. Clayton M. Christensen, *The Innovator's Dilemma: The Revolutionary Book That Will Change the Way You Do Business* (New York: HarperBusiness, 2011).

8. Ben Thompson, "What Clayton Christensen Got Wrong," *Stratechery* (blog), September 22, 2013, http://stratechery.com/2013/clayton-christensen-got-wrong/.

9. Jena McGregor, "Clayton Christensen's Innovation Brain," *Businessweek*, June 15, 2007, http://www.bloomberg.com/bw/stories/2007-06-15/clayton-christensens-innovation-brainbusinessweek-business-news-stock-market-and-financial-advice.

10. Larissa MacFarquhar, "When Giants Fail," *New Yorker*, May 14, 2012, http://www.newyorker.com/magazine/2012/05/14/when-giants-fail.

11. A valuable survey of the varying definitions and applications of business models is provided by Christoph Zott, Raphael Amit, and Lorenzo Massa in "The Business Model: Recent Developments and Future Research" (working paper, IESE Business School, University of Navarra, Pamplona, Spain, 2010), http://www.iese.edu/research/pdfs/DI-0862-E.pdf.

12. Alexander Osterwalder and Yves Pigneur, *Business Model Generation: A Handbook for Visionaries, Game Changers, and Challengers* (Hoboken, N.J.: Wiley, 2010).

13. Mark W. Johnson, Clayton M. Christensen, and Henning Kagermann, "Reinventing Your Business Model," *Harvard Business Review*, December 2008, https://hbr.org/2008/12/reinventing-your-business-model.

14. Ibid.

15. Alexander Osterwalder, Yves Pigneur, Gregory Bernarda, Alan Smith, and Trish Papadakos, *Value Proposition Design: How to Create Products and Services Customers Want* (Hoboken, N.J.: Wiley, 2014).

16. In 2002, Verna Allee described *value networks* as "a complex set of social and technical resources that work together via relationships to create economic value" in the book *The Future of Knowledge* (London: Routledge, 2011). In 1999, Cinzia Parolloni had used a similar term, *value net*—defined as "a set of activities linked together to deliver a value proposition at the end consumer"—in the book *The Value Net: A Tool for Competitive Strategy* (New York: Wiley, 1999).

17. Kevin Kelly lays out a list of generatives specifically for information and media businesses looking to charge customers in a digital world where their core products are easily replicated for free. "Better than Free," *The Technium* (blog), January 31, 2008, http://kk.org/thetechnium/better-than-fre/.

18. Kristina Shampanier and Dan Ariely, "Zero as a Special Price: The True Value of Free Products," *Marketing Science* 26, no. 6 (2007): 742–57. doi:10.1287/mksc.1060.0254.

19. Kevin Kelly, "Immortal Technologies," *The Technium* (blog), February 9, 2006, http://kk.org/thetechnium/immortal-techno/.

20. Laura Hazard Owen cites a PwC study predicting that e-books would surpass print books in 2016 in "What Will the Global E-book Market Look Like by 2016?" Gigaom, June 12, 2012, http://gigaom.com/2012/06/11/what-will-the-global-e-book-market-look-like-by-2016/.

21. The 30 percent figure was cited in George Packer, "Cheap Words," *New Yorker*, February 17, 2014, http://www.newyorker.com/magazine/2014/02/17/cheap-words.

22. Olga Kharif, Amy Thompson, and Patricia Laya, "WhatsApp Shows How Phone Carriers Lost Out on $33 Billion," Bloomberg, February 21, 2014, http://www.bloomberg.com/news/articles/2014-02-21/whatsapp-shows-how-phone-carriers-lost-out-on-33-billion.

23. Courtney Rubin, "Last Call for College Bars," *New York Times*, September 26, 2012, http://www.nytimes.com/2012/09/27/fashion/for-college-students-social-media-tops-the-bar-scene.html.

24. Clayton M. Christensen and Derek van Bever, "The Capitalist's Dilemma," *Harvard Business Review*, June 1, 2014, https://hbr.org/product/the-capitalists-dilemma/R1406C-PDF-ENG.

25. Greg Sandoval, "Blockbuster Laughed at Netflix Partnership Offer," CNET, December 9, 2010, http://www.cnet.com/news/blockbuster-laughed-at-netflix-partnership-offer/.

26. Maxwell Wessel and Clayton M. Christensen, "Surviving Disruption," *Harvard Business Review*, December 2012, http://hbr.org/2012/12/surviving-disruption.

27. Clark Gilbert, Matthew Eyring, and Richard N. Foster have written about how to most effectively coordinate a two-pronged strategy of repositioning your core business while launching an independent disrupter of your own in "Two Routes to Resilience," *Harvard Business Review*, December 2012, http://hbr.org/2012/12/two-routes-to-resilience.

28. Ibid.

29. Kana Inagaki and Juro Osawa, "Fujifilm Thrived by Changing Focus," *Wall Street Journal*, January 20, 2012, http://www.wsj.com/articles/SB10001424052970203750404577170481473958516.

Conclusion

1. Jo Boswell, telephone interview with author, August 9, 2015.

2. Peter F. Drucker, *The Practice of Management* (Oxford, UK: Elsevier, 1955), 31–32.

3. Theodore Levitt, *The Marketing Imagination* (New York: Free Press, 1983), 48.

INDEX

Page numbers in italic indicate figures or tables.

ABOUT THE AUTHOR

David L. Rogers, a member of the faculty at Columbia Business School, is a globally recognized leader on brands and digital strategy, known for his pioneering model of customer networks and his work on digital transformation. He is the author of three previous books, including *The Network Is Your Customer: Five Strategies to Thrive in a Digital Age.*

At Columbia Business School, Rogers teaches global executives as the faculty director of Executive Education programs on Digital Business Strategy and Digital Marketing. His recent research with Columbia's Center on Global Brand Leadership has focused on big data, the Internet of Things, in-store mobile shoppers, digital marketing ROI, and data sharing. Rogers is also the founder and cohost of Columbia's acclaimed BRITE conference on brands, innovation, and technology, where global CEOs and CMOs come together with leading technology firms, media companies, and entrepreneurs to address the challenges of building strong brands in the digital age.

Rogers has consulted and developed executive programs for global companies such as Google, GE, Toyota, Pernod Ricard, Visa, SAP, Lilly, Combiphar, IBM, China Eastern Airlines, Kohler, Saint-Gobain, and MacMillan, among many others. He has delivered strategic workshops for executives in hundreds of companies from sixty-four countries.

Rogers delivers keynotes at conferences worldwide on digital transformation, digital marketing, big data, and the impact of emerging technologies on business. He has appeared on CNN, ABC News, CNBC, Marketplace, Channel News Asia, and in the *Financial Times*, the *Wall Street Journal*, *Forbes*, and the *Economist*. He received the 2009 Award for Brand Leadership at the World Brand Congress, is a board member of the Marketing Hall of Fame, and is president of the New York American Marketing Association.

For more tools and content from Rogers, visit http://www.davidrogers.biz.